INVENTING THE EGGHEAD

INVENTING
THE EGGHEAD

The Battle over Brainpower
in American Culture

AARON LECKLIDER

PENN

UNIVERSITY OF PENNSYLVANIA PRESS

PHILADELPHIA

Published by
University of Pennsylvania Press
Philadelphia, Pennsylvania 19104-4112
www.upenn.edu/pennpress

Printed in the United States of America
on acid-free paper
2 4 6 8 10 9 7 5 3 1

Library of Congress Cataloging-in-Publication Data
Lecklider, Aaron.
Inventing the egghead : the battle over brainpower in American culture /
Aaron Lecklider. — 1st ed.
    p.   cm.
Includes bibliographical references and index.
ISBN 978-0-8122-4486-1 (hardcover : alk. paper)
1. United States—Intellectual life—20th century.   2. Intellectuals—
United States—History—20th century.   3. Popular culture—United States—
History—20th century.   I. Title.
E169.12.L393   2013
306.0973—dc23
                                                              2012032987

For Evelyn Clark, and for Brian

CONTENTS

Introduction: Or, They Think We're Stupid

> It is the glory of America that it believes that all that anybody
> knows everybody should know.
>
> —Joseph Cook

George W. Bush's presidential election in 2000 left American liberals dumb-struck. The shame of defeat was one piece of the election's humiliation: that Bush had been awarded the presidency in spite of losing the popular vote was troubling, and the unprecedented role of the Supreme Court in his victory was difficult to reconcile with American ideals of democracy. But it was not simply the fiasco of the election itself that was so unsettling. It was also what the newly elected president represented: wealth, political power, avarice, and—perhaps most important—mind-numbing stupidity. Following Democratic contender Al Gore's concession, American liberals mourned the defeat of their candidate, but they also loudly bemoaned the death of intelligence in American culture, society, and politics. "The presidential campaign ended, effectively, in a tie, but it did speak clearly about the value accorded intellectuals and intellectuality in American culture," complained Todd Gitlin in the *Chronicle of Higher Education*. "What it declared is, to say the least, inauspicious."[1]

The 2000 election transformed the United States into a cultural combat zone of red against blue. The new map divided the country by region—sectional division between North and South experienced a renaissance—but also by degree of cosmopolitanism, lifestyle, taste, and gender. Overwhelmingly, though, the nation appeared to be divided by intelligence. Books began appearing that exposed with humor or with horror the gross incompetence of the new commander-in-chief. Late night television unleashed a torrent of bon mots about dim-witted politicos. A cavalcade of pundits battled over the pros and cons of installing an idiot in the Oval Office. Celebrities attacked the stupid president; politicians assailed vapid celebrities. A short-lived comedy series even made it onto cable television in 2001, coyly titled *That's My Bush!*, revolving around one central joke: a fool is elected president of the United States and turns out to be as dumb as a typical sitcom dad. The narrative of victory by incompetents would be repeated in 2004, when a presidential campaign that had been focused largely on issues of combating terrorism and an ongoing war in Iraq was again transformed into a contest over intelligence. That the two candidates for executive office, George W. Bush and John F. Kerry, were both graduates of Yale who had performed at the C-level during their undistinguished undergraduate careers was not important. From their first debate, the election again turned to the apparently contrasting role of intelligence—and sometimes competence—in their leadership.

The perceived victory of anti-intellectualism in the Oval Office was by no means new in 2000, even less so in 2004. George H. W. Bush had received similarly disapproving treatment in his grammatically challenged campaigns for president (marred even further by V.P. Dan Quayle's persona, epitomized in his unfortunate p-o-t-a-t-o-e mishap). Ronald Reagan was well known—even respected by some—for his frequent speaking gaffes. Richard Nixon's distaste for "the establishment" and the "Elite" was the stuff of legend, and his favorite targets were those with useless degrees from highly reputable colleges. In such distinguished company, attacks on George W. Bush's brains appeared as just another volley in a long-standing game of American attack-politics. Mark Crispin Miller declared confidently in his impertinent 2001 compendium of Bush misspeak, *The Bush Dyslexicon: Observations on a National Disorder*, that "anti-intellectual appeal goes way back in American history and is still a potent one; and the Bush team made it with enormous skill, alleging W's rusticity and hyping Gore's aggressive braininess with due unanimity and vehemence."[2]

But this was only one side of the story. On the right, pundits began fighting back against charges of their neoconservative hero's "anti-intellectual appeal" with vigor—and their chosen strategy was not to merely affirm the "rusticity" of their president, as Miller and countless others anticipated. Rather, they retaliated by affirming the soundness of Bush's mental capacities, the fecundity of the Republican intellectual landscape, and the robust intelligence of conservative politics. They also went on the defensive against liberal claims of conservative stupidity, effectively reframing a debate that seemed to be about dismantling intellectual culture into a defense of intelligence. "Bush occasionally misspeaks and therefore he's an idiot," complained Ann

Coulter in a chapter called "The Joy of Arguing with Liberals: *You're Stupid!*" "Reagan spoke mellifluously, which proved he was an idiot, except the one time he finally fumbled a word—which also demonstrated he was an idiot. You can't win with these people; all a Republican can do is die."[3] Rightwing radio host Laura Ingraham railed against representations of the smart liberal/dumb conservative divide:

> They think we're stupid. They think our patriotism is stupid. They think our churchgoing is stupid. They think our flag-flying is stupid. They think having more than two children is stupid. They think where we live—anywhere but near or in a few major cities—is stupid. They think our SUVs are stupid. They think owning a gun is stupid. They think our abiding belief in the goodness of America and its founding principles is stupid. They think the choices we make at the ballot box are stupid. They think George W. Bush is stupid. And without a doubt, they will think this book is stupid.[4]

Radio personality Michael Savage went even farther in his typically bombastic tirades by defending the intellectual pedigree of the Bush administration. "President Bush's formal education includes graduating from Yale and then completing a master's of business administration from Harvard's business school," Savage declared. Furthermore, the vice president, "Dick Cheney, is also a learned man. He holds both a BA and MA in political science. Secretary of State Colin Powell went to George Washington University where he earned an MBA. Not to mention his collection of distinguished military awards. Condoleezza Rice, who serves as the national security advisor, graduated cum laude from the University of Denver." By contrast, Savage reveled in revealing the lack of distinction in the academic records of those smug anti-Bush haters in Hollywood. "Many have no formal college education," Savage seethed. "Yet these hollow souls come before the microphones to lecture us over issues that they don't know the first thing about. And we're supposed to take them seriously?"[5]

The obsession with intelligence (or lack thereof) in Bush's presidency has been widely interpreted as evidence for the persistence of anti-intellectualism in American life.[6] Yet the cranky conflict between pundits on the left and the right cannot be easily split into intellectual and anti-intellectual camps, and the polarized red-blue debates are curiously united in their appeals to intelligence: both sides fight over who is smarter; both charge the other side with narrow-mindedness; both refuse to submit to character-izations of their ideas and identities as stupid. Though it is tempting to in-terpret the early 2000s as having been defined by rampant anti-intellectualism, close attention to media discussion reveals a more complicated picture. Representations of intelligence in the Bush era were, of course, shaped by their immediate cultural and political contexts, but their basic structure conformed to that first produced in the early to mid-twentieth century un-der the signs of modernity, industrialization, and the emergence of mass culture.

It is against the backdrop of this contentious political and cultural scene that this volume was conceived and written. Here I explore representations of intelligence in twentieth-century American culture. Over the past hun-dred years or so, popular songs, magazine articles, plays, posters, and novels in the United States vacillated between representing intelligence as empow-ering and threatening, often refusing to settle on a simple definition. Close study of these sources reveals how Americans who were not part of the tra-ditional intellectual class negotiated the complicated politics of intelligence within an accelerating mass culture. Americans were encouraged through their engagement with popular culture to conceive themselves as intellectu-ally gifted while deflating the pretensions of those who were labeled as overly intelligent. Representations of intelligence thus embodied a stubborn para-dox in American society, which this book seeks to uncover.

Central to this study is the concept of brainpower as a tool for laying claim to intelligence and the authority that came with it. I use the term "brainpower" to reference the complicated ways in which intelligence was invoked to empower the wide swath of Americans who did not necessarily have access to the institutions of higher education.[7] Brainpower encom-passed efforts by ordinary Americans to seize cultural capital from an intel-lectual elite by positioning themselves as intelligent and by deflating the intellectual pretensions of others.[8] The building blocks of brainpower as a form of cultural politics were forged in the newly modern United States as changes in work, leisure, and domestic life introduced various means for challenging traditional social and political hierarchies. Moreover, changes in the industrial workplace, the rise of the labor movement, and the birth of mass media at the beginning of the twentieth century made available a new vocabulary as well as new avenues through which to define intelligence in relation to social, cultural, and political power.[9]

Representations of intelligence in the twentieth century engendered an uncomfortable paradox: they diminished the value of intellectuals while establishing claims to intellectual authority among ordinary women and men. Yet in spite of the perceived impossibility of this position, these paradoxical representations nonetheless managed to exert a powerful influence in American culture, shaping the invocations of intelligence on the part of labor activists, women workers, and African Americans alike. To be sure, appeals to brainpower were particularly visible within mass culture, but brainpower's reach also extended to Harlem Renaissance literature, autobiographies of working women at summer schools administered by labor unions, and mass-produced posters of the New Deal. Though the paradox at the heart of brainpower's representations of intelligence was perpetually unresolved, brainpower's appeal was widespread, and its influence in American culture would be difficult to overestimate.

The role of popular culture in this study is of vital significance. It was largely through popular culture that ordinary Americans expressed and affirmed their brainpower. The politics of intelligence have too often been relegated to the workplace, universities, and halls of government. Yet the lives of ordinary Americans, especially among the working class, have been structured by cultural practices that extend far beyond this limited range of venues, and the meaning and power of intelligence has been determined in no small measure by everyday cultural practices.[10] In recent years historians have become more attentive to the significance of the culture industries in structuring ordinary lives and everyday politics.[11] When considering the cultural implications of intelligence within the modern United States, popular culture represents an important site for analysis because ordinary intelligence was situated as both powerful and empowering within the culture industries.[12] Indeed, such popular expressions of intelligence were shaped within the structure of an emerging industry producing mass culture in the United States. By the dawn of the twentieth century, few could deny that mass-produced commodities were impacting the way information was produced, distributed, and consumed; leisure was sought; and politics were enacted.[13] With the rise of industrialized media and mass production, assisted by advancing technology and the division of intellectual labor, Americans were exposed to more information than ever before, and the shape of American culture was accordingly changed. Ordinary Americans were placed at the center of cultural production and consumption at this moment, and they were exposed to a dazzling amount of information they were entrusted to process, decode, and filter.

Historian Richard Ohmann defines the mass culture that emerged at the turn of the twentieth century as "voluntary experiences, produced by a relatively small number of specialists, for millions across the nation to share, in similar or identical form, either simultaneously or nearly so; with dependable frequency."[14] Central to this historical rendering are two features that impacted representations of intelligence: first, mass culture's broad dispersal, and second, the specialized production demanded by the evolving culture industries. Embedded within mass culture was a leveling impulse that brought consumers together as mass audiences. At the same time, the culture industry positioned the production of mass culture as requiring specialized intellectual labor. The rise of mass media invoked the conditions that made paradoxical representations of brainpower possible. It created both a division of intellectual labor and a mass movement. Popular culture increasingly relied upon audiences recognizing both the power of the masses and the growth of professionalization within the culture industries.

Changes in media production and consumption were themselves inseparable from transformations in the industrial workplace. By the turn of the twentieth century, the United States was a largely industrialized nation. The manufacturing sector represented the lifeblood of the state, and workers struggled for control over their jobs and lives as managers moved further from the floor of the shop. As scientific management took hold in the workplace and professionalization reshaped occupations, managers were divorced from the everyday drudgeries of work and working-class communities while workers found themselves subjected to greater surveillance by bosses and shareholders.[15] Decision making in the workplace was deferred to experts defined by both class and education, and workers found themselves in the awkward position of adhering to the demands of bosses who lacked their overall comprehension of work. Brainpower was thus invoked to resist workplace hierarchies and empower workers while disrupting a tendency to assume intelligence as a unique attribute of the middle class.

Though workers were largely on the losing end of changes in the industrial workplace, they also took advantage of new possibilities as they organized into labor unions and challenged these oppressive structures.[16] Harry Braverman, one of scientific management's most outspoken opponents, famously characterized these innovations as the "degradation of work," but these conditions also instantiated the modern labor movement.[17] The new division of labor that rewarded managers while degrading workers was met with a widespread collective movement within a radicalizing working class. In the words of historian David Montgomery, "the machinists' answer to 'scientific management' was to demand a 'truly scientific' reorganization of society on a collectivist basis."[18] Rather than simply opposing science and professionalism with salt-of-the-earth rusticity, Montgomery's machinists appropriated the tools of scientific rationalism to oppose their managers. They objected to the notion that they could not understand their industry and challenged the value of managerial intelligence. Discussions about science were made inextricable from conversations about work, class, and the politics of brainpower.

Education also underwent a series of significant changes in the United States at this time. Beginning in the late nineteenth century, school attendance became compulsory, a process that was completed by 1918 when every state in the union had enacted laws requiring public education. In a study of education published in 1934, Edward Cubberley noted that "after about 1900, new courses of study and new teaching directions appeared," and that "the excess of drill which had characterized earlier school work came to be replaced by lessons in subjects involving expression and appreciation, such as art, music, manual work, domestic training, play, and humane education."[19] Education was both expanding its reach and was becoming more organized around comprehensive ideas about intelligence. Higher education was also extending to more of the population, as new colleges appeared at a rapid clip in the early 1900s and the student population swelled. Yet higher education remained relatively inaccessible to the vast majority of Americans until the latter half of the twentieth century. Though public universities were growing in the early twentieth century, it took some time for them to take root.

The dawn of the twentieth century also witnessed a period of major progressive political reform that was particularly significant in challenging hierarchies of sex and class. "Everyone who has studied the history of American reform," historian Christopher Lasch writes, "agrees that the reform tradition underwent a fundamental change around 1900." This change entailed a variety of new approaches by which ordinary women and men could access and claim political power.[20] Underlying these changes in American political life was a renewed sense of empowerment for populations who had found themselves on the losing end of many of the changes in the rapidly industrializing and modernizing United States. At the turn of the century political reform was increasingly claimed by and for the people.[21] Against whom this progressive spirit was directed depended on contingencies of community and ideology, but there was certainly no mistaking the fresh face of political resistance finding new forms of visibility. Given this distinctive collision of scientific, labor, educational, and political change, it follows that the turn of the century is a particularly revealing period for the developing cultural politics of brainpower in the United States. Indeed, it was a moment when anti-intellectualism coexisted with representations of an intellectually gifted working class. By the mid-twentieth century, this paradox had become naturalized. "Being an egghead," claimed philosopher Charles Frankel in 1956, "seems to be a station in life to which no one aspires but which everyone would like to think himself natively qualified."[22] The cases I highlight point to both the persistence of brainpower as a discursive strategy for empowering ordinary women and men within popular culture and the availability of new vocabularies for representing intelligence at various key moments in the twentieth century.

That brainpower was inflected by the language of race, ethnicity, and gender comprised an important feature of its representations, and it is impossible to study intelligence during these decades without attending to such inflections. The lives of women, African Americans, immigrants, and working-class women and men were marked by profound struggle as these communities fought against multiple forms of social inequality. Though marginalized communities could not always access institutions that had the potential to improve their conditions, they frequently capitalized on the transformative potential of brainpower by identifying themselves as smart and their oppressors as unintelligent. At the center of the story of brainpower is the conflict between Americans who wielded tremendous social power and those who were excluded from accessing this power yet found enterprising channels for pushing against their conditions.

Although the book follows a roughly chronological sequence, it is structured around the examination of especially potent cultural texts, figures, and social movements. I begin the story at Coney Island at the dawn of the twentieth century, broadly exploring the politics of brainpower in relation to the growth of mass culture at this time. I then turn to Albert Einstein, a significant and widely celebrated individual who, I propose, embodied post-World War I shifts in representations of science and intelligence. I follow this by focusing on the role of brainpower in shaping political and cultural movements aimed at working-class women and African Americans. In each of these cases the tension between affirming the intelligence of marginalized groups and resisting the narrowly defined labeling of intellectuals in the United States is navigated and charted. I then turn my attention to the impact of the Great Depression and the growth of the New Deal through shifting representations of intelligence. Lastly, I analyze representations of intelligence in the postwar years when Cold War attacks on brainpower were reshaping American society, culture, and politics while the black civil rights, homophile, and labor movements advanced efforts to counter these threats.

Acknowledging the centrality of brainpower as a tool for articulating various political identities in twentieth-century American culture has the potential to answer—or at least reframe—a series of questions about the history of the United States that are in need of revisiting. Why have Americans been so conflicted in their relationship with intelligence? Why has the vocabulary of anti-intellectualism so often demanded acknowledgment of populist heroes' brainpower rather than promoting their rusticity? How have organizations working to advance African American, working class, and women's political standing represented their collective intelligence to achieve these goals? How have representations of intelligence in American popular culture mediated the organic intellectual tradition in U.S. political and social life? And how did representations of intelligence shape culture and politics in the twentieth-century United States?

Whether serving the goal of expanding the intellectual tools of the working class, promoting black cultural achievement, or puncturing the social privileges of America's elite, representations of intelligence have been critical to the project of defining, deploying, and defending ordinary American interests in public life. Popular culture represented an important site for exploring the messy politics of brainpower in the twentieth century. Cultural texts consumed by millions of ordinary women and men between 1900 and 1960 suggested all Americans were intellectually gifted while deflating the presumptuous grandstanding of the traditional intellectual elite. The idea of "intelligence"—both access to it and the danger in acquiring too much of it—was employed in various and contradictory ways throughout the twentieth century. These representations were not simply scattershot and without ideological resonance; on the contrary, they served clear purposes across a wide spectrum of political and social perspectives—from radical to conservative and from working-class to elite. Even at their most paradoxical, representations of intelligence in American culture suggest the complicated network of meanings attached to brainpower and the wide range of strategies adopted by ordinary women and men to express frustration and refusal when somebody in a powerful position tells them they think they're stupid.

1

"Aren't We Educational Here Too?": Brainpower and the Emergence of Mass Culture

You make a big mistake when you set the workingman aside for a numbskull.

—Horace Traubel

In May 1909, Luna Park, one of three amusement parks at Coney Island, was transformed into Luna Park Institute of Science. Employees of the park, from ticket-takers to performance barkers, donned badges identifying themselves as professors. Fred Thompson, Luna Park's proprietor, was greeted by police inspecting the grounds as "President of the Faculty."[1] Recounting his nobly educational mission when he conceived the park, Thompson straight-facedly proclaimed that "to have advertised them at that time as educational amusements would have been fatal, so I gave the park a sugar coating with a title that implied frivolous pastimes." In response to challenges by the law, Thompson declared, "I am disrobing it of its sugar coating."[2] Rides and shows that had generated suspicion from authorities enforcing laws prohibiting amusement on Sundays were rebranded as educational demonstrations. The Mountain Torrent, a roller coaster promising to jolt intrepid ticket-holders in rickety cars following a windy mountainous track, became an "institute for the practical illustration of a mountain logging sluice."[3] The Red Mill, a waterborne ride, was rechristened "a model for the study of sea-level canals as applied to Panama."[4] Even the stands where visitors purchased their famed Coney Island hot dogs were now "home of our educated dogs."[5]

George Tilyou, the eccentric owner of Steeplechase, invoked a similar defense of his pedagogic mission as he issued beleaguered statements to stave off Sunday shutdowns. "Aren't we educational here too?" begged the wounded businessman. "Look at those persons riding on our mechanical ponies. They go as fast as thirty miles an hour, quite as fast as most horses. A few times around and a man will know how to ride. Then on our dancing floor we always have a professor to teach those who don't know how to." In what proved to be a more or less successful effort to convince authorities they were complying with New York statutes, women working at both Luna Park and Dreamland cash registers were outfitted in "collegiate caps and gowns of maroon and blue."[6] The daily newspapers reported with great pleasure as spectacular shows such as "Saved by the Wireless" were reborn with preposterous names like "Prof. Jack Binn's College for the Study of Wireless Telegraphy." Visitors meanwhile defied authorities as they descended upon the threatened parks in massive numbers. Mass culture, endlessly disparaged by middle-class reformers and politicians as uncouth and dangerous, was kept afloat by representing working-class leisure as a means to intelligence, and the many guests visiting Luna Park Institute of Science were too smart to miss out.[7]

Though the rationale behind rebranding Coney Island as educational represented a rather straightforward effort to take advantage of a loophole in New York's draconian blue laws, the discourse in which the park owners participated is not nearly so transparent. Why, for example, did Luna Park's transformation specifically brand the park an institute of science? Why not a center for the study of humanity? There was plenty of evidence that visitors might have made convincing armchair ethnographers. What compelled the owners of all three parks to assume the character of universities complete with "professors"? Why not simply reference teachers and leave it at that?[8] And why did appeals to brainpower have the capacity to offset charges of moral depravity anyway? Each of these questions can be answered by looking closely at the relationship between mass culture and representations of intelligence in the early twentieth century. The immediate circumstances confronting Coney Island in the midst of a police crackdown forced spokespeople such as Thompson and Tilyou to enter into conversations about brainpower that were already in progress. Debates about the value of education, new science, and intelligence in relation to working-class politics became, by the turn of the century, typical within a wide variety of popular cultural texts. Coney Island's overnight accreditation fits into a larger narrative about brainpower that was a regular feature of popular culture in a rapidly modernizing United States.

In what would become a familiar pattern, turn-of-the-century mass culture was accused of appealing to base instincts. The discontinuity between its broad accessibility and the restrictions on institutions of higher education seem at first glance to suggest that pleasure palaces and amusement parks would have represented sites of escape from brainpower. "Usually, when an intelligent man comes back from Coney Island," wrote one critic in 1917, "he knows it isn't so. He concludes that it was something he ate which didn't digest."[9] Yet a closer look at the popular culture consumed by ordinary Americans reveals how deeply interwoven appeals to intelligence and popular amusements were within mass culture. Some of the entertainments audiences sought out made explicit claims to expanding their intelligence. Salons, public lectures, traveling science exhibits, and Chautauqua assemblies appealed to large audiences with their explicitly educational mission. The idea that intelligence was desirable and attainable was familiar to audiences seeking out this kind of entertainment. Yet even the amusements that were least inclined toward education—roller coasters, Tin Pan Alley songs, and cartoons—participated in shaping the discourse of brainpower at this critical historical moment. Though some of the more overtly educational circuits collapsed lectures and popular entertainments into the same evening's entertainment, a far wider range of turn-of-the-century mass culture bespoke an educational impulse.

This chapter considers brainpower as a central feature within the emergence of the mass culture industries. The growth in American mass culture was met with an emergent critical discourse that lamented the death of high culture as an opportunity for uplift and spiritual transcendence. Yet at the same time that popular culture was being maligned for abandoning ordinary Americans' intellectual potential, the mass culture industries offered myriad culture outlets that made available all manner of intellectual entertainments targeting working-class consumers. Rather than simply appealing to the lowest common denominator of consumers, the cultural texts produced and consumed during this transformative moment represented a mainstreaming of intelligence among ordinary women and men. Brainpower was incorporated into even the most bemoaned songs, magazines, and amusements, and popular culture was upheld as a significant site for working out the complicated cultural politics of American intelligence.

Incorporating brainpower into Coney Island's popular amusements was, in fact, part of the park owners' formula even before they became "universities." Though they are most often remembered for their thrilling and occasionally salacious amusements, these parks were just as often celebrated in their time for promoting cutting-edge scientific exhibits and prestigious lectures. Observed in a longer historical context, this is not surprising; scientific and technological achievement had been the subjects of many popular amusements from the nineteenth century forward. Prolific inventors such as Alexander Graham Bell and Thomas Edison had become cherished American celebrities, and the public's fascination with science had built up what historian Glenn Scott Allen smartly refers to as a contradiction between representations of the "heroic figure with mastery over technology who utilizes that skill in the service of his community to achieve relatively limited goals of reform; or that of a villain whose arrogance is rooted in the intellect and who seeks, to the detriment of his community, some sort of totalizing revolution."[10] Coney Island represented a unique case in the emergence of mass-culture intelligence only because of the unrelenting torrent of rancor and scorn it precipitated among social reformers and cultural critics who held the parks as representative of the hopeless dumbing down (and sexing up) of American popular entertainment. It was a locus, in other words, for the paradoxes of brainpower in twentieth-century American culture.

Mass Culture and the Cultural Power of Intelligence

In 1903, amid the stomach-churning rides, carnival games promising unwinnable prizes, and spectacular freak-show displays, Dr. Martin A. Couney introduced Dreamland visitors to his experimental baby incubators holding tiny premature infants being kept alive through a complex network of glass cases, tubes, and antiseptic machinery. Dr. Couney's exhibition, displayed at Coney Island after the doctor failed to interest the scientific community in his offbeat research, dazzled visitors with a vision of folk whimsy and modern technological achievement. In an article about the exhibit, the *New York Times* described for readers a "scientific demonstration of how the lives of babies can be saved" within a building "designed in farmhouse style, the first story being of brick—and the upper part in half timber. The tiled roof has a gable with a large stork overlooking a nest of cherubs."[11] The building's architecture and its journalistic description equally emphasized scientific rationality, cultural myth, childlike wonder, and banal Americana, resolving anxiety about this dazzling and potentially terrifying new science with appeals to its mass accessibility. The technological marvel found its most positive reception in an amusement park celebrated as a place where, according to one visitor's description, "bare human nature, naïve and unashamed, stands up . . . and cries out 'Brother' and the unanimity with which human nature responds is hopeful though disconcerting."[12] In 1904, the *New York Times* reported that Dr. Couney's first batch of babies, the "graduates" and "alumnae" of the display, had returned to Dreamland for a reunion at "Incubator College."[13]

Turn-of-the-twentieth-century mass culture offered a site where aspiration to intellectual heights and celebration of working-class spectatorship coexisted, if not always comfortably then at least in a tentatively peaceable entente. Coney Island's incubator exhibits afforded audiences an opportunity to conceive themselves as scientific peers colluding with Dr. Couney and his colleagues. Walking through the exhibit leveled the playing field of intelligence by making visitors colleagues and peers, and Couney contained anxiety about the technological changes altering American lives by staging scientific demonstrations and lectures that also featured adorably tiny infants. Dr. Couney was celebrated for having defied scientific institutions in favor of mass culture, and his incubators became the most popular attraction at Coney Island. It was Couney's expulsion from respectable scientific circles that brought him to Dreamland (by way of several expositions), and the audience for the preemie exhibit was reminded that their intuitive thrill-seeking was preferable over the stodgy, inaccessible intellectualism of academic science. Visitors to the incubators could both affirm their interest in scientific progress and their skepticism toward intellectual institutions. As historian Jeffrey Baker notes, "the elaborate 'scientific' appearance of the incubator doubtless explained its persisting attraction to the American public, much as static electricity machines had mystified and excited the previous generation."[14] In a self-professed "affectionate history of Coney Island" tantalizingly titled *Sodom by the Sea*, Oliver Pilat and Jo Ransom lovingly recalled entering "a large clean room where almost motionless prematures dozed in incubators day and night" while "a lecturer explained the machines in detail."[15] For these visitors Coney Island brought charm, education, showmanship, spectacle, and intelligence into alignment.

It was precisely this form of cultural practice—engaging brainpower while dismantling intellectual hierarchies—that structured the relationship of ordinary Americans with intelligence in early twentieth-century mass culture. Though they had already begun to shape American culture in the mid-nineteenth century, the modern culture industries expanded exponentially in the early twentieth. The technology that instantiated mass culture's emergence, including printing presses capable of producing books, magazines, and sheet music on a massive scale and a state-of-the-art infrastructure for distributing products nationally with remarkable speed, became more efficient with each passing year. Alongside accelerating cultural production and streamlined distribution networks came decreases in production costs and increased output. The volume of consumers purchasing or otherwise accessing mass-produced cultural products swelled, and with the growing market for cultural objects, producers became more skilled at capturing widening groups of consumers. The broad appeal of these new cultural texts was read by critics of mass culture as indicative of the culture industry's pandering to the lowest common denominator. While social reformers bemoaned the excessive drawing power of working-class taste and the attendant failure of America's moral compass, popular culture continued to appear that defied genteel respectability in favor of what critics decried as gut experience. Even middle-class audiences happily pursued cultural amusements that targeted working-class tastes, provoking even more apoplexy among critics.[16] Yet these same texts that were dismissed as frivolous, mind-numbing entertainment just as often attracted consumers by appealing to their intelligence. At the same time that anti-intellectualism was on the rise, ordinary women and men were positioning themselves as intelligent by seeking out organic-intellectual amusements. As a site for thinking through the meanings of brainpower in modern American culture, mass culture offered turn-of-the-century audiences a tentative resolution to this implicit paradox by popularizing working-class intelligence.

This hunger for educational amusements alongside an unquenchable thirst for mass entertainment was made into an occasion for celebrating American exceptionalism. Nowhere was this more apparent than in the discourse surrounding the Chautauqua circuit, about which the British ambassador to the United States boldly stated that no "country in the world but America could produce such gatherings."[17] The assemblies began in Chautauqua, New York, in 1874 primarily as a forum for religious instruction, but they quickly expanded into a national movement that brought lectures about current events, vaudevillian performances, and debates on contemporary topics onto a common stage. Lecturers included university professors and prominent politicians; at the same time, one particularly popular performer was Mascot, "the educated horse," who held chalk in his teeth and who could "add, subtract, and do many other mathematical stunts."[18]

Though Chautauqua lectures dabbled in highbrow themes that advocated for the uplift typical of religious ecumenicalism, they also clearly played to their audience, offering large arenas jammed full of spectators as evidence for American intelligence while diminishing the value of traditional educational achievement. Americans were imagined as always-already intellectuals; those who sought amusement at the Chautauquas could signify both their intelligence and their distinctively American identity. The Chautauqua assemblies also tended to replicate the lurid thrills and intellectual appeal of mass culture. A 1909 poem by Walt Mason titled "Plans of a Chautauqua Promoter" from *Collier's Weekly* satirized the promoter's blurring of education and amusement:

I want to beat my record, and I'm hunting freaks today,
Who will elevate the platform when I open up next spring!
With the Higher Life in mind,
And the Uplift well defined,
Oh, I'll educate the masses—educate 'em till they're blind![19]

As the speakers at the Chautauqua assembly expanded to include a broad cross section of dynamic lecturers speaking on topics ranging from religion to art and comedy, the increasingly national Chautauqua circuit became associated with programming that incorporated educational content into mass cultural entertainment. Popular culture was defined at these assemblies in no small measure by its association with brainpower. Audiences for the Chautauquas were comprised of women and men without any particular standing as intellectuals or claims to expertise, and though they were occasionally glossed with the narrative sheen of social uplift, the assembly programs were designed to offer education to undistinguished audiences and to imbue mass culture with a gleam of shimmering smartness. The assemblies illustrate how intellectual pursuits and popular leisure were inextricable for turn-of-the-century audiences.

As the assemblies grew in popularity, American intelligence became itself a central topic on the Chautauqua circuit, and audiences grew accustomed to hearing lectures with titles such as "Work and Play as Factors in Education," delivered by Jane Addams in 1905; "Knowledge and Power," delivered by E. H. Hughes in 1907; and "America's Contribution to Civilization," delivered by C. W. Eliot in 1896, alongside the usual popular songs and vaudevillian skits. By participating in a Chautauqua assembly, audiences could simultaneously become smarter, more powerful, and more American. Theodore Roosevelt could hardly contain his excitement when he triumphantly declared, "Chautauqua is the most American thing in America." The U.S. Commissioner of Education enthusiastically envisioned the Chautauqua as a model for celebrating American brainpower. "Think of one hundred thousand persons of mature age following up a well-selected course of reading for four years in science and literature," he exclaimed, "kindling their torches at a central flame!" Populist hero William Jennings Bryan celebrated the experience of speaking at a Chautauqua by claiming that "this privilege and this opportunity is one of the greatest that any patriotic American could ask"; similar praise was offered on the other end of the intellectual spectrum by Hjalmar H. Boyesen, a professor at the Ivy League Columbia University. "Nowhere else have I had such a vivid contact with what is really and truly American," Boyesen proudly announced.[20] Americanness, it seemed, was synonymous with the pursuit of intelligence: the broad array of ordinary women and men eagerly expanding their intelligence became symptomatic of the exuberant American's national identity, and brainpower was pursued within, rather than in opposition to, a rapidly expanding mass culture.

The Chautauqua circuit was instrumental in eliminating dividing lines between popular entertainment, education, and edification. As mass culture expanded the range of venues where educational lectures and lowbrow entertainment could share the stage, popular culture that engaged brainpower for mass audiences similarly flourished. In magazines, popular songs, newspapers, and books, as well as on vaudeville stages, complicated discussions about brainpower were plotted through reference to two interrelated subjects that functioned as metonyms for intelligence: science and education.

Becoming Scientific

That "scientific" functioned as shorthand for "intelligent" in popular culture is unsurprising when taking into account the rapid modernization—much of which turned on scientific discovery—affecting turn-of-the-century Americans at home, work, and school.[21] The influence of modern science was felt in multiple registers: physics was incorporated into the college curriculum, technical ingenuity reshaped home and industry, and scientific management affected the daily lives of workers and homemakers by introducing mathematical measures of efficiency. Alongside its increasing presence in the lives of all Americans, science was incorporated into popular culture as an opportunity to work out complex ideas about the meanings of brainpower in the United States. Though signifiers of elitism that had been attached to the practice of nineteenth-century science persisted into the twentieth century, it was also recognized as ever more essential to the ongoing development of U.S. capitalism. Working-class audiences sought educational entertainments that allowed them to identify with the creative intelligence of the scientist while challenging representations that put scientists on a pedestal. Popular culture offered a site where these contradictory concerns could coexist. As was evident at the Coney Island baby incubator exhibits, science represented both danger and hope; it was terribly banal, yet cutting-edge developments were moving the pursuit of science hopelessly out of reach of ordinary women and men. Within popular culture, consumers and scientists could coexist.

Though science had been a wildly popular topic of conversation and object of leisure in nineteenth-century American culture through lectures, lyceums, World Fairs, and displays of technological wizardry, the easy availability and kaleidoscopic variety of nationally circulating magazines both jump-started the mass-culture industries and provided an occasion for popular culture to engage an ongoing conversation about brainpower. Rising literacy rates—though these varied widely by region, race, and class—combined with compulsory education that raised high school graduation rates exponentially beginning in 1900 further expanded the audience for print culture and the range of venues through which Americans could consume science.[22] Even as general-interest serials regularly covered scientific topics, magazines devoted to writing about science were also popular turn-of-the-century subscriptions. These publications negotiated between fascination with the peculiar and unordinary world of scientific work and the more modest lives of their ordinary readers. The task of bridging this gap became an explicit subject in a variety of self-referential articles written for scientific magazines. In 1915, for example, T. Brailsford Robertson, a contributor to the newly re-titled publication *Scientific Monthly,* translated the seemingly intangible contributions of contemporary scientists into bluntly economic terms that would have been familiar to even the most unscientific reader. In an article matter-of-factly titled "The Cash Value of Scientific Research," Robertson argued for the centrality of science in American industrial and economic life, connecting an academic subject with the world of work. "The average man in the street or man of affairs," Robertson wrote in a bold appeal to his undoubtedly smarter-than-average readers, "has no very clear conception of what manner of man a 'scientist' may be. No especial significance attaches in his mind to the term. No picture of a personality or his work arises in the imagination when the word 'scientist' is pronounced."[23] Yet without these under-appreciated scientists' invaluable contributions, Robertson argued, American capitalism would struggle and eventually die. Science was useful insofar as its value to industry could be mathematically calculated into a neatly profitable sum. Robertson vindicated the unknown scientist by transforming him into a capitalist.

Robertson's representation of scientists as both invisible and in need of social respect was typical of pop culture representations at this time and points to a long-standing tension between embrace of the technical wizard and fear of the abstract theorist.[24] His ambivalence about the "average man in the street" reflected a tension between the audiences for mass culture, the specialized intellectual labor required for its production, and the rarified spaces where scientific work was actually being performed.[25] The early twentieth-century culture industry expanded access to science for many nonspecialists. A growing audience of consumers created a demand for informed writers to fill popular magazines, lecture halls, and amusement parks with specialized knowledge made accessible to mass audiences. These audiences were comprised of women and men who were themselves working in industries experiencing massive transformation through modern machinery and corporate organization or participating in a growing consumer economy. The representations of science within mass culture thus reflected the contradictions of a society that was becoming both more culturally democratic and technologically and scientifically advanced.

Science represented both a type of intelligence and a form of labor that operated at a distinct remove from the vernacular experiences of most Americans. Periodicals such as *Scientific Monthly* were placed in an awkward position: their attractiveness to consumers depended upon acknowledging the curiously compelling world of scientific work, yet their audience could not be made to feel alienated or stupid for working outside it. In Robertson's article this tension was resolved by highlighting those aspects of scientific work that were most familiar to readers through appeals to the universality of work and remuneration while diminishing the class privilege implied in educational achievement. This job was made easier by the economics of magazine publishing: unlike Coney Island, which attracted many working-class visitors, magazines were read primarily by middle-class consumers who were far more likely to have access to higher education than their roller-coasting comrades.[26] The very fact of having picked up a magazine did important work in associating scientific knowledge with class privilege. Audiences became middle-class both by reading magazines and becoming scientific.

At the same time, science also provided an opportunity for challenging cultural hierarchies in the midst of a modernizing society. Appeals to brainpower entailed affirming ordinary Americans' interest in science while deflating the cultural, social, and economic power attributed to scientists. *Scientific Monthly* could only push its criticism of scientists so far. The magazine's audience was, after all, consuming a magazine about science. Other media outlets, especially those targeting working-class consumers, were less constrained in this regard and unabashedly needled scientists as hopelessly odd. An 1895 song titled "The Scientific Man" described the scientist as emphatically weird and inassimilable in American society. Though he was obviously smart and indicatively American, the scientific man was also a decidedly unappealing character.[27]

That this depiction appeared in the form of a song rather than within a magazine points to its intended audience, but understanding its appeal also demands a basic recognition of the particularities of the sheet music industry. In early twentieth-century American culture, commercial sheet music was almost exclusively produced on Tin Pan Alley, described by historian Jeffrey Melnick as "a place of business (actually a few places), a time, and a style (or a number of related styles)." The songs, produced quickly and efficiently in the songwriting factories of New York by a handful of prolific songwriters, were formulaic, topical, and immensely popular; this is where, according to Melnick, "American music came into its own."[28] It was here as well that scientific management's influence was felt most acutely within the culture industry. Songwriters on Tin Pan Alley were caught up in both the lucrative possibilities in mass culture and the productivity demanded within a scientifically managed workplace.

Employing the goofy wordplay and corny humor that was Tin Pan Alley's stock in trade, "The Scientific Man" featured a highly educated and unreasonably smart man.

He could tell you the weight of the moon to an ounce
And the name of ev'ry star;
He'd stand on a slope,
With a big telescope,
And squint at Venus bright.[29]

This man was "scientific" insofar as he was able to recall trivial quantities, establish weights and measures, and maintain highly specialized information, most of which was literally otherworldly.[30] His cosmic intelligence was complemented with highly unpredictable personal behavior and a bizarre physical appearance:

He'd a beak like a parrot
The color of a carrot,
With a Roman wart on top;
A swan-like throat,
Like an old mud boat,
And breath like a chemist shop;
A long mustache, like weeds in a marsh,
And a temper sour and crabby;
He'd nap and scrap with a Russian or a Jap,
And swear like a drunken cabby.[31]

In this song the scientist was awkward and unattractive, but when push came to shove, he behaved like any red-blooded American man, ready and able to "scrap" with a robust xenophobic fervor. Though he could never be of Russian or Japanese descent, the scientific man did bear a number of physical burdens: his oddly shaped nose, his strange coloration, his narrow neck, and his halitosis.[32] His body was described in obsessively repellent detail, and his most distasteful feature was his profound unattractiveness. The scientific man's body stretched and contorted to contain the surplus of information it contained. The song's final stanza described the scientific man's spontaneous combustion under the pressure of all that knowledge, emitting a smell "like a brimstone match" and exploding the man's house. Intelligence colonized the scientific man's body until there was nothing left.

The different characterization of scientists in Robertson's article and "The Scientific Man" illustrates the unresolved paradoxes in representations of intelligence when science was at the center: both imagined a scientist who engendered paradoxically banal and fantastic, desirable and dangerous, and American and alien characteristics.[33] The scientific man was masculine, intelligent, capitalist, and eager to defend his American identity; he was also unattractive, short-tempered, and strange. He was, in sum, both representative of dominant characteristics in American society and unworthy of his powerful position. Yet the texts also point to a shift in the discourse surrounding intelligence in American culture between the 1890s and the 1910s: as science affected even the most ordinary lives through its influence on industrial labor, working-class consumers were more likely to identify with scientists rather than to assume their most unsavory aspects. By consuming cultural texts that treated ordinary Americans as scientifically inclined peers and scientists as ideal capitalists, American consumers could close the gap between the powerful elite and ordinary women and men. Devaluing scientific labor as the product of strange, socially awkward creeps reminded audiences that they were fortunate that they were not truly scientific but that they were just as capable as any scientist. Cultural representations of scientists positioned ordinary women and men as entitled to brainpower's rewards without demanding audiences fully embrace the building of an intellectual class.

One factor contributing to the popularization of scientific knowledge was a contradictory development: academic science was becoming increasingly inaccessible precisely as scientific management was directly affecting working-class lives at work and home. By the turn of the century, scientific theories developed in laboratories and universities had been complicated far beyond what could be easily verified or refuted through common sense or naked observation. The comfortably quaint image of Louis Pasteur breeding fruit flies in his home with a Mason jar and a swatch of cheesecloth to prove that meat did not organically generate maggots was replaced with the massive and threatening specter of large, impersonal institutions or individual scientists who had somehow acquired the unfathomable capital necessary to perform the new science.[34] Audiences could access the prestige of an elite community with incomprehensible capital at their disposal by simply picking up a magazine. Consuming popular science thus became a marker of social status. "Only the very young may be excused for being philosophers," an author in the lifestyle magazine *Good Morning* wrote in 1919. "Growing older, we should become scientific. Philosophy is the groping; science the finding. Philosophy moves out when science moves in."[35]

Though popular science allowed ordinary audiences to access the social power intelligence offered, it also functioned as a means for reinforcing gender hierarchies.[36] Though brainpower undermined class conflict, it often also affirmed patriarchy. "Speaking with a young lady," recounted a joke in *The Half-Century* magazine in 1917, "a gentleman mentioned that he had failed to keep abreast of the scientific advance of the age. 'For instance,' he said, 'I don't know at all how the incandescent electric light is produced.' 'Oh, it is very simple,' said the lady. 'You just press a button and the light appears.'"[37] Such humor made ordinary Americans confident that they were not alone in their ignorance and inability to gain access to the world of new science, even as it muted the anxiety implied in its own punch line by replacing the truly specialized discoveries of the day with a far more familiar and comforting discovery: the electric light.[38] This joke also revealed the gendered implications of interest in scientific developments: though the man acknowledged his lack of scientific insight, the woman was unable to even recognize her own ignorance. As science was invested with social and economic power it was increasingly conceived as the reserve of men.

The other side of science was its direct impact on the world of labor. There were plenty of compelling reasons for working-class Americans to feel unresolved in their attitudes toward scientists when they went to work or worked around the home. One of the most significant factors confronting ordinary Americans as they negotiated the increased demand for intelligence in the modern world was the industrial change brought about through the rise of "scientific" management.[39] Though the actual scientific qualities of Frederick W. Taylor's revolutionary approach to management were specious—it was not until after his system caught on that Taylor retroactively labeled it scientific—Taylorism's associations with science in American culture, and the potential for massive social change that its quick absorption in industry implied, dominated discourse about science and industry in these opening decades of the twentieth century. As we have seen, science was taken as shorthand for intelligence in American culture at this time. Under scientific management, the cultural value of brainpower assumed a distinctly capitalist hue, and those who were attuned to the unequal distribution of capital and power saw in the divided workplace the foreshadowing of a dark new age when labor was not only alienated from intelligence, but labor's value disproportionately favored those who were least inclined to work simply because they were considered scientific. Accessing brainpower could challenge the division of labor in the modern workplace, but it could also legitimize class conflict.

Frederick Winslow Taylor, an engineer and a consultant and expert on industrial machinery, began his experiments with scientific management in the late nineteenth century.[40] Drawing on his belief in systematic management and efficiency, he began to conceive of a more organized and hierarchical system of management as a means to maximum efficiency in American industry. Taylor himself did not settle on the term "scientific management" as a label for his management system until 1910. In that year, the famous lawyer Louis Brandeis argued a case before the Interstate Commerce Commission, during which he devoted considerable time to a discussion of scientific management in the Eastern Rate Case.[41] The term caught on immediately and showed up in the popular media: in 1911 alone, twenty-six widely circulated magazine articles casually employed the phrase.[42]

It was only after the adjective "scientific" was used by others to describe Taylor's work that he began to use it himself, having earlier assigned no particular significance to this label. Yet Taylor quickly championed the credibility this retroactively applied name lent his ideas. In his 1911 book *The Principles of Scientific Management*, Taylor confidently wrote that "the best management is a true science, resting upon clearly defined laws, rules, and principles, as a foundation."[43] Rather than relying on the scientific community to establish standards for management, Taylor called on the authority of science to justify his management practices. A 1915 textbook made the scientific basis of Taylorism even more explicit:

> Just as the scientist in a laboratory tears apart a complex substance, finds its different constituents, writes down the proportionate amount of each, then puts them together again—so the man who would practice "scientific" management analyzes his work. For scientific management simply is the laboratory method of studying work instead of the rule-of-thumb procedure.[44]

Science appeared, by all accounts, to be the fundamental grounding for Taylor's management.[45] Taylorism enshrined a cultural belief that managers performed scientific (that is, intelligent) work while workers simply followed orders to perform mindless tasks (Figure 1). The worker thus became replaceable precisely because the value of his knowledge about his labor was diminished. Frederick Taylor justified this division between workplace theorists

Figure 1. Illustration from *How Scientific Management Is Applied* (1915).

and laborers, noting that "in practically all of the mechanic arts the science which underlies each workman's act is so great and amounts to so much that the workman who is best suited to actually doing the work is incapable, either through lack of education or through insufficient mental capacity, of understanding this science."[46] As managers were transformed into scientists, worker intelligence was belittled, in spite of the fact that many workers knew far more about their jobs than the dispassionate "scientists" observing their every movement. For many Americans, scientific management was the first place science entered into their daily lives in a way that was not limited to school textbooks or quirky anecdotes about Newton's apple; its appearance was tied intimately into workplace politics. Brainpower—that is, obtaining knowledge about science through the scientific entertainments that were available to them—offered the working class an opportunity to offset the imbalance of a scientifically managed workplace and increasing class division; small wonder so many working-class women and men sought opportunities in mass culture to affirm their interest in science even as they resisted its incursions into the workplace.[47]

Representations of intelligence that emboldened and empowered workers also counteracted the gendered implications of science as indicatively male. The influence of scientific management extended far beyond industrial workplaces. A number of prominent women introduced scientific management into the domestic sphere, opening the doors of their homes to a usable scientific process and inaugurating a new site for expanding access to brainpower. Three popular books on the subject—*Household Engineering: Scientific Management in the Home*; *The New Housekeeping: Efficiency Studies in Home Management*; and *Principles of Domestic Engineering, or the What, Why and How of a Home*—appeared between 1913 and 1915. Each of these titles applied the techniques of scientific management to housework, covering such topics as designing the efficient kitchen and chopping for maximum productivity[48] (Figure 2). The women who wrote these books were uniformly insistent about the direct relationship between the scientific value of housework and the elevation of women—socially and psychologically—in the United States. As Christine Frederick wrote:

> I felt that in spite of any difficulty or trying conditions, that I *could* master my house problems—that there *were* solutions, and that there was no such word as "fail" in the whole language of scientific management. I cannot express how much poise and determination came from this efficiency attitude—the attitude of being superior to conditions, of having faith in myself and in my work, to feel that it was drudgery or degrading only if I allowed myself to think so. I felt I was working hand in hand with the efficiency engineers in business, and that what they were accomplishing in industry, I too was accomplishing in the home.[49]

For this author, as for her fellow house workers, scientific management in the home elevated not only the value of her labor but also, by acquiring knowledge of science, her position in society and her sense of self-worth.[50] The introduction of scientific management into the home threatened to upset the gendered division of labor that severely limited the variety of women's work by offering a professional validation for domestic work and promoting

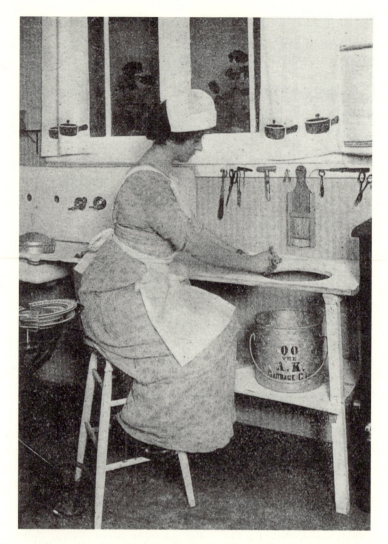

Figure 2. Illustration from Christine Frederick, *Efficient Housekeeping* (1915).

the status of women's labor by legitimizing such work as scientific.[51] The
ideal purpose of scientific management, wrote the author of the 1915 book
Principles of Domestic Engineering, was "to bring the masculine and feminine mind more closely together in the industry of home-making."[52] It was
the mind that could resolve the conflicts of the body, and in brainpower
women found a tool that placed a premium on their domestic labor.

Scientific management reorganized the relationship between intelligence, class, and gender in American society by treating the division of labor born out of modern industry as a natural byproduct of differences in intelligence. According to the literature of scientific management, managers were given their positions because they were intelligent; workers were simply ill-equipped to be managers and insufficiently scientific. Work, it seemed, was for the unintelligent. Yet this was a precarious position to maintain, and working-class popular culture spared no opportunity to offer alternative readings of the scientifically managed shop. By simply representing non-management jobs as intelligent, and by suggesting managers were less smart than they believed themselves to be, ordinary women and men could undermine the logic of class division and position themselves as the true bearers of American brainpower. The latter could be affirmed by reading magazines about science, riding Coney Island roller coasters or visiting baby incubator exhibits, even while discussing math with a horse named Mascot. It could also be affirmed by incorporating scientific management into the practice of everyday life.

Terms for Students

As representations of science in popular culture were becoming more complicated, the popular view of higher education also changed and became inextricably associated with brainpower. At the turn of the century, college students and college life were largely maligned within popular cultural representations, though the characteristics of these representations reveal something at once more complicated and ambiguous. In part, taking jabs at higher education offered another opportunity for ordinary women and men to imagine themselves as capable peers of the intellectual elite and to challenge the dominant assumption that college degrees, unavailable to most Americans, denoted intelligence. Less than 5 percent of eighteen- to twenty-four-year-olds were enrolled in college before 1920.[53] If education was imagined to make students stupider rather than smarter, ordinary women and men who did not have access to colleges and universities might more convincingly imagine themselves to be intelligent. Yet representations of the charm, ease, and pleasures of college life counterbalanced mockery of educational institutions.[54] Higher education was invoked within mass culture to articulate both the promise and anxiety attending to brainpower at this moment: even as popular culture thrashed against America's educational elitism, the underlying belief in brainpower as an equalizer for working-class people exerted a powerful influence over the entertainments ordinary women and men sought.

The turn of the twentieth century witnessed what historian Christopher Lasch has characterized as "a tendency to see cultural issues as inseparable from political ones; so that 'education,' conceived very broadly, came to be seen not merely as a means of raising up an enlightened electorate but as an instrument of social change in its own right."[55] Yet popular songwriters never seemed to tire of mocking and celebrating higher education. "There's a Lot of Things You Never Learn at School," a Tin Pan Alley song published in 1902, took aim at college education in the United States at the turn of the century, poking fun at the middle-class presumption that a college degree would be met with praise, success, and public recognition of a job well done:

> I confess when I left college
> With a bunch of high class knowledge,
> My cranium was not the normal size;
> All the high degrees I'd won them
> All the toughest problems done them
> I simply thought the earth would be my prize.
> But I find my education
> didn't seem to jar the nation
> I find no streets named after me today.[56]

As representations of higher education go, the song offered a decidedly jaded perspective. Though the lyrics made comic light of the assumption that a college education denoted social prestige, audiences were also expected to recognize that this was an arrogant presumption typical of the college graduate, who was both saddled with a massive amount of knowledge and literally big-headed. The narrator confronted twin difficulties in his relationship with knowledge: first, an unimpressed populace that did not particularly care about one's educational background, and second, the failure of higher education to adequately prepare students for modern life.

The song's narrator continued to humorously catalogue examples of scenarios where education resulted in folly. In one verse the song attacked physicians for their frequent failure to cure common ailments and the inferiority of their medical knowledge to folk remedies.

Although Doctors are prolific with their knowledge scientific,
a visit to our home they seldom take,
for dearest old grandmother has a cure somehow or other,
for every kind of ailment pain or ache.

This verse launched a critique of professionalism and elitism, all under the rubric of parodying education. Neither is the gendered dimension incidental here: just as education seemed to confirm class privilege, the growing need for knowledge in navigating modern society, signified through educational institutions whose student bodies largely consisted of men, also diminished and marginalized women's social contributions. The traditional curatives passed down by generations of women were pushed to the peripheries as modern medicine applied scientific methods to the growing business of health. Mothers were replaced with incubators; grandmothers were supplanted with male medical doctors. Popular culture at the turn of the century mocked higher education's exclusivity but also challenged the assumption that education in its present form promoted intelligence. Popular culture dared to ask provocative questions: does education equal intelligence? Is it possible to be educated and unintelligent? Is it possible to be uneducated and intelligent? And finally, how effectively did education provide access to brainpower?

Popular culture tended to fall back on a stock set of representational strategies for depicting the pursuit of higher education. First, representations depicted education as accessible only to the most elite, privileged members of society. Second, and paradoxically, education was also represented as too widely accessible, its value diminished through its democratization. Without any concern for consistency, and sometimes within the same source, cultural representations attacked the inaccessible elitism of the college educated, then commenced to criticizing the devaluation of college education. Third, representations of education focused on the lack of a particular kind of intelligence among even those who had achieved advanced degrees. Fourth, there was an increase in representations of brainpower among African Americans, as black activists and intellectuals such as W. E. B. Du Bois advanced civil rights goals through increasing access to education. Through each of these strategies, popular representations of intelligence, even when they appeared to advance an anti-intellectual position, reinforced the value of brainpower and positioned working-class audiences at the center of discourse about intelligence in popular culture.

Songs depicting higher education in a negative light reached wider audiences, while racial, ethnic, and religious minorities—many of whom comprised the audience for these songs—continued to position themselves as legitimate citizens of the United States by demanding access to education and promoting brainpower among their ranks as a means to equal citizenship. Popular culture's skewering of higher education emerged within a broad reform effort that sought to transform American higher education into a populist project; it is not incidental, then, that representations of intelligence maligning education appeared precisely as education was demanded by the same marginalized groups who seemed most inclined to resent it. Representations belittling educated people destabilized the ideological underpinnings used to keep an intellectual aristocracy in place, upsetting the assumption that education belonged in the hands of the elite because they naturally deserved it or had legitimately earned such privilege. By pointing out the failure of educated people to live up to their promise, popular culture that laughed at college life, incompetent professors, fancy language, and frivolous degrees imagined ordinary women and men as more deserving of education's rewards than the gentlemen who populated the nation's elite universities.

Popular representations of the overly educated gave voice to fantasies about education's decadence and put college graduates on an equal level with their less privileged peers. *The Freshman and the Sophomore*, a 1907 vaudeville skit by Ed Wynn, a writer and performer whose simpleton character was often billed as "The Perfect Fool" and who penned a Broadway show by that name in 1921, entertained audiences with a spirited comic sketch featuring two college students whose malapropisms, puns, and combative wit neatly collapsed cultural anxiety about the failure of a college education to provide job opportunities into a critique of the ineffectiveness of colleges to provide a real education. An educational system that was widely criticized for sanctioning class and racial privilege was revealed to be little more than an instrument for promoting ignorance. "A sophomore is a fellow," explained one character in the skit, "who has been to college a year longer than a Freshman, and in consequence knows much less."[57] In a further articulation of a fantasy where education had no effect on intelligence or financial reward, criticism of the ignorance of college graduates was accompanied with pointed jokes about lack of any increase in wages for college graduates:

S. M. — Yes, and when you graduate with high honors, you become a
    clerk in an office at $5.00 per.
C. — And the errand boy gets $6.00.

Wynn's connection drawn between higher education and lower wages—an
obvious fiction that diverted attention from the actual linkage between
educational achievement and increased wages—indulged a fantasy in which
ordinary audiences could imagine themselves as more valuable (and
wealthy) than their educated comrades. The diminished value of education,
here made into a literal disparity in pay, reinforced working-class women's
and men's sense of their own intelligence; one would have to be a fool to
pursue education instead of financial gain. The brainpower of the working
class was being built up even as the value of education was being knocked
down, and a critical tool for evening social inequalities was disparaged as
frivolous but also accessible. By dissociating college from financial gain or
privilege, *The Freshman and the Sophomore* made higher education into a
mere commodity and signifier of decadence. Education's value was reduced
to conspicuous superficiality, and it took the intelligence of the working
class to uncover this terrible ruse. At the same time, seeing through the
mystique of education's allure made brainpower into a common stock, a step
that had the effect of rendering education accessible and desirable.

Along similar lines, many politically progressive voices targeted the expense of college and the elitism of educated people as a reason for diminishing the value of education. A *Scientific Monthly* article in 1916 charged that
the "jealous guarding of titles and honors, by academics is, in part at least,
due to an ideal which is developing in this democracy of ours, the ideal of an
intellectual aristocracy."[58] Contrasted with the democratic promise imagined in the collapse of high and low culture at the Coney Island Institute or
alongside the Chautauqua's arithmetically gifted horses, higher education
was imagined in popular culture as an archaic reminder of class privilege.
This perspective took on an added political dimension as critics juxtaposed
working-class resourcefulness and college-educated coddling. A 1916 letter
from a self-identified "railroad worker" published in the radical bohemian
magazine *The Masses* suggested how education, as opposed to work, could
reinscribe social inequality rather than undermining it. "A few students work
their way through College," noted this concerned reader, "but most students
are in College because they were lucky in picking out their parents."[59]

The railroad worker's critique debunked the prestige of college by foregrounding higher education's tendency to reinforce class privilege. Far from merely attending to an impulse for anti-intellectualism, exposing the social fact of wealth begetting education facilitated a charge to expand educational opportunities for the working class. Brainpower was thus exacted from the educated elite and reassigned to a working class that lacked not intelligence but access to tools that might allow them to reach their intellectual and social potential—tools that were jealously guarded by the wealthy beneficiaries of the capitalist system. "I believe that our educational system is rotten from the bottom to the top," wrote radical magazine editor William J. Robinson in 1919. "It crushes, in the vast majority of cases, all initiative and power of independent rational thinking. Our universities are the worst in the world, and the presidents of our universities are not chosen for their scholarship but for their success in begging money from the rich."[60]

Divorced from such critique, however, negative assessments of the state of higher education could easily drift into a more reflexive mocking that internalized the rhetorical strategy of diminishing educational value without attaching it to progressive efforts at building brainpower. In 1917, *Half-Century* a black lifestyle magazine launched the previous year, poked light fun at college students.

Student — What are your terms for students?
Landlady — Dead beats and bums.[61]

The joke's humorous play on the landlady's derogatory "terms" relates a suspicion of college students that parallels the railroad worker's complaint, albeit without the social clues that grounded the *Masses* letter in the language of class critique. Still, even when distilled down to their essential scorn, negative assessments of college students tended to highlight the inequality that prevented higher education from being accessible to all. Even the exchange between the student and landlady cast its negative tone in economic terms, critiquing the college student's easy-going idleness. Popular magazines routinely attempted to resuscitate college's reputation alongside efforts to knock entitled university students down a peg. "Ill fares our educational system," warned an editor in the progressive magazine *Good Morning*, "when the impression gains currency that no good can come out of a college unless it is kicked out."[62]

Representations of college students as privileged, decadent, unambitious, intellectually challenged, and frivolous thus walked a fine line between deriding the unmistakable class privilege implicit in the nation's unequal educational system and praising the real social benefits of higher education that had the potential to redress precisely this inequality. A piece of doggerel in *Good Morning* sidestepped this conflict by taking on the university president rather than professors and students:

The college president makes a show
Of shrewd and erudite avowments,
But yet he's careful not to know
Too much to scare off fat endowments.[63]

Representing a cynically sagacious president allowed that brainpower legitimately threatened the corporate structure of American colleges and universities; to "know too much" was to challenge the power of wealth housed in the university's administrative offices. Though this poem was critical of the class privilege preserved in American colleges, it also did the work of acknowledging brainpower's potential threat.

Though many cultural texts oscillated ambiguously between affirming brainpower's radical potential and criticizing the class inequality housed in U.S. colleges and universities, others affirmed brainpower by resolving conflicted representations through reference to heteronormative sexuality in university life. These representations asserted that intelligence was organically connected to heterosexuality. One such text, a popular song from 1907 teasingly titled "Watch the Professor," proffered a bold claim that professors made excellent lovers, at least in the bedroom. "There is a certain knack, / Most people seem to lack / In making love," the song chided. "Watch the professor, and you'll learn a thing or two, / Watch the Professor and you'll know just what to do." Linking knowledge with sexuality had roots going back to at least the nineteenth century, when access to sexual knowledge was suppressed out of fear that it would lead to carnal activity.[64] In early twentieth-century representations, however, the presumed sexual knowledge of professors was treated as a healthy and vigorous quality, and positioning educated people as robust lovers suggested that one did not have to choose between intelligence or sex; brain or body. Brainpower could be met with and even demanded physical exertion. "Yes, I am watching," replied the student upon being directed to watch the professor, "and it makes me very tired."[65]

The emphasis upon sexual prowess in "Watch the Professor" overlapped with another popular musical form of the early twentieth century:

the college song. Dozens of these appeared between 1900 and 1920 to celebrate the dashing young college student, who was represented as bold, ambitious, and fun-loving.[66] Though these songs focused on the carefree and
licentious proclivities of the college student, they did important work in coun-
tering representations of intelligence that conceived brainpower as emasculating, intelligence as de-sexing, and mental labor as disembodied. Most
often these songs depicted confident, robust, and sexually appealing college
men. A 1909 song celebrated the college boy's brash temerity: "He'll rush in
where angels fear to tread / He's a college boy / With his college walk / and
his college talk." The carefree, privileged college boy was represented as
sexually adventurous and irresistible. "Girlies shout for joy / life for him is a
toy."[67] The college song aligned college with sexual conquest, eliminating
signifiers connecting college class and social privilege in favor of extolling
male virility. These songs were conflicted in their celebrations; if life was a
"toy" for the college boy, this also meant that he was in a privileged position
where labor was unnecessary. The solidarity of maleness trumped the anxieties precipitated by the class stratification found and reified in the nation's
educational institutions, and representations of college as a sexual play-
ground diminished the social division between those who could and could
not attend a university. Yet in a society that valued work, the reckless pursuit
of leisure represented by the college boy also suggested his exceptionalism.

Though most of the college songs focused on ribald young men, there
was also a sub-category that focused specifically on women—most often the
new co-ed.[68] Women in the early twentieth century were enrolling in colleges and universities at a rate that outpaced their male counterparts, and by
the time of World War I they had nearly achieved numerical proportional-
ity.[69] Between 1907 and 1915, the number of male students enrolled in U.S.
colleges increased from 91,344 to 141,679, a 55 percent increase. Women
students, on the other hand, increased their ranks from 31,187 enrolled in
1907 to 79,763 in 1915, a 156 percent increase. These numbers were similar
for professors: male professors increased 39 percent, whereas women increased 117 percent. Among graduate students, the statistics are even more
staggering. Male graduate students increased 100 percent, whereas females
increased 207 percent.[70] Though the total figures still showed a dispropor-
tionate number of male students, women were affecting the shape of college
life, a reality that was reflected in cultural representations. Though the
academic achievement of women was often overlooked, a number of songs
balanced cheerful discussion of women's sexual appeal with celebrations

of their intelligence. "Here's to the girl in college / here's to her charming ways!" one song, bluntly titled "Co-Ed," pronounced. "Here's to the girl of knowledge / pride of our student days."[71] The song might have lacked substance—the woman was rewarded not for her groundbreaking work in neurology, but rather for her feminine charm—but it did recognize that her charm was supplemented with knowledge.[72] Brainpower was acknowledged and normalized in even these conflicted texts.

The college song appeared at a moment when universities were opening their doors to women in co-education environments and single-sex schools. This resulted in both celebratory and condemnatory cultural texts. Those texts that mocked educated women recognized that brainpower had the potential to disrupt gender inequality. In 1916 Maurice Becker published a cartoon in *The Masses*, a popular magazine appealing to bohemian, radical, and intellectual audiences (Figure 3). Two contemporary-looking women were depicted conversing while holding stacks of oversized books. "Let's go out to central park and look at the animals," suggests one. "I can't, I've got to study my zoology," the other replies. The central joke in this cartoon highlighted the irony attached to a student's immersion in books at the expense of enjoying real life. Though his tone was not especially caustic, Becker's cartoon nonetheless gently nudged at the consequences of book learning. The joke channeled anxiety about the potential for education, not incidentally about a scientific subject, to distract from real-world pursuits. At the same time, the cartoon casually incorporated gender and higher education into its analysis. The sex of the characters in the cartoon was made explicit. These smartly dressed women were also demonstrably beyond high school age, and their massive textbooks bespoke a highly academic book learning. Though *The Masses* ostensibly attempted to challenge the sexism that was dominant in American culture and society, the magazine was still a largely male-driven affair, and this cartoon articulated a widespread cultural anxiety about educated women. Education had the potential to upset gender hierarchies, just as it had the potential to undo the algorithm of class. Brainpower's threat was celebrated and contained within mass culture, where educated women were both visible and dangerous.

Representations of educated women often made their intelligence symptomatic of a refusal to be satisfied with the simple expectations of normative gender behavior. Representations of intelligent women undermined efforts to exclude women from participating in the discourse around brainpower while also exposing its limits. A joke printed in the *Michigan Baptist*

Figure 3. Cartoon from *The Masses*, February 1916, by Maurice Becker.

Advance in 1916 illustrates the tendency for representations of educated women to stop short of making radical demands:

> FIRST CO-ED: I've lost a diminutive, argentous, truncated cone, convex on its summit, and semi-perforated with symmetrical indentations.
>   SECOND CO-ED: Here's your thimble.[73]

This joke capitalized on the humor in using fancy words to describe something simple and ordinary. It also specifically targeted co-eds trying out big words to describe simple feminine pursuits. Representations of education, then, acknowledged the increased visibility of women in higher education. Even when mocking women, however, these representations made visible the potential for brainpower to fundamentally shift women's vernacular culture and bring male and female knowledge into alignment.

African American reformers explicitly represented education as a tool for social advancement. Compared with white women, African Americans had fewer inroads into existing American universities; this was a period just emerging from what historian Rayford Logan has referred to as the "nadir" of American race relations.[74] African Americans formed groups such as the Niagara Movement, NAACP, and Negro Academy to address grievances against racism and segregation, and public intellectuals, including Du Bois and Hubert Harrison, educated the masses about the tragic consequences of white racial hegemony.[75] Popular representations of education among African Americans tended to complement formal education with the intelligence one gained from surviving racism. "Plain it is to us," wrote Du Bois, "that what the world seeks through desert and wild we have within our threshold."[76] This knowledge offered opportunities to black women and men that could be used as a political weapon—and to fend off the ignorance of institutionalized knowledge. "Get education," wrote the social reformer and black education activist Hubert Harrison in 1919. "Get it not only in school and college, but in books and newspapers, in market-places, institutions, and movements. Prepare by knowing; and never think you know until you have listened to ten others who know differently—and have survived the shock."[77] Intelligence, as Harrison conceived it, moved beyond simply participating in the practices of the nation's educational institutions. In order to truly confront racism, intelligence was required, and this was only possible through the accretion of knowledge outside the self-perpetuating institutions of schools and colleges. "New leadership must come," wrote Chandler Owen in *The Messenger*, "leadership of intelligence and character. Leaders must not only have good intentions, but information. Virtuous, but ignorant leadership, is fatal."[78] Brainpower was connected to race consciousness.

Yet less intellectually ambitious black periodicals also continued to criticize intelligence and education for appealing to so-called race leaders and talented-tenthers detached from the experiences of ordinary women and men. These discussions accentuated the accumulated wisdom of African Americans while expressing skepticism about the capacity for institutional knowledge to centralize black concerns. Popular periodicals in particular were critical of elite journals such as *The Crisis* and *The Messenger* that demanded African Americans constantly theorize the effects of racism and celebrate educational achievement as a sign of racial progress. The relatively short-lived *Half-Century*, drafted its editorial policy to counter the grandiose rhetoric of highbrow black magazines. "It will not be our sole ambition," wrote Katherine E. Williams in the inaugural issue of 1916, "to make this magazine a 'literary gem' either for our own gratification or to suit the fancy of the 'high-brows,' but to present facts in plain, commonsense language, so that the masses may read and understand . . . we propose to call a 'spade a *spade*' and not an 'excavating instrument for manual manipulation.'"[79] This populist call for vernacular language was articulated even more bluntly two issues later, when the editors wrote that

> *The Half-Century Magazine* founded its policy on the outstart of not desiring manuscripts with indigestible 'philosophy, science, sociology and eloquence.' The folks who write such stuff are evidently animated with a desire to display the profundity of their wisdom and knowledge. Far be it from our motives to detract from the importance and worth of such knowledge—but from the standpoint of our own interests, our business welfare and success, we have not been able to see as yet where a discussion of, say, *The Psychological Effect of Heat Waves on Jelly Fish* would contribute even remotely, not to say directly, towards increasing the circulation of *Half-Century*.[80]

Still, such viewpoints did not exist in isolation. It was only because other "literary gems" had saturated the marketplace that a space for less explicitly intellectual fare such as *The Half-Century* could exist. Magazines such as *The Messenger* continued to publish articles celebrating intelligence and education as the primary tools of black liberation.[81] For African Americans living in a nation founded on their exclusion from institutionalized political and social empowerment, brainpower represented a tool well suited to challenging the illogic of racism.

Mass Culture's Radical Arsenal

The emphasis upon intelligence's potential for liberation and brainpower as an essential weapon for waging class warfare mobilized radical communities and accelerated leftist cultural production. With an increased prominence, through their ability to manufacture and distribute mass-produced magazines, tracts, and books, early twentieth-century radicals questioned the notion that intelligence could ever be apolitical, while attempting to harness the potential for brainpower to advance explicitly leftist political goals. Mass culture represented a venue through which radicals could reach large audiences of ordinary women and men who were conversant in the language of popular consumption. Rather than using these outlets as an elevating mechanism for uplifting the masses, radical magazines and popular presses became key sites for asserting the intelligence of the ordinary women and men who would form the backbone of the socialist movement.

In a 1905 issue of *The Comrade*, a slick, mass-produced socialist magazine, one writer complained that "the chief function of colleges like Columbia is to train and let loose upon society a swarm of brutal and cowardly bullies, which, we take it, is the accredited equipment for a young man who expects to make his way under the capitalist system of industry."[82] Mass culture was offered up as a counter-institution valuable for offsetting universities' capitalization of brainpower. The Appeal Book Department in Girard, Kansas, placed advertisements in radical magazines in 1915 stating that they were "fully prepared to supply you with books, pamphlets and leaflets on Socialism." The language in this advertisement illustrates how brainpower was being promoted as an ideological weapon: to "supply" meant that the books would constitute part of an arsenal. Yet it was not only propaganda that would advance the socialist cause; the purchase of any cheap, mass-produced books would promote brainpower. "We also handle books on science, literature, and history," the advertisement continued. "In fact, we can supply you with any book on the market."[83] Though socialism might have comprised the most critical form of knowledge, brainpower itself was promoted as a political intervention regardless of subject.[84] Similarly, equipping a cadre of socialists and workers with books could both diminish the class distinctions implicit in the currency of an intellectual class and force intellectuals who believed themselves at a comfortable remove from mass culture to recognize the common beliefs and intelligence of their radical comrades.

Cheap, mass-produced editions of classic works of literature were also marketed at bargain prices to working-class consumers as a tool for advancing brainpower and diminishing the class inequality that separated the privileged educated class from working-class women and men. In his 1903 review of a mass-produced Shakespeare companion, prominent socialist theorist John Spargo optimistically announced that "with it the humble possessor of a cheap copy of Shakespeare's works is on an intellectual level with the owner of any of the expensive annotated editions."[85] Consuming mass-produced books about Shakespeare was conceived as crumbling the foundation of class hierarchies; brainpower, accessible through the wide circulation of mass-produced books, had the potential to dismantle the logic of capitalism and to free workers from the chains of ignorance that drove them to supinely accept a marginal share in American political, social, cultural, and economic life.

A 1916 book review of a socialist program in *The Masses* suggests how mass culture acted as a catalyst for producing brainpower much as a scientist generated results in a laboratory:

> We may conceive our scientists as producing this revolutionizing substance [knowledge] in their laboratories and libraries—as yet only in small quantities, like radium. And we like to think of ourselves as putting little bits of it here and there in people's minds where it will have the most effect in disintegrating established modes of thought. But after people have suffered the first pains of seeing their old ideas destroyed, they commence to enjoy the process, and the best service we can render them is to send them straight to the storehouses where this revolutionalizing substance is piled up.[86]

The most immediate concern of most radicals, of course, was educating the masses about the specific goals and strategies for advancing their party's stature and numbers. To this end, the Socialist Party built up a cadre among their ranks skilled in the ways of teaching ordinary men and women the principles of socialism. Yet the persistent socialist concern with producing knowledge more generally, chiefly through producing and consuming mass-produced books, meant that brainpower was rhetorically linked with radical ideas.

Not all magazines embraced brainpower as truly radical. An editorial in *Why?* magazine castigated those who restricted their efforts to promoting brainpower as "goody-goody, pious, sissified, scientific Socialists."[87] The editors decried education and reading as inferior to direct action, strikes, and public demonstrations. This brand of socialism conceived radical interest in brainpower as a dangerous feminization of the movement and a turning away from the hard edge of immediate demands for action. Representations of brainpower as feminine emerged largely within radical communities, an unfortunate irony that had deleterious consequences when conservatives glommed onto this idea in the 1950s. Within radical popular culture, brainpower was paradoxically depicted as both indicative of clearthinking masculinity but also as a sentimental softening of political action into feminine idealism.[88]

Radicalism shifted the parameters of brainpower and representations of intelligence in various significant ways. Socialist strategies emphasizing working-class brainpower indelibly marked intelligence with the tint of radical ideas: intelligent women and men were represented as likely radicals, and the allure of brainpower was inextricable from the seductions of socialism, anarchism, and one-big-unionism. Radicalism also brought brainpower more closely in alignment with ordinary women and men. Socialists, anarchists, and other radicals challenged the cultural capital afforded intelligence, promoted programs and courses to educate the working class, and placed hope in an intellectual revolution. In so doing, they brought a characteristic largely associated with the elite into the purview of ordinary folk. This representational strategy limited the potential for brainpower to be blindly criticized as a tool of class oppression and presented ideal conditions for expanding intellectual democracy.

*   *   *

Throughout this chapter I have suggested how popular culture at the turn of the twentieth century already tended toward a high-spirited engagement with brainpower. In songs about science, cartoons about college, and handbooks on housekeeping, mass culture audiences were treated as colleagues and specialists; they were represented as intelligent and their interest in developing their brainpower was virtually assumed. Coney Island's Sabbath-day denizens followed a script that was repeated throughout popular culture at this moment; no wonder the 300,000 visitors that first Sunday were willing to play along with the fundamental supposition that mass culture could be a serious site for education and brainpower could legitimize working-class taste.

Mass culture represented a critical site for establishing and shaping an organic intellectual tradition in the United States. The story of brainpower speaks to the relationship between those possessing power and those seeking social, cultural, and political empowerment. The familiar narrative of intellectual uplift, whether in the form of intellectuals lifting up common folk or of working-class people accessing educational institutions, hardly factors into popular culture at this time. The texts produced for mass audiences in the early twentieth century were as likely to defy the narrative of uplift as they were to seek it. Neither was anti-intellectualism a dominant trope. When it appeared it was in contrast to the organic intellectualism of ordinary women and men. A preponderance of cultural texts acknowledged the value of brainpower by conceiving ordinary women and men as intelligent; the cultural politics of intelligence became in turn an important site for working out politics.

Taken together, the cultural texts discussed in this chapter reveal a striking set of contradictory impulses, ambivalences, and ill-conceived strategies embedded within popular culture. Brainpower was evidently a concept that was very much in flux, and Americans' fascination with popular culture was inextricable from their interest in intellectual pursuits which in turn were filtered through mass culture. These cultural texts also suggest how representations of intelligence were being used and created to challenge hierarchies of power in the United States, articulate the values of the working class, and cultivate sites of political action among minoritized groups. Popular songs and amusement parks became highly politicized sites in which marginalized Americans could have their voices heard, their ideas respected, and their intellect rewarded. The early decades of the twentieth century represented a time of tremendous flux in representations, and the diffuse channels through which intelligence was being conceived rendered a simple representational strategy more elusive. Yet by the end of this period, particularly following World War I, many of these divergent ideas moved into closer alignment. The appearance of Albert Einstein presented an occasion for working out the contradictory representational strategies applied to intelligence. Though Einstein would not resolve the conflicts and paradoxes, he was made into a common subject for exploring the relation between class, intelligence, science, mass culture, and American identity. Professor Einstein introduced popular culture audiences to the strangely alluring world of theoretical physics.

2

The Force of Complicated
Mathematics: Einstein Enters American Culture

Einstein has come by force of
complicated mathematics
among the tormented fruit trees
to buy freedom for the daffodils
till the unchained orchards
shake their tufted flowers

—William Carlos Williams

Albert Einstein first visited the United States in 1921, two years after the experiments confirming his theory of relativity made him an American celebrity. In honor of his appearance on U.S. soil, the *New York Call Magazine*, a supplement to a socialist newspaper, published a cartoon featuring the scientist engaged in a perplexing conflict with President Warren G. Harding (Figure 4). In this two-panel cartoon, Einstein confounded Harding with his hopelessly complex theory of relativity, only to find himself similarly confused by the knotty language of Harding's speeches. This humorous comic made light of Einstein's intellectual sophistication while also targeting Harding's tangled political pronouncements. Though Harding's inability to grasp Einstein's theory was based on an actual event—the *New York Times* reported on April 6 that Harding had "failed to grasp the relativity idea"—the cartoon capitalized upon Einstein's genius to conceive readers' confusion as political.[1] The apparent consensus about his extraordinary brainpower made Einstein into an ironic populist figure: though he was

Figure 4. Cartoon from *New York Call Magazine*, May 1, 1921.

hardly ordinary, his befuddlement at Harding's speech legitimized ordinary Americans' confusion and transformed Einstein into one of the masses. Americans who had never advanced in their studies beyond basic arithmetic could now imagine themselves as little Einsteins.

On its most overt level the *New York Call* cartoon employed Einstein as an archetypal genius, used by the cartoonist to illustrate both the complexity of Harding's speeches and the inability of even the most intelligent to understand him. Yet the value of Einstein as a figure for articulating (and occasionally resolving) paradoxical ideas about brainpower in the United States is further complicated in another cartoon published in *American*

WHEN PROFESSOR EINSTEIN CALLED
ON PRESIDENT HARDING

Figure 5. Cartoon from *American Monthly*, July 1921.

Monthly's July 1921 issue featuring Harding and Einstein similarly locked in mutual confusion, this time over Harding's use of the neologism "normalcy" (Figure 5). Though Harding and Einstein were not publicly linked in any but a handful of articles, their entanglements in popular representation illustrate how Einstein was used to stand in for American ideas about intelligence, citizenship, and identity in the postwar years.[2] He might have been most famous as a scientist, but representations of Einstein reveal that

Americans also imagined him as a foreigner and a fellow citizen; a dangerous enemy and a beloved friend. He was rarely depicted alongside other
scientists. Instead he was represented accompanying political figures, ordinary women and men, or, most often, alone. Because of his complicated national, ethnic, and political identity and oversized brain, Einstein was
uniquely available to be used by Americans to embody, without fully resolving, contradictory impulses about the relationship between intelligence and
modern American identities. Einstein became, in short, a key figure for
working out the politics of brainpower in American culture.

Relativity for the Masses

The backdrop of World War I shaped attitudes toward Einstein's theory in
a number of complicated ways. In 1917 few Americans remained neutral
about the decision to enter World War I. Though Woodrow Wilson's foreign
policy was initially founded upon his commitment to neutrality, by spring
1917 his mood had changed. "Woe be to the man or group of men," he
boldly declared in a 1917 speech, "that seek to stand in our way."[3] Wilson's
transformation from spokesman for national neutrality to mouthpiece of
hawkish resolve has been widely documented.[4] Yet as surely as his official
policy shifted slowly from neutral ambiguity to hard-line determination, so
the American people needed a good deal of coaxing to shift their support
from isolationism to advocacy for a world war with incalculable human
costs.[5] This transformation was initiated in part through national politics:
speeches and policy resolutions; congressional acts; and presidential orders. But such efforts never fully swayed national sentiment. Capitol Hill
had much greater success in changing minds than in changing hearts, and
minds alone could not convince a nation to go to war.

American military success in World War I depended in part upon a
wholesale myth of national unity.[6] "Many of the spokesmen who cried for
greater military strength" during the war, historian David Kennedy has
written, "frequently spoke in the next breath about the necessity to create—by
coercion if necessary—a strong, unifying nationalist sentiment among the
immigrant masses where no such sentiment appeared to exist."[7] The question confronting leaders about to bring the United States into a war that
barely touched most Americans in their daily lives was crystal clear. How
would the requisite unity ever come to a nation struggling with its own

internal dissension in the forms of ethnic tension and racial segregation? The experience of war also precipitated an intensive redefinition of American identity. One element of this discussion was an investigation of the meanings, effects, and implications of brainpower in American culture. Would providing tools for Americans to pursue their education or represent themselves as intelligent offset other forms of oppression? Or would intelligence exacerbate social inequality and make unity impossible?

Three historical factors served to reorganize cultural understandings of brainpower in the United States between 1919 and 1924. First, the experiments supporting Einstein's theory of relativity simultaneously introduced a new popular image of the theoretical scientist and rendered scientific theories wholly inaccessible to mass culture. The scientific manager, the professor, and the college boy were supplanted with the Einstein: the archetypal genius. Second, the advent and conclusion of World War I introduced new technology and modern systems of war that reframed discussions of intelligence on American soil; no one could any longer doubt that brainpower had unfathomable potential to wreak global havoc. This expansion of technology during the war created a need for experts to navigate the modern world and introduced anxiety about the dangerous potential for new forms of mass destruction. Third, the Russian revolution offered a real example of what theory could mean for nations. Though concerns about Bolshevism were substantially different from fears of relativity, the spirit of modern warfare and political revolution pointed to the need to diffuse the power of intellectuals, affirm the brainpower of ordinary women and men (lest they be swayed by dangerous ideologies), and expose the dangers of radical intelligence.

Einstein developed his theory of relativity in 1905, but his findings did not appear in American popular culture until his highly technical mathematical calculations of planetary measurements were confirmed during a 1919 lunar eclipse. Even then relativity was a curious media story: the theory had no immediate potential for practical application; Einstein's theory merely described the physical world in a particular way. The anxiety relativity provoked, then, is unusual within the history of scientific developments in the United States. Contrasted with Freud or Edison, for example, whose theories were met with a new set of practices and a popular usage, Einstein's theory had very little everyday impact. One *New York Times* author mused, "while Edison was an inventor who dealt with practical and material things, [Einstein] was a theorist who dealt with problems of space and of the universe."[8] Americans nonetheless greeted the theory with a hysterical frenzy of interest. Books and articles attempted to put relativity in layperson's terms.[9] In 1920, Eugene Higgins cooperated with *Scientific American* to offer a $5,000 award to any author who could explain relativity to the ordinary reader in fewer than 3,000 words. The editors of the magazine observed that "the whole subject had caught the popular attention so strongly, that even complete initial failure to discover what it was all about did not discourage the general reader from pursuing the matter."[10]

Readers of the *New York Times* had opened their newspapers on Sunday, November 6, 1919, to a perplexing headline: "Eclipse Showed Gravity Variation / Diversion of Light Rays Accepted as Affecting Newton's Principles / HAILED AS EPOCHMAKING / British scientist calls the discovery one of the greatest achievements." In a relatively balanced and cautious article, the *Times* reported that the results of an experiment conducted earlier in the year had confirmed Albert Einstein's theory of relativity. The article cautioned, "the effects on practical astronomy . . . of the verification of Einstein's theory were not very great. It was chiefly in the field of philosophic thought that the change would be felt." The precise features of the Einstein theory, as of the experiment that confirmed it, were left vague. The possibility that the findings "would completely revolutionize the accepted fundamentals of physics" was mentioned, but this claim was muted by the abstract complexity of the experiment's findings. References to Einstein himself or doubts as to the experiment's veracity were entirely absent. Readers were instead presented with what was considered the vital, newsworthy information about an esoteric scientific experiment: it had taken place, its results had been announced, and scientists would adjust their hypotheses accordingly.[11]

By the following day, the *Times*'s cool approach to the story was giving way to decidedly more apocalyptic headlines. "Lights All Askew in the Heavens," one announced on November 10: "Men of science more or less agog over results of eclipse observations / EINSTEIN THEORY TRIUMPHS / Stars Not Where They Seemed or Were Calculated to Be, But Nobody Need Worry. / A BOOK FOR 12 WISE MEN / No More in All the World Could Comprehend it, Said Einstein When His Daring Publishers Accepted It."[12] On November 16, one short week after the initial report of the experiment, the *Times* published an editorial by Columbia University professor Charles Lane Poor that disputed Einstein's theory as evidence for the influence of Bolshevism in physics.[13]

The urgent desire among nonspecialized audiences to understand relativity was in part driven by a populist impulse toward obscuring the division between the educated elite and the common masses. Particularly troubling was the fact that Einstein's theory of relativity openly defied common sense; it implied that ordinary people's observations were always wrong. The theory created a fissure between ordinary and intelligent Americans at the same time as it revealed the simple wrongness of ordinary people's knowledge. It was not simply a matter of inequality, then; the brainpower of the intellectual class was suddenly revealed to be objectively better, more honest, and totally inaccessible to all but the most elite dozen. One (very) amateur poet described this challenge to common observation in the form of a cracked nursery rhyme, a familiar form associated with literal infants that invoked the anxiety surrounding the revelation that ordinary women and men were no more sophisticated in their observations of the world than small children:

> Twinkle, Twinkle little star
> Give us answer from afar . . .
> Tell us why you have of late
> Turned from pathways that are straight . . .
> Little star don't make us guess!
> Rather wouldn't you confess
> Why you try with all your might
> To deflect your starry light?[14]

The appearance of relativity concentrated scientific knowledge in the minds of experts as it questioned the ability of everyday folk to trust their own powers of observation. Who could ever again trust the masses to be empowered with self-government when their understanding of the natural world was so hopelessly misguided? Ordinary Americans were instructed that they could not believe their own eyes—relativity dismantled the ability of ordinary intelligence to see and describe reality accurately—at the precise moment when a more accurate model was limited to only the most educated Americans. "Albert Einstein has come around," wrote another would-be poet in 1921, "to tell Princeton what he's found / That Isaac Newton had unsound / Ideas of gravitation."[15] Relativity did not merely compartmentalize a particular field of specialization that was inaccessible to ordinary folk; it rendered all ordinary intelligence false.

Many representations of Einstein belonged to broader efforts to restore the power of observation to ordinary women and men and affirm the rightfulness of their intelligence. Two strategies for restoring ordinary Americans' brainpower emerged in early discussion of the theory. The first emphasized the infuriating complexity of relativity to highlight the overlap between ordinary women and men and intellectuals' equally deficient and defiantly commonsensical understanding of the world. These representations imagined relativity as a site of mutual ignorance, a critical gap in knowledge shared by both advanced scientists and the uneducated masses. There was certainly no denying that the theory of relativity was so complicated it left both trained scientists and ordinary Americans—alongside President Harding—hopelessly perplexed. The *New York Times* description of scientists as "agog," for example, served to align highly intelligent scientists with common folk: physicists were confused and surprised, just like the masses. Though Einstein's emphasis upon the theory's complicated math might have exacerbated the division between ordinary and very intelligent Americans, popular media also emphasized the inaccessibility of the theory to all but the most elite dozen; ignorance and disbelief were conceived as overwhelmingly unifying rather than dividing. Rather than accentuating the distance between the intelligence of ordinary women and men and their highly educated counterparts, such representations emphasized their shared confusion.

Second, the seemingly endless discussions of Einstein and relativity within American popular media further bridged the division between experts and ordinary folk by representing both as eager consumers of knowledge. A fictional dialogue placed at the beginning of famous science writer Edwin Slosson's 1920 book, *Easy Lessons on Einstein*, illustrates the important role of newspapers in popularizing relativity and bringing together the intellectual elite and the lowbrow audiences:

> *The Reader* (looking over the top of a morning paper): Here's something queer—a whole page taken with a new discovery in physics—"Eclipse Observations Confirm Einstein's Theory of Relativity." Anything about it in your paper?
>
> *The Author*: Yes. Here's a cartoon on it by McCutcheon.
>
> *The Reader*: Must be something to it then. McCutcheon always knows what's news.[16]

Slosson's vignette envisioned a conversation that placed Einstein's theory in the hands of ordinary women and men at the precise moment when theoretical developments in physics demanded a specialized vocabulary.

The visibility of relativity in newspapers and comic strips suggested the curious interest of the masses in expanding their brainpower and pointed to the intellectual potential within mass culture. Slosson's exchange positioned Einstein as a liminal figure straddling the threshold between elite specialists and mass audiences, and much of the discussion about relativity that appeared in popular culture focused equally on dissecting what meaning could be derived from its persistent fashionability. "With their columns crowded with news of grave economic and political disturbances at home and abroad," an author noted in a 1920 article in the liberal news-magazine *New Republic*, "it was a rather liberal conception of what is really important that prompted our daily newspapers to find room for a report of a discussion on the nature of light and gravitation."[17] Liberal it certainly was, though not only in the sense this author intended. The interest in relativity was motivated in no small measure by a liberal myth of American democracy that protested the appearance of any form of elitism or exclusion. Liberalism was offered as explanation for Einstein's mass appeal and justification for the frenzied pursuit of accessible explanations of Einstein's theory. "Prof. Einstein may be considered the greatest living scientist," sniped the editors of the City College of New York's student newspaper, "but don't forget that we passed Physics 3 the second time we took it."[18] If the United States were truly a democratic republic, the ordinary and the intellectual elite had to find common ground.

Efforts at representing relativity as a theory that appealed to the masses were conceived within popular culture as reflecting a liberal political strategy for reprieving inequality in the United States. A 1921 *New York Times* article explicitly addressed the pressing question why relativity should find such a large popular audience specifically in the United States. "The true answer," the author determined, "is democracy. The Declaration of Independence itself is outraged that there is anything on earth, or in interstellar space, that can be understood only by the chosen few."[19] The Declaration of Independence was invoked here as a document that gestured toward the brainpower of the masses and the need to cultivate intelligence among ordinary women and men. Popular representations of Einstein were necessary for a functioning republic; neglecting relativity would lead the masses into tyranny. The author's appeal to the Declaration of Independence also hints at how relativity presented an occasion for a defense of American exceptionalism; as will become evident later, the ongoing discussion about relativity was offered as evidence for U.S. superiority not only internationally, but intergalactically as well.[20] In this article, the surprising anthropomorphism of the Declaration of

Independence preserved the uniquely national character of the quest for intelligence as a signifier of freedom, equality, and, of course, independence.

The link between U.S. democracy, brainpower, and the desire of the masses to understand relativity was repeatedly invoked in magazines and newspapers as the only possible explanation for what the poet William Carlos Williams memorably termed the "force of complicated mathematics." A *New Republic* article from 1921 described the American quest to understand relativity as the termination point of Western Enlightenment:

> Western civilization, beginning with Greek rationalism, is opposed to the oriental caste distinction between the esoteric and the exoteric. Free civilization means that everyone's reason is competent to explore the facts of nature for himself. But the recent development of science, involving even greater mastery of complicated technique, means in effect a return to an artificial barrier between the uninitiated layman and the initiated expert. If, therefore, the essence of western civilization is to be preserved, we need not only a higher level of general education but a class of general popularizers who will aim not to humor tired minds but to guide man's thirst for knowledge to the sources of its deepest satisfaction.[21]

Not content merely to attribute the pursuit of relativity to the Declaration of Independence, the *New Republic* universalized interest in relativity as a natural product of "liberal western civilization," "Greek rationalism," and "free civilization." In short, American hunger to understand relativity, and, correlatively, the U.S. media's stalwart efforts to deliver digestible explanations of it, were conceived as carving a prominent space for American intelligence within the history of "western" progress.[22] Americans reading about relativity were envisaged as the natural heirs to those great minds who paved the way for the bold democratic experiment that became the United States of America, and the brainpower of the masses seemed symptomatic of the natural order of democratic progress.

Though many media reports conceived popular interest in relativity as an auspicious sign for American liberalism, others capitalized on the occasion as a long-awaited opportunity to attack other nations as incompetent, aggrandizing the brainpower of the American masses to advance a nationalist project. John Malcolm Bird, editor of *Einstein's Theories*, a popular anthology featuring essays entered into a contest to render relativity understandable for the masses, mocked the submissions of "foreigners" who entered the contest because "most of them were distinctly below par as literary composition," and their authors' "English was so execrable as to make them quite out of the question."[23] An editor at *Scientific American* similarly attacked one would-be popularizer's "colossal ignorance of the English language."[24] The discourse surrounding relativity was used to conceive scientific understanding as uniquely available to those who already had a clear point of entry into American cultural citizenship.

In contrast to the "colossal ignorance" of foreigners, Americans were represented as having been organically inclined toward intellectual pursuits even before Einstein's theory hit the news. Kenneth W. Payne, editor of *Popular Science Monthly*, reflected in 1921 on Americans' passion for relativity by contrasting it with "the appalling ignorance of the European masses." Payne continued in an effort to defend and explain America's interest in Einstein:

> We have over a million and a half readers of the popular scientific magazines—over three and a half million if engineering and technical magazines are included. What European nation can even approach such figures showing widespread popular interest in science? We have over 50,000,000 readers of the daily and Sunday papers. And where are the European papers that give the same consistent play to scientific developments that ours do?[25]

Payne's statistics were staggering. His massive numbers dazzled with their incontrovertible evidence for the intellectual superiority of Americans over Europeans. Significantly, Payne's evidence also foregrounded mass culture as a site for asserting American intelligence. Rather than positioning mass culture against intellectual pursuits in a defensive gesture, Payne instead offered mass culture consumption as symptomatic of American brainpower. Noting the many readers of "popular scientific magazines" and the prodigious base of American newspaper subscribers, Payne suggested that Americans were exceptionally intelligent precisely because of their rabid consumption of mass culture. One can almost hear in Payne's defensive statistics George Tilyou's plaintive cry, "aren't we educational here too?" That magazine consumption was mentioned before statistics of educational achievement indicates how central mass culture was in organizing American ideas about Einstein and relativity, as well as affirming the value of brainpower in the culture industries.[26]

Media discussions about relativity appeared in the same newspapers, and often on the same pages, as stories about national politics. The collapse of science and politics in the headlines further connected relativity with the growth of liberal democracy for mass audiences. A debate about Einstein on the floor of the U.S. House of Representatives in 1921 made relativity's implications for democracy explicit. When New York representative John J. Kindred began to address relativity, Representative Joseph Walsh of Massachusetts declared, "ordinarily we confine matters that are to appear in the Congressional Record to things that one of average intelligence can understand." Kindred, unconvinced, responded that relativity "may bear upon the legislations of the future as to general relations of the cosmos."[27] In what was framed by Walsh as a stark disruption of the populist nature of congressional debate—an ironic claim given how frequently congressional debate dipped into the arcane banality of legal jargon—it was incumbent on all who valued the future of American government to understand Einstein's complicated mathematics.

In keeping with emerging appeals to raise the level of average intelligence, popular media stories about relativity pointed to the shared enthusiasm and common language adopted by armchair enthusiasts and scientific specialists as they grappled with Einstein's theory. These reports offered opportunities for newspaper readers to align their intellects with highly trained physicists, in part by allowing common sense to creep into mass-cultural discussions of relativity. "Some cynics suggest," allowed one newspaper writer, "that the Einstein theory is only a scientific version of the well known phenomenon that a coin in a basin of water is not on the spot where it seems to be and ask what is new in the refraction of light."[28] The inclusion of "cynical" viewpoints in discussions of theoretical physics, especially those based on quotidian observations familiar to all, implied that ordinary readers would be permitted skepticism toward relativity, a critical posture shared with prestigious scientists shuttered in ivory towers. Einstein's theory uniformly alienated both the masses and the overly smart. Characterizing critics of relativity as "cynics" implied that the theory could be discussed without resorting to the unnecessarily rigorous jargon of academic science.

In fact, media stories fusing theoretical physics with American vernacular suggested that far from being mathematically complex and alienating to common folk, Einstein in fact drew his relativity theory from observations of everyday life. Without ordinary women and men, scientists would have had no metaphors from which to draw their conclusions. One newspaper story claimed that Einstein "was drawn to this research through the fact that iron and wooden balls fall to the ground with the same degree of acceleration in spite of the law of gravitation."[29] Another article describing Einstein's discovery of relativity reported a silent-movie-like scene where the physicist "observed years ago a man dropping from a neighborhood roof—luckily onto a piece of soft rubbish—and escaping almost without injury. The man told Dr. Einstein that in falling he experienced no sensation commonly considered as the effect of gravity."[30] These banal explanations of relativity's development both brought Einstein's complicated mathematics down to the level of the ordinary and allowed audiences to imagine themselves making similar scientific conjectures. The slapstick anecdote of the fall into a garbage pail transformed Einstein's serious scientific work into the corniest of mass culture entertainment; it also revealed that those base elements of mass culture that seemed most vacuous—in this case a comical trash-heap plunge—could be mined for evidence of American genius nonetheless.

Still, efforts at simplifying and popularizing relativity could not fully mitigate concerns that Einstein's theory represented a terrifying example of specialized knowledge and that those who did understand it were just too smart. Understanding relativity allowed ordinary Americans to imagine themselves building up intelligence that promoted democracy, but it also threatened to cut off those who claimed comprehension from their ordinary peers. A chorus of skeptics argued that the claim that only a dozen could understand relativity was un-American. The fact that a tiny cluster was uniquely capable of comprehending the theory of relativity meant that the principles upholding democracy—especially the belief that every citizen was supposed to have an equally informed voice—were under threat. Representations of relativity balanced celebrating the theory's mass appeal and challenging those aspects that resisted popularization.

Populist dismissals of theoretical physics were offered as legitimate responses to relativity's brainy excess: ordinary Americans who resisted the call to understand relativity could position themselves as heirs to the democratic principles of the United States by boldly, proudly staking their ground among the unlearned masses.[31] Discussions about relativity's limited appeal hinged on the complexity of the theory's promoting and advancing elitism, and scientists and other intellectuals were accused of using relativity to sustain intellectual inequality. An especially vitriolic author in the *New York Times* berated the scientific community's refusal to discuss Einstein's theory in accessible language, attacking scientists for their maddening "inclination to keep a particularly interesting thing to themselves."[32] As for relativity itself, the theory was being disseminated by scientists in such a way as to be interesting to only "a rather haughty minority of Superior Persons."[33] Ordinary women and men demanded that the media salve this danger by cultivating alliances between the educated and the uneducated. They also set up defensive representational strategies that preempted those who believed they truly understood relativity from wielding their knowledge as a weapon.

In response to the suggestion that ordinary Americans could never understand relativity, some journalists vilified scientists, battered the theory of relativity, and attacked the suggestion that ordinary women and men were not capable of understanding it. The push to understand relativity and decrease the gap between ordinary and scientific Americans was offered up in one newspaper editorial as a reasonable rationale for an assassination attempt upon Einstein in 1922:

> It takes not a little thought to arrive at even a suspicion why anybody wants to attack Dr. Einstein. . . . Not long ago he announced, or at least allowed somebody else, without denial, to announce, that there were not more than 12 people in the world who could understand his new theory of relativity. That, come to think of it, did waken something of animosity in every mind whose possessor lacked the self-confidence to number himself among the so exceptional dozen. . . . This may not be the basis of the rumored plot against Dr. Einstein, but it is a working hypothesis that will stand until facts are brought forward to prove it untenable.[34]

Though the editorial's author stopped short of actually advocating Einstein's murder, the author's defensive tone conceived the scientist as a man who was walking into danger with brazen defiance and scandalous disregard for American equality. One might not murder for math, but one certainly could, it seemed, attempt an assassination in the interest of preserving American democracy. The proper balance of brainpower was conceived as essential to the proper functioning of American political life.

Reports of global events sharing headlines with Einstein also informed Americans' understanding of relativity. Particularly significant in this regard was the Bolshevik revolution in the emerging Soviet Union that appeared in newspapers alongside reports on Einstein's revolution in physics. Representations of relativity often contrasted Americans' liberalism and thirst for intelligence through mass culture with the profoundly un-democratic Bolsheviks' apparent disinterest in Einstein and attraction to developing an intellectual class.[35] They also suggested a potential parallel between Einstein's theory and the Marxist theories that had culminated with the implementation of a communist state.[36] In his self-professed "Non-Technical Explanation of the Fundamental Principles of Gravitational Astronomy," Columbia University professor, political conservative, and relativity skeptic Charles Lane Poor attacked relativity as a symptom of Bolshevism in an unstable world:

> For some years now the entire world has been in a state of unrest; mental as well as physical. The physical aspects of this unrest, the strikes, the socialistic uprisings, the war, are vivid memories; the deep mental disturbances are evidenced by the widespread interest in social problems, by the futuristic movements in art, by the light and easy way in which many cast aside the well tested theories of finance and government in favor of radical and untried experiments. Can it be that the same spirit of unrest has invaded science?[37]

By comparing relativity unfavorably with the stability of "finance and government" and associating relativity with leftist political tactics including "strikes" and "socialistic uprisings," Poor suggested that the quest for popular understanding of relativity was symptomatic of broader social unrest and agitation by the masses and framed relativity as itself a form of Bolshevism. "When is space curved?" Poor asked. "Why, when Bolshevism enters the world of science of course!"[38] Both relativity and Bolshevism favored the "radical" over the practical or the expedient, and both seemed to weirdly empower the masses. American capitalism and appropriate levels of inequality could best be upheld through a return to Newtonian physics. Relativity seemed to bespeak a refusal of the masses to shun experts who did not have their best interests in mind; it was precisely this trust in intellectuals and striving for theoretical knowledge that threatened to bring a Bolshevik-style revolution to the United States.

Inventing an American Einstein

At the top of the hierarchy of experts weighing in on relativity sat one figure whose unparalleled brilliance served as an important barometer for American brainpower: Albert Einstein himself. Though complicated discussions about relativity in the popular media offered opportunities for ordinary Americans to align themselves with the very smart while exacerbating the divisions intelligence created, representations of Einstein also articulated evolving ideas about the relationship between intelligence and emerging American identities. The fetishistic media rehearsals of Einstein's biographical details ensured that Einstein himself was represented as an exceptional, oftentimes problematic, but also charming figure. The compulsive dissections of Einstein in the mass media allowed the relationship between brainpower and liberalism to be discussed specifically through reference to an individual rather than purely as a theoretical concept.[39] Einstein embedded science within a body, allowing discussions about the theory of relativity to slip into conversations about nationality, race, religion, and other social locations. Einstein's intelligence was recognized to be inextricable from the other aspects of his national and ethnic identity, thus rendering future discussions of brainpower, intelligence, and science similarly invested in identity discourse.

Representations of Einstein departed from reports on relativity as they shifted the focus away from abstract theory and pure brainpower and attempted to unravel the physicist's tangled national identity.[40] "Albert Einstein is a Swiss citizen about 50 years of age," wrote one author in a 1919 *New York Times* piece. "After occupying a position as professor of Mathematical Physics at the Zurich Polytechnic school and afterward at Prague University, he was elected a member of Emperor William's Scientific Academy in Berlin at the outbreak of the war."[41] Though his German origins could not be denied, Einstein's nomadic life offered a more complicated narrative that allowed audiences to grab at a veritable smorgasbord of social locations. An article in the *New York American* in 1921 offered another tangled effort that resisted neatly defining Einstein's nationality. "Although a Swiss citizen," this author wrote, "Professor Einstein spoke in his native German, and it was difficult for him to convey his technical discussion to lay hearers through an interpreter."[42] Einstein's position during World War I offered few additional clues to his national affiliations. "Einstein no longer could be ignored, but he kept on working during the war," declared Oliver Lodge in a 1920 lecture; "I don't know how he did, but I think he must have been a pacifist. At any rate, since he wrote from Zurich, we called Einstein by politeness a Swiss."[43]

Though these representations all emphasized the multiplicity of Einstein's identities, thus rendering it easier to assimilate him into an American narrative of the "melting pot," they also eliminated the possibility of claiming him as belonging to one particular national or ethnic group. "Einstein comes as a distinguished and somewhat mysterious foreigner to partake of our insatiable hospitality," wrote an author in *The Freeman* ambiguously in an article given the further exoticizing, weirdly Orientalist title "Aladdin Einstein."[44] A *New York Evening Post* author was less vague with his intentions: "One could hardly allude to the lineaments of this Swiss Jew as Semitic," he wrote. "They are hard to classify, racially—and still more difficult professionally."[45]

This concern about Einstein's body concealing his dangerous ideas often took on resonances of the anxiety about immigrants wracking the United States after the end of World War I. These concerns were particularly attached to Jewish immigrants. Some descriptions emphasized physiognomic features that emphasized his nonwhite embodiment.[46] Though these accounts often celebrated Einstein, they recycled the narrative of his foreign body, using descriptive language to both accentuate his otherness and to assimilate him easily into a comfortable neighborly essence. "His coloring is warmly brown," one writer noted, "the features prominent, the eyes and mouth friendly."[47] Einstein's Jewish features factored into his body, ideas, and character. His Jewishness was also conceived as symptomatic of a high-functioning intelligence. Edwin Slosson noted that "the Jews have more men of genius in proportion to their numbers than any other race since the ancient Greeks."[48] Yet Einstein's Jewish intelligence was also represented as potentially pathological.[49] Slosson continued by claiming that given this Jewish propensity toward genius, "they could afford to be generous with them." His undeniable Jewish features notwithstanding, media discussions of Einstein suggested another opportunity to capitalize on his genius to transcend difference in favor of shared humanity. "It is to be hoped that Einstein's theories will be judged objectively on their own merits," according to Slosson, "without prejudice in their favor or against on grounds of race."[50] Einstein's brilliance pointed to both his identity as a Jew and Americans' noble enthusiasm to completely overlook that fact.

Swiss, Jewish, or mysteriously foreign, Einstein was insistently represented as defying neat compartmentalization. Just as his theory of relativity united a variety of Americans in a common ignorance while building up dissent from its more unsavory features, so Einstein's complicated body frustrated efforts to depict him as belonging to any one group and allowed Americans flexibility to alternately conceive him as foreign or familiar as suited their broader cultural preferences. Einstein's brilliance rendered him appealing to mass consumers seeking to stake out their own positions in American society. Yet he also represented a dangerous foreign force that could, in 100 percent Americanist hands, be used to achieve the objectives of a growing nativist movement that cast suspicion on all who were foreign born. A 1919 article by Edward Slosson in the *Independent* acknowledged the intense pressure placed on Einstein to be represented as a national subject in this contentious climate. In an article discussing the reception of Einstein and relativity within scientific circles, Slosson suggested that

> the controversy it precipitated has not altogether been confined to the realm of pure reason, for scientists are but human and as such are not entirely uninfluenced by patriotic prejudice. It cannot be denied that Einstein is a Berlin professor, but any latent hostility we may harbor against his theories on that score may be alleviated by recalling that he is also a Swiss Jew.[51]

In Slosson's analysis, the complicated mathematics of Einstein's national and ethnic identity offered both a problem and a solution to the (il)legibility of immigrant bodies. Einstein's German residency was represented as a problem—this was a period, after all, when "sauerkraut" had been renamed "liberty cabbage" to excise all Germanic influence from the English language—but his "real" identity was identified as the more neutral Swiss, and his ethnic identification Jewish.[52] Einstein himself recognized the American distaste for his German identity. An article following his 1921 visit to the United States found that "Einstein says he found America violently anti-German, although with evidence of a change of heart taking place."[53] Discussion of Einstein's intelligence negotiated between defining his national identity and celebrating the potential for genius to dissolve national boundaries altogether.[54]

In a period characterized by heightened U.S. nationalism and spreading waves of anti-immigrant resentment, some popular media descriptions of Einstein began to move away from the thorny politics of ethnic identity and troubling nativist rhetoric, instead deemphasizing Einstein's nationality in favor of universalizing aspects of his intelligence that dissociated him from foreign bodies. These representations reframed Einstein's alien status by centralizing his otherworldliness, a strategy made palatable thanks to the cosmic implications of his theory of relativity. "The doctor lives on the top floor of a fashionable apartment house on one of the few elevated spots in Berlin," noted one author in a profile of the scientist, "close to the stars which he studies, not with a telescope, but rather with the mental eye."[55] This author placed Einstein in closer proximity to the stars than to the earth, as though celestial space were where his body fit most naturally. Such characterizations sidestepped Einstein's national identity, instead highlighting his ability to transcend borders and positioning him as beyond citizenship. In the process he became instead a literal alien.[56] Representations of Einstein's disembodied and deracinated identity were reinforced through reference to two entwined problems: the indecipherability of relativity and Einstein's inability to explain it adequately. In an article describing the impossible task of determining who would sit next to Einstein at a Boston breakfast, a *Boston Journal Transcript* author noted that "it was generally known that he cannot speak English and equally well known that nobody understood his 'relativity' theory which has made the man famous."[57]

The alien was not an entirely fictional construct, especially in the anti-immigrant fervor of the 1920s United States.[58] It is unsurprising, then, that one feature common to early representations of Einstein was his depiction as an American immigrant.[59] Though he did not take up residence in the United States until 1932 and was not naturalized as an American citizen until 1940, this detail did not prevent early representations of Einstein from adopting descriptive language that expressed an eagerness to treat him as a fellow American, albeit not a native one. Popular representations of Einstein's contested nationality reached a fever pitch when Einstein first landed on U.S. soil in 1921 as part of a visit advocating the creation of a Jewish state. Though he claimed he would not entertain interviews on this trip that were unrelated to his Zionism, Einstein could not hold against the tide of interest in his scientific theories; much of his time in the U.S. was spent extemporizing on relativity whether he wanted to or not. His visit insured that relativity would be long associated with Einstein in American popular representations, and that Einstein himself would stand in as the archetypal genius and American celebrity.

The frenzy to reimagine Einstein as uniquely American in orientation (if not in origin) played out across media. A writer in the *Hartford Daily*

Courant triumphantly announced following his appearance that Einstein had declared that "baseball unites the spirit of democracy, the 'movies' are a grand thing and prohibition is good."[60] Such a concentrated effort at aligning Einstein with American cultural interests, values, and leisure suggests how representations of Einstein cast him as nonthreatening by highlighting his eager consumption of U.S. popular culture.[61] "Baseball, baseball," Einstein enthused, "I've seen the game here. That's fine. It makes everybody concentrate on what is going on. It helps to unite the spirit of democracy."[62] Though he was maligned at points for his foreign national identity, Einstein was also inclined toward sporting American pastimes, and his appearance in the United States was folded into a narrative of becoming American.[63] This Americanized Einstein served the double purposes of bringing the foreign scientist closer into alignment with ordinary women and men while also raising the profile of American cultural interests. Americans watching baseball and screening movies were behaving like their iconic genius. Mass culture was once again aligned with intellectual pursuits.

Representations of Einstein nonetheless highlighted the underlying conflict between those who conceived his intelligence as freakish and others who sought to diminish distinctions between the ordinary and the smart. One common narrative that appeared in many physical descriptions of Einstein placed him alongside the American stereotype of intellectual long-hairs. The OED defines the "long-hair" as "a 'brainy' person, an aesthete, an intellectual; also a devotee of classical (as opp. to popular) music," and dates the term's appearance to 1920.[64] Though this recognizable cultural type was most often identified with an overinvestment in the arts—especially classical music—creative writers insinuated that Einstein was essentially a physicist's longhair. For one thing, Einstein's hair was literally quite long according to American male fashion of the day. Sometimes the unruliness of his hair made Einstein appear more ordinary. "His long, bushy hair," one writer claimed, was "worn a la the William Jennings Bryan of other days."[65] Bryan, a populist hero, had hair that was unruly, suggesting a salt-of-the-earth physicality that, when transplanted onto Einstein, disrupted unsavory associations with effete sensibility by making an explicit parallel to the earnest everyman. The Einstein/Bryan reading of Einstein's hair reinforced the utility of Einstein in promoting brainpower as a social equalizer through his populist embodiment.

Yet the similarities between Einstein and the stereotypical longhair were not always so easily redirected to populist aims. "The long hair that

ended in tight curls and the chalk balanced between his fingers like the baton gave him the appearance of an orchestra leader when not at the black-
board," wrote one author in an account of a series of Einstein lectures.[66]
Another similarly declared that his "long wavy hair gave him the appearance of a music master."[67] A third indicated that "Professor Albert Einstein
has commenced one of the greatest pro and con discussions in the world of
science, but to his wife, he is just a plain, music-loving husband."[68] Just as
the longhair's sensitive tastes were culturally maligned for having exuded
a female essence juxtaposed with the vulgar tastes of common men, so Einstein was made to seem somehow feminine in the manly world of physics.
His ability to move seamlessly between highbrow discourses made him less
of a myopic expert, but his musical ability was a sign of his feminine taste.
"He plays the violin," noted one author, adding for emphasis, "He has his
violin with him."[69] Another announced that Einstein's wife controlled "the
number of cigars he smokes but there is no control over the amount of time
he chooses to spend at the piano or with his violin."[70] Albert Einstein
seemed pleased by these associations, even, on occasion, identifying himself
with longhair sensibility. "The sculptor, the artist, the musician, the scientist
work because of love for their work," he was quoted as saying. "Fame and
honor are secondary."[71] Einstein's longhair tastes and appearance presented an obstacle for those who attempted to make him an unconflicted
symbol of populist intelligence, but they also broadened his audience by dissociating him from narrow-minded experts. His femininity defused anxiety
about the threat posed by his scientific brilliance.

Efforts to domesticate Einstein emphasized features that characterized
him as a comfortingly familiar, disarmingly feminine oddball. By most accounts, Einstein possessed a charming, nonthreatening, avuncular presence—
"most pleasant and affable," according to one local reporter.[72] When he was
not treated as feminine, he was often characterized as childlike. "He seemed
to take a childlike amusement in the whole process of questioning and
scribbling and interpreting that was going on before him," wrote one author.[73] His eyes were particularly suggestive of his warm, disarming nature.
"His eyes are brown and bright," wrote a Boston reporter.[74] In Cleveland,
another invoked the childlike character of his "large, luminous eyes."[75] Vera
Weizmann, one of Einstein's traveling companions in the United States, was
observed declaring that "I never thought a great genius could be so childish!"[76] Emphasizing Einstein's childlike wonder again disrupted fears about
his intimidating intellect and highlighted features familiar to ordinary

women and men. His overwhelmingly childlike qualities crystallized his intellect into representations that rendered his vast brainpower nonthreatening, banal, and even appealing.

Einstein's childlike characteristics morphed easily into depictions of advanced age. Whether childish or elderly, Einstein was could be unintimidating and delightful. Though he was just barely over forty when he became an American celebrity, a common picture of him that emerged in the media was as a somewhat doddering elderly man. One author bemoaned that "this eminent German has found one thing since he came to America about which there is nothing relative. That is weariness." Sleepy, weak, and elderly, Einstein engendered a profoundly nonthreatening image. Some accounts treated him as frail as he struggled to behave with the proper comportment of an able-minded, relatively young man. A student newspaper at the City University of New York took apparent pleasure in widening the generation gap by recounting their witnessing of "a world-famous scientist frantically dodging in and out along motor cars and trucks on crowded upper Seventh Avenue in pursuit of what an American would have called his 'lid.'"[77] A series of articles in the *New York Times* delighted in describing how Einstein miscounted his change on a streetcar, a story given the satisfyingly succinct headline "Einstein Counted Wrong."[78]

The archetype for American genius was thus represented in popular culture as a character who not only resembled ordinary Americans but might even call upon them for assistance in basic tasks such as counting his change and fetching his "lid." Representations of Einstein's impossibly placid demeanor and nonthreatening disposition offset startling descriptions of his seldom-seen monstrous side. Though these depictions tended not to represent him as an unbridled maniac (he was not, to be sure, a ravenous Victorian monster along the lines of Dr. Jekyll/Mr. Hyde), they nonetheless transformed Einstein's quiet body into a cage containing a dangerous mind. "His hair was disheveled," recounted one author, "and his eye had a roving look. His wife told me that when the professor is seized by a problem the fact becomes known to her by this peculiar wandering look which comes into his eyes and by his feverish pacing up and down the room. At such times, she said, the professor is never disturbed."[79] This description conceived Einstein as something of a sheep in wolf's clothing, his placid exterior concealing a deeper—possibly sinister—unconscious that "seized" him unwarned. Such representations emphasized the danger of implicitly trusting Einstein's inscrutable body. He might have appeared avuncular, "but underneath his shaggy locks was a scientific mind whose deductions have staggered the ablest intellects of Europe."[80] The warning was clear: genius might present as ordinary, and Einstein represented a character who had a unique degree of mass appeal, but about whom popular opinion was largely unsettled. Though representing his body as childlike, avuncular, or elderly did make Einstein's brilliance less threatening, such representations failed to defuse the dangerous potential of his theories; the revolutionary potential of brainpower, while in some ways advanced through Einstein's appearance, seemed also to be fundamentally undermined by his own ordinariness.

*   *   *

Einstein became a celebrity in part because he served as a lightning rod for so many concerns, questions, and criticisms about the relationship between ordinary Americans and intelligence. Rather than resolving the paradoxes of brainpower in American culture, Einstein embodied its contradictions. The complexity of his theory was represented as furthering the division between the very smart and the ordinary, yet it was also seen as so complicated it could unite everyone in mutual ignorance. Einstein's complicated national identity allowed him to be represented as an American, buttressing claims to U.S. intellectual exceptionalism, but his foreignness also introduced representational strategies that conceived his brainpower as unwelcome in a liberal state. Einstein's revolutionary theories were conceived as typical of brainpower's dangerous potential, but they were also depicted as representative of American creativity and ingenuity. Finally, Einstein's body was alternately portrayed as nonthreatening and as monstrous, articulating complicated narratives about sex, race, and ethnicity underlying the politics of brainpower. Though representations of Einstein failed to resolve the contradictions at stake in defining American identities following World War I, his brainpower was used to filter these contradictions through a fascinating individual whose legacy was the subject of contentious division.

If Einstein represented concerns and hopes about the concentration of brainpower in exceptional bodies that issued from mass culture, the workers' education movement offered counter-representations of intelligence that attempted to explicitly politicize brainpower in the interests of building a militant working-class movement. Their representations of working-class intelligence undermined efforts to imagine brainpower as apolitical or unappealing to ordinary women and men. The workers' education movement began at the same time as discussions of Einstein were exploding in mass culture. Representations of Einstein in mass culture and intelligence in the workers' education movement set the stage for the debates about brainpower in American life that acknowledged the undeniable impact intelligence had on ordinary women and men. While working-class people grabbed at these tools for social advancement as they became available, a counter discourse also emerged to prevent radical elements from unleashing brainpower's dangerous potential.

3

Knowledge Is Power: Women, Workers' Education,
and Brainpower in the 1920s

Where buildings steeply climb
And tower cleft sky is seen,
The worker races time
Above her swift machine,
But here with folks from every land
She learns to think and understand.
—Author unknown, Poem for Bryn Mawr Summer School
for Women Workers

Bryn Mawr College first opened its doors to women working in factories in 1921. Throughout a six-week summer session, women who were usually found laboring at jobs that did not reward their intelligence—working for bosses who hardly recognized them as human, let alone as thinkers—assembled to study history, art, culture, literature, ethnicity, and other subjects commonly found in a liberal arts education. During their time at the Bryn Mawr Summer School for Women Workers, the students began to envisage themselves as intelligent and learned to conceptualize the world around them in ways that challenged the notion that brainpower was accessible only to the managerial class. Education gave these women access to a form of power that was rightfully theirs, and the strength they found through intelligence translated into a large-scale, organized battle against the forces of intellectual oppression that threatened to derail an accelerating labor movement by diminishing the value of women's brains.

Working-class women capitalized on the growth of progressive education initiatives and grassroots labor organizing to envision classrooms as
spaces primed for promoting workers' power in the workplace and society.
Though participating in the Bryn Mawr Summer School for Women Workers
(BMSS) offered a life-changing opportunity for each of the women who participated, many of whom risked job termination and other forms of retalia-
tion from their bosses to participate in the program, the Summer School
was relatively short-lived. By 1928, BMSS had shifted its emphasis toward
"practical" subjects such as English language and trade unionism, a change in
focus that was typical of workers' education programs over this period and
marked a decided turn away from brainpower as the center of labor organizing. By 1938, the school had ceased operation and the progressive idea of liberal education as a right, a spiritual necessity, and a critical tool for social
change by workers was supplanted with programs that conceived education as
a utilitarian concern designed primarily to accrue skills that would promote
occupational advances. The workers' education movement represented both
an expansion of brainpower's reach to the working class in its early years and
an attenuation of the politics of brainpower in the labor movement toward
narrowly pragmatic organizing goals by the end of the 1920s.

The progression of the workers' education movement through organization, institutionalization, and finally centralization, the sequence for this
chapter, directly affected the framing of the labor movement in relation to
the discourse of working-class intelligence. Though the workers' education
movement began by highlighting a radical perspective, increased centralization corresponded with a shift toward a more liberal understanding of
brainpower in American culture. The move to centralize control with the
growth of the Workers Education Bureau of America (WEB) fundamentally
undermined the progressive goals and democratic flavor of educational efforts that were favored by grassroots organizations and the union rank and
file. By examining this critical period in working-class educational initiatives through the stories of the International Ladies' Garment Workers'
Union Educational Department (ILGWU-ED), the BMSS, and the Workers
Education Bureau of America, I seek to place these educational efforts at the
center of the story of brainpower's shifting definition in 1914–1929. I also
foreground women—in their various roles as students, organizers, and
instructors—as the most significant figures in the fight for workers' education. That many of these women were first-generation immigrants laboring
during a period of heightened nativist sentiment in the United States further

accounts for both their successes and their gradual exclusion from positions of influence within the movement and outside mainstream representations of intelligence.

In contrast to earlier labor organizers' belief that worker control over industrial skills should be at the center of their political strategies, the organization of a workers' education movement represented a critical departure from earlier battles in favor of an embrace of education as a vital weapon of class warfare. Over the years 1914–1929, educational institutes appeared rapidly throughout the country, each offering classes and programs to a component of the working population that otherwise might have been ignored. Some prominent figures within the workers' education movement conceived education as merely useful for training workers in basic skills (reading, writing, and labor organization) or to awaken political consciousness. Many others believed workers' education comprised a formal effort to wrench control of the cultural capital of intelligence from the managerial class. From the ILGWU-ED's adopting "Knowledge Is Power" as a slogan in the 1910s to the formation of the Art Workshop for College and Industrial Women in New York in 1929, the workers' education movement introduced a compelling discursive strategy that sought to place progressive politics under the control—and in the minds—of working-class women (Figure 6). By 1926 there were over 400 workers' education initiatives throughout the United States.[1] Even as conservative forces in the industrial labor movement and the Republican administrations of the 1920s succeeded in containing the radical impulses of labor by bringing it into closer alignment with management on an organizational level, workers' education represented a radical alternative where workers could reinscribe labor with workers' needs and interests at the center.

Organization: International Ladies' Garment Workers' Union

The American workers' education movement took shape in 1914 with discussion about forming an Educational Department of the International Ladies' Garment Workers' Union.[2] Since its founding in 1900, the International Ladies' Garment Workers' Union (ILGWU) had emblematized a militant approach to labor organization. "The Jewish young women, who took an active part in organizing the unions," wrote Louis Levine describing the ILGWU in 1924, "demanded that the union be something more than a mere business organization, that it have a 'soul' as well as a 'body,' and that

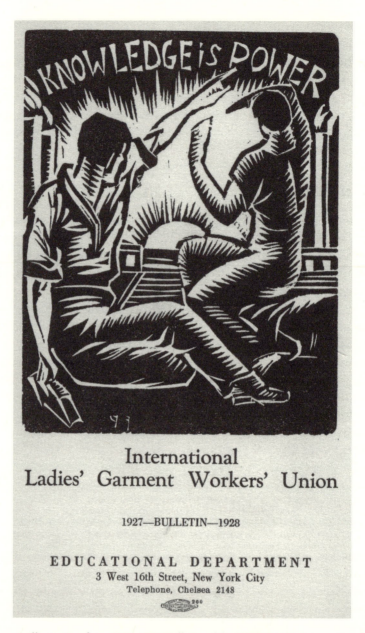

Figure 6. Illustration from 1927–1928 Bulletin of the ILGWU-ED. International Ladies Garment Workers Union Publications Education Department Files, 1920–1979, 5780 PUBS, Kheel Center for Labor-Management Documentation and Archives, M. P. Catherwood Library, Cornell University.

it provide for the 'intellectual' and 'emotional' life of its members."[3] This radical spirit was largely motivated by the determined women working in the garment industry, many of them immigrants, who were committed to creating a better world for themselves and their society by expanding their brainpower. Among ILGWU members the insurgent women of New York Local 25 were especially rabid in their demands for union-sponsored activities, strong negotiation, and initiatives for empowering and expanding their ranks. Given its alchemy of radical energy and shared identity, it is unsurprising that this Educational Department acted as a catalyst and model for workers' education programs across the nation.[4]

Though there had been a number of experiments with educational programs targeting laborers prior to the ILGWU's efforts, most of these had either been imported from Europe with the hopes of fomenting a shift toward European-style working-class politics—most notable among these was the Rand School of Social Science, established in New York as a Socialist school in 1906—or were controlled by political groups aiming to teach the specific contours of their system to workers. At a 1914 meeting held in Cleveland, Ohio, ILGWU president Benjamin Schlesinger approved calls by delegates to "dwell particularly upon the more solid and preparatory work of education and not to devote much time to the more superficial forms of agitation and propaganda."[5] Education threatened to overhaul the whole system that devalued workers' intellectual interests and divorced their minds from their bodies. The cadre marching in the streets would be more powerful if they also posed a formidable intellectual force.

In accordance with Schlesinger's call, the ILGWU began to offer courses through the Rand School during the 1914–1915 season. Schlesinger advocated a program that was primarily concerned with teaching rank-and-file members the basic tenets of trade unionism. Education was largely conceived as a utilitarian concern; it provided the foundation for an informed union membership. Yet this definition conflicted with the demands of workers themselves, who sought a more fundamental restructuring of the division of intellectual labor. "Our International found out that teaching girls how to picket a shop was not sufficient," recalled Mollie Friedman, a member of Local 25, who was among those agitating for an expansive educational program, "and they taught us how to read books."[6]

The ILGWU made an overture toward endorsing a comprehensive education program when Local 25 appointed Juliet S. Poyntz, a history instructor from Barnard College, as director of the local's educational activities in 1915.[7] Poyntz, who remained in this position until 1918, championed a comprehensive educational program. Selecting a director who was trained in the liberal arts, as opposed to one with on-the-ground experience in union organizing, brought to the surface the philosophical division separating those who saw education as promoting the accretion of organizing skills and those who conceived it as advancing working-class brainpower. It was under Poyntz's influence that the ILGWU formed a centralized Educational Department at their 1916 convention.[8] The Department began its official activities by opening Workers' University at the Washington Irving High School, offering four courses that emphasized industrial and labor problems. The budget appropriation allotted for education was significantly increased over the next two years.[9]

Though her official title was executive secretary, the development of an even more comprehensive education program within the ILGWU was largely the work of Fannia M. Cohn. Cohn, a Russian Jewish immigrant who had been active in the National Women's Trade Union League where she had herself attended courses in English and organizing, was committed to the idea that working women deserved an education that exposed them to culture, philosophy, and history. From the beginning of her involvement with the ILGWU, Cohn conceived knowledge as the most valuable weapon available to workers. She believed education programs promoted solidarity within unions, but she also argued that education could overcome the social obstacles preventing working-class women from challenging bosses and political leaders and confront gender obstacles in the process. "Our girls need never feel ashamed of being factory workers," she stated. "They can meet socially with any young man and know as much of art and literature and other cultural values of our society."[10]

The appeal of workers' education as a site of labor agitation reflected an approach to radical politics that was aligned with feminism during this period. Historian Nancy Cott has described the 1910s and 1920s as a period when feminism developed as a movement distinct from the "woman movement" that had led the charge for suffrage and temperance. Feminism situated a politics of collectivism and unity uniquely accessible by women at its center, emphasizing "women's collective self-understanding or action."[11] The workers' education movement represented a similar site where the strong-armed rhetoric of class warfare could be replaced with a more utopian and shared vision. As workers' education activist Thomas R. Adam noted, these programs "represen[t] the major alternative to force in overcoming the injustices of society; through reconciliation based on under-standing, it promises relief from hated strife between nations or classes. Idealism is capable of producing solid, practical results when it is related to needs as instinctive to womankind as peace and social stability."[12] Similarly, Maud Schwartz, president of the Women's Trade Union League, conceived educational efforts' most important responsibility as including women. De-scribing the germination of her commitment to sponsoring education ini-tiatives within the National Women's Trade Union League (NWTUL), Schwartz recalled that "it was because of our efforts to organize women that we met such tremendously discouraging conditions that we felt that we must take other methods and that we were driven to seek some way by which we could attract women and bring them into the labor movement and to working in the labor movement by another way."[13]

Building education initiatives supplanted the masculinist organizing strategies of male-dominated crafts unions as a means for attracting women to the cause of labor, but feminist contributions to workers' education con-tinued to meet with hostility from men within the labor movement and the educational establishment[14] In a typical screed from 1925, a New School professor complained bitterly about how "solemn-eyed senior flappers from women's colleges solemnly sought consultations on the choice of 'la-bor education' as a career."[15] Workers' education threatened not only the division of labor, but also posed a serious challenge to the organization of gender within the labor movement, the workplace, and in society at large.

The fact that the ILGWU, alongside others of the more radical garment industry unions, was controlled and populated largely by Jewish immi-grants from countries in Eastern Europe helps account for their notably progressive Educational Department and the range of responses they elic-ited both inside and outside the union rank and file.[16] A combination of historical contingencies—reasons for migrating; opportunities for assimila-tion; founding of ethnic trades, involvement in communities and benevo-lent associations—brought to bear on the values and politics of the Jewish population of the United States. Many shared a commitment to both social-ist ideas and education. Particularly among the new Jewish immigrants, the formation of educational departments within the labor movement brought community values and politics together in a common struggle for advance-ment in American society.[17]

An emblematic moment in the campaign to articulate the role of educa-tion was found in a 1921 report authored by Fannia Cohn describing the

ILGWU-ED's work to the leadership of the WEB. On the one hand, the report defined workers' education as offering workers tools to enact the power given them through their unions. "The work of the Educational Department of the I.L.G.W.U," Cohn wrote, "is based on a conviction that the aims and aspirations of the workers can be realized only through their own efforts on the economic and educational fields. While organization gives them power, education gives them the ability to use that power intelligently and effectively." Education, in other words, was useful insofar as it taught workers to channel their power in effective ways. Yet the report also allowed that the department sought "to cultivate in [students] an appreciation for beauty and art, which tends so much to increase the enjoyment of life. Their longing for beauty should be awakened to such an extent that they will despise the dirty tenements, oppose unsanitary conditions in their shops and abolish slums."[18] The intelligent worker was expected to be enlightened and attentive to beauty to such an extent that she would be inclined to abhor what was not beautiful in the world.

As the 1920s progressed, the ILGWU-ED became an increasingly visible and vital model for other workers' education programs, and internal debates about the purpose of the education gave way to a consensus that saw educational work as primarily invested in imbuing workers with cultural capital.[19] The ILGWU-ED adopted official slogans that included "knowledge is power" and "the future of the world lies in the hands of intelligent and well-informed workers."[20] These slogans underscored the politics of education espoused by Cohn, who argued that "the hope of the labor movement is based upon the increasing intelligence of the rank and file. Education and information must be the cornerstone of the society of the future. It is the intelligent citizenship in the unions—the rank and file—that will bring about an intelligent leadership."[21] More than recreation, more than solidarity, and more than an inclination to organize, education offered the only hope for a fully realized, politically incorporated, intelligent working class—and it placed such radical notions about brainpower in the hands of the workers, not the labor leaders.

Institutionalization: Bryn Mawr Summer School for Women Workers

The ILGWU model for workers' education defined workers' intelligence broadly enough to incorporate both practical and theoretical knowledge. Yet most of their surviving records reveal the debates and initiatives among the union's leadership. The experiences of workers in the classroom are harder to come by. This is not the case with the Bryn Mawr Summer School for Women Workers, a program that responded to a similar set of concerns among working-class women and brought them into close alignment with a traditional liberal arts college. Following a 1916 call by the National Women's Trade Union League to use existing college campuses to educate women workers, the president of Bryn Mawr College, M. Carey Thomas, began discussing her idea for a summer school with Professor Susan M. Kingsbury and Hilda Worthington Smith, then dean of the college.[22] These talks led to the opening of Bryn Mawr's campus to women working in factories in 1921.[23] Under the direction of Thomas and Smith, the BMSS offered working women an opportunity to study a variety of subjects during the summer on a bucolic campus in Pennsylvania, replete with cloisters, lawns, and fountains.[24] "Classes are often out of doors," Smith recalled, "each appropriating a tree, a corner of the cloister, or a shady stretch of lawn as well as a place indoors."[25] A pamphlet describing the school emphasized both its focus on industry and the rewards of a liberal arts education, encapsulating the school's mission to offer working women "opportunities to study liberal subjects and to train themselves in clear thinking; to stimulate an active and continued interest in the problems of our economic order; [and] to develop a desire for study as a means to understanding and of enjoyment of life."[26] The school admitted up to one hundred students a year.

That BMSS was a residential program proved to be one of its most attractive features. The inclusion of room and board—and the lack of need for work during the days—eliminated a significant obstacle for women trying to juggle work and school. "It was hard in evening classes after a long day of monotonius [*sic*] work in uninspiring surroundings to spend our few remaining hours at intense studying," wrote one student of her failed experiences taking night classes such as those offered through the ILGWU-ED. Yet in contrast, her leisurely schedule at Bryn Mawr filled her with energy and enthusiasm for both her work and her studies. "After each lesson," the student recounted, "and often even a single instance of a new fact revealed, something in me wanted to cry aloud, 'for this, for this, alone it has been worth while losing eight weeks pay and chancing the loss of my job.'"[27]

Still, though risking unemployment might have at times felt to be "worth while," the advantages of an intensive summer session were certainly offset by this occupational hazard, and the women who were willing to assume such a risk were undoubtedly an unusually eager and ambitious group. The aim of the Summer School to offer education to working women introduced another obstacle by divorcing their classroom experiences from everyday life in the workplace, thus compartmentalizing intellectual labor as distinct from working in industry—a danger that the ILGWU had been cautious to avoid. "Where are all the factories?" Hilda Worthington Smith recalled one student bemusedly asking upon arriving on the lush campus. "It seems strange for a factory worker to be in a place without any factories."[28]

Yet for most of the students who found their way to BMSS, the benefits afforded by the program outweighed both the lost pay and the risk of termination from their jobs, and they resisted any inclination to conceive their experiences at Bryn Mawr as undermining their working-class identities. Indeed, there is significant evidence that the students returned from the BMSS more invested in their identities as workers. The program's ignominy as a breeding ground for working-class militancy introduced yet another challenge: as the Summer School became better known, employers were reluctant to permit workers time off only to return with a newfound radicalism concerning workplace matters. The media fanned these flames. "Of course, the Philadelphia newspapers . . . saw the school as a Communist revolution," recalled Lillian Herstein, a teacher in the program. "We had a time!"[29] Such concerns also eventually fell on Bryn Mawr College, which began withdrawing its support for the Summer School in the 1930s.

One of the central issues confronting students and administrators of BMSS was their shared concern about the relationship between education and embourgeoisment. For administrators, most of whom were middle-class women and were otherwise involved in the day-to-day affairs of Bryn Mawr, itself a rather polite college, the temptation to require genteel behavior of the Summer School students was sometimes too great to resist.[30] An image used in promotional materials for BMSS illustrates the paradoxes embedded in this challenge: the illustration features a serene scene of properly dressed women converging around a tasteful fountain as they meditate on their studies (Figure 7).[31] The allure of the Bryn Mawr campus with its lush greenery, cloisters, and ornamentation invited associations with bourgeois values, which many working women found repellent. For Hilda Shapiro, a member of the Amalgamated Clothing Workers of America who was a student of the first summer at Bryn Mawr, the school seemed an obvious plot. "Do you think we working women would fall for a fake like you're talking about?" she skeptically protested. "We know all about the welfare plans of employers. The game is to break up unions. I'm on to your

Figure 7. Illustration from a 1939 pamphlet for the BMSS. Box 3, American Labor Education Service, Pearl L. Willen Memorial, 1927–1962, 5225, Kheel Center for Labor-Management Documentation and Archives, M. P. Catherwood Library, Cornell University.

game."[32] The paradoxical attraction to bourgeois standards of intelligence and liberation of the working class was a site of conflict for some students; the distribution of intelligence among the working class had not prepared these students to conceptualize brainpower as comprising a tool for class warfare. Many were deeply conflicted by their impulses to both oppose the bourgeois values of education while also gaining access to the power of intelligence in American culture. BMSS introduced the radical idea that college students could be workers and workers could be thinkers.

The refined lifestyle of the Summer School was overwhelming for some of the factory women. They worried that the attempts to focus on workers' needs might be insufficient and that efforts to educate working women were doomed to be mere indoctrination into middle-class values. One student, Sorell Balazowsky, expressed a lively distaste for the dull etiquette prized at the Summer School, contrasted with the excitement of her ordinary life:

> The faculty and staff is very polite, in fact too polite for me. I can't digest too much politeness. When politeness reaches excess it becomes stupidity. I am afraid we have such a case in Bryn Mawr. I wonder how much they pay Miss Ferguson, our housekeeper, for smiling all the time, when you look at her? I would contribute to a fund to pay her to remove that constant smile of hers. Every time I see her smiling I have a great desire to tickle her very hard to see how will she react to it. Will she laugh extravagantly with a full mouth? I would appreciate good genuine anger more than that frozen smile.[33]

Though Balazowsky openly resisted the gentility promoted by the Summer School, two factors dampened the impact of her complaint. First, her willingness to write such a trenchant critique in a student paper suggests she assumed a sympathetic audience among her teachers. Second, Balazowsky's specific criticism of a housekeeper rather than a teacher indicates that part of her concern stemmed from a fear that she was being treated by the school's workers as a manager, rather than simply concern that she was surrounded by too many women adhering to middle-class values.[34]

Other students struggled terribly to resolve their contradictory attraction to middle-class standards of intelligence and the liberation of the working class. In order to resolve this paradox, a few students affirmed the education they felt they had secured through working in factories while resisting society's demand that they articulate their ideas in crude, folksy language. One such student wrote an elegant short poem expressing her feelings of inadequacy when confronting middle-class education that might also be read as an affirmation of a specifically working-class form of intelligence:

I would like to write a poem
But I have no words.
My grammar was ladies' waists
    And my schooling skirts.[35]

For some students, the lack of factories and basic knowledge presented less of an obstacle to their education than the associations they brought with them toward elitist undergraduates. "I will never forget how prejudiced I was against college students," one student wrote. "I always thought they were rich, snobbish [sic] young folks."[36] Rebellion against the politeness of the institute flared up regularly. One student was expelled after sending a cake to an overweight teacher, a hairdresser to a bald teacher, and having wine and spirits sent to a teacher whose personal habits might be surmised. Other workers such as Minnie Hoskins found Bryn Mawr's middle-class setting a challenge, but met the challenge head on. "Can you picture me sitting still for an hour or an hour and a half listening to a speaker on labor problems?" she wrote in 1929. "That is exactly what I have been doing for the past seven weeks which I consider have been as interesting and valuable as some of the classes."[37]

One of the most significant ways students at BMSS were able to resist as-similating to middle-class values and behaviors was by taking an active role in developing the BMSS curriculum and taking charge of discussion within the program. Students had a significant role in shaping BMSS's educational direction by suggesting course offerings, which Hilda Worthington Smith noted were "largely decided by the wishes of the women workers. The course in the appreciation of music, for example, was included at the urgent wish of the workers themselves." Class discussions at the Summer School were also worker centered: rather than replicating an alienating factory with the teacher as "boss" and the students as "workers," BMSS insistently empha-sized a cooperative classroom. "The workers think of their instructors not as superior officers," Smith noted, "but as human beings, and as fellow human beings take a kindly interest in all that concerns them." One student emphasized how her experiences at BMSS "taught me to *think* for myself, to use my own mind. This perhaps has meant more than anything for I have been called upon many times since to use my own mind."[38]

The courses offered at BMSS were also designed to be interdisciplinary, holistic, and non-intimidating. "The study of the boll weevil offered unexpected opportunities for correlation in economics, science, and English," Hilda Smith recalled, "and the 'Boll Weevil Song' was often heard on the campus."[39] Any division of knowledge that privileged some subjects at the expense of others came to be seen as replicating the division of labor found in the workplace, and both were to be resisted. By demanding that the program accommodate the students in curriculum, pedagogy, and admissions, the students were able to resist the institutionalization of the program, instead conceiving their education as a collective enterprise. Student learning emphasized knowledge acquired from work, personal experience, book learning, and cultural practices.

The students themselves also considered the ethnic and racial composition of the student body at Bryn Mawr integral to student education and expected diversity to be subject to their input. Bryn Mawr's immigrant students agitated for the admission of African American women, a campaign that was successful by 1926. Women working in some of the more marginalized industries were also included in the Summer School after encountering initial resistance from other students. "At first I thought my mother would have a fit if she knew I was going around with the cotton mill girls," one woman recalled. "Now I see that they are just as nice girls as anyone else, and I am trying to get them to come to our club."[40] Another struggle concerned admitting waitresses, who some women believed were bad influences.[41] The students ultimately decided to include them. Decisions concerning the diversity of the student body were conceived as an important part of students' education at the school.

Though students took control of these efforts toward inclusion, a central feature of the educational plan for BMSS, advocated by all the program's administrators, was promoting a pluralistic definition of American identity. "Can you imagine a little hick like me," wrote a student, "born and reared in the same community, with not only race prejudices but nationalities included?" After spending a summer at Bryn Mawr, this same student observed how ethnic diversity was "a source of experience and an education in itself."[42] Coming into contact with women from a variety of backgrounds created a climate in which students critically reevaluated their identity as Americans, their status as workers, and their relations with other women. "Do you remember my telling you that I just couldn't stand the foreign girls?" wrote Beatrice Kercher after spending some time at Bryn Mawr. "Wasn't I silly? I have learned to forget the nationality and get to know the girl."[43] Other students referenced their experiences at Bryn Mawr to promote the advancement of their racial or ethnic group. "Coming to Bryn Mawr Summer School has been a dream unfolded and a definite gain for me," wrote Helen Brooks, an African American student. "In the first place, I hope I have furthered the path through which other colored girls might enter, instead of hindering it. Then my thoughts of an opportunity to do something for my race has been strengthened."[44] A poem by Tessie Frankalangia reinforced the education at Bryn Mawr as consciousness-raising in an evocative poem:

Bryn Mawr has opened my eyes,
I no longer see darkness but see light,
Light in friendship, beauty and knowledge.
Bryn Mawr has taught me to make friends with
    The other nationalities and races.
Bryn Mawr has taught me the study of birds,
    Trees, flowers and the beauties of the sky.
Bryn Mawr has opened the key of my heart to Art,
    Music, books, and poetry.
Bryn Mawr has opened my eyes,
I no longer see darkness, but see light,
Light in friendship, beauty and knowledge.[45]

Frankalangia's poem emphasized the qualities of intelligence and solidarity, as did the very fact of her composing a poem. Her education did not deny difference, and it was not pragmatically designed to educate workers about their unions; rather, it was conceived as "enlightening" workers to their shared goals and obstacles. Education was valued at Bryn Mawr for its potential to strengthen ethnic and racial identifications, rather than to simply erase them, and education was envisioned as a tool for promoting equality across racial, ethnic, and national borders.

As was the case with the ILGWU-ED, the goal of the Summer School was always largely to educate students in such a way as to encourage a transformation outside the walls of the classroom. Floyd Joyce, a 1926 student, articulated exactly how her education translated into social change following her summer at Bryn Mawr. "All cannot be executives of trade unions, or head up great activities," Joyce writes, "but in our own local cities, with our own group of workers, the feeling of unity and solidarity can fire others with enthusiasm." Though she conceded that participation in workers' Summer School did not necessarily create a new cadre of union leaders, Joyce still depicted education as a vital component in a broader political struggle:

> Education is one tool which will help workers to build a better world. Not the kind of education that is for self advancement alone, but the kind of education which will help the individual worker to think for himself and go back into the shop to help other workers face the difficult tasks which confront them. Muscles without brains can never change the present social order. The Summer Schools, Vineyard Shore, and Brookwood are places where workers are taught not what to think but how to think and do and at all times to face the truth squarely and fearlessly.[46]

Joyce's rumination on the meaning of her Summer School experience reveals a remarkably nuanced understanding of the relationship between education and social change and illustrates the high level of investment working women had in representing their class as an intelligent group. "There are no weapons like words," another student confidently declared. "Many causes have been won through words; the lives of many millions are changed through words. Words have incited man to fight for freedom. Time will come when battles will be won by words."[47]

Centralization: Workers Education Bureau of America

The success of the ILGWU-ED and the Bryn Mawr Summer School as well as the programs they inspired, including the educational division of the Amalgamated and the Barnard School, in turn influenced a broader labor education movement. Settling lingering debates about the specific goals of labor education and the role of brainpower within the broader labor movement became increasingly critical as the workers' education movement was centralized through the formation of two national agencies: the Workers Education Bureau (WEB) in 1921, and the Affiliated Schools for

Workers (ASW), founded in 1926, which changed its name to the American Labor Education Service (ALES) in 1939. Though the latter organization had a national leadership, it was a loosely organized clearinghouse for the local organizations. The WEB, on the other hand, represented a model for workers' education that opposed in principle and spirit the idea of localized control. Earlier workers' education programs had been designed and managed within trade unions and their locals, a structure that preserved flexibility and responded to many constituencies. The form of education offered reflected the goals of limited groups and the demands of the workers themselves. The garment unions, with their militant leadership and rank and file, had conceived workers' education in radical terms that saw liberal arts education as important as—sometimes even more important than—developing trade or organizing skills. The BMSS was comprised of two-thirds garment workers; even though among those only about half belonged to unions.[48] The Amalgamated Clothing Workers of America unanimously passed a resolution implementing an educational department at their 1920 convention in Boston with J. B. Salutsky named national director. This official resolution stated explicitly "education is the basis of permanent and responsible organization among workers," but did not seek only to create workers amenable to organization. The resolution determined that "the purpose of this educational department of our organization be confined not only to economic and industrial instruction, but that it also include art, science and culture generally."[49] In another document, the Amalgamated asserted that "EDUCATION AT LARGE is the first task to which the Department proposes to devote itself. That is education for the largest numbers."[50] Brainpower was assumed to be an effective tool for advancing labor politics regardless whether the specific content in educational programs promoted organizing skills; and cultivating organic intellectuals, it was assumed, led inexorably to freedom.

The centralization of workers' education shifted discussions about comprehensively educating the working class to narrower conversations that limited the impact of education by referencing its practical contribution to the organization of labor unions. Centralization put workers' education in the hands of people who were heavily invested in furthering the goals of a craft-oriented labor movement, rather than in creating and promoting an intelligent working class. This distinction is small but important. The decentralized early years of women workers' education meant that control of educational initiatives was often placed wholly in the hands of administrators who were not otherwise entrenched in the morass of a massive labor organization.

Though the centralization of workers' education in the Workers Education Bureau continued to plot a track for education within a healthy labor movement, the founders of the WEB drew more from traditional American Federation of Labor (AFL)-style organizing than from the lessons taught by women who headed educational initiatives within the garment industry locals that prefigured it. The WEB was formed at a New York City workers' education conference on April 3, 1921, at the urging of the AFL.[51] The AFL had, according to one participant in the Bureau, "urgently called upon international and local unions, state and central bodies, to work actively for adequate representation of organized labor on all boards of education."[52] Clearly, the emphasis was upon control and centralization of the growing workers' education movement, which was in its current state diffuse and threatening the hegemony of the AFL's craft unionism. Though the AFL had, since 1918, claimed to support educational efforts, these were evidently seen as corollary to the more important organizing and negotiating efforts of the leadership.[53]

The Bureau set up offices at the New School for Social Research, itself a center for establishing the power of education for New York's working-class women and men. The following year, the Bureau formalized its relationship with the AFL at the labor federation's Forty-Second Annual Convention. In 1923, the Bureau again reorganized its executive committee to accommodate the AFL leadership. "Identification with official trade unions," wrote workers' education advocate Thomas R. Adam in 1940, "gave workers' education an opportunity to found itself on the habits and needs of organized labor, instead of the shifting sands of advanced intellectual theory."[54] It might be added that the WEB, under the direction of Spencer Miller, Jr., also placed the control of the movement firmly in the hands of men who comprised the AFL's leadership, displacing the radical women and militant immigrant rank and file who had shaped the movement's early years. The AFL began withdrawing support for the WEB's efforts by 1929 as they responded to the mounting economic crisis with an emphasis upon expanding their organizational reach.[55]

From its inception, the Bureau sought to centralize and bureaucratize the various rogue workers' education initiatives scattered throughout the country, similar to the way the AFL sought to centralize labor through crafts unions.[56] This muted the voices of the rank and file and excluded unskilled workers from the conversation; both factors effectively silenced women's voices within the movement. The constitution adopted at the AFL 1921 convention laid out several goals for the Bureau: to "act as a clearing house for information," to "act as a publicity organization," to "function as a registration bureau for supplying teachers to the different educational centers," to reform textbooks that were biased against labor, and to establish "a more or less clearly defined curriculum."[57] No mention was made of knowledge being power or the experiences of students in functioning workers' education programs.

The proceedings for the 1921 conference reveal the underlying division between those who favored a progressive educational program as the basis for working-class empowerment in keeping with the movement that had taken shape with women at the helm and those who saw education only as a means to create a skilled working class sympathetic to labor organization. This latter group saw comprehensive intelligence as less important than practical skills. Algernon Lee, educational director for the Rand School of Social Science, was a particularly vocal proponent of this view. "Education is a means to power—workers' education is a means to develop the workers' power to emancipate themselves. And every question as to what should be taught and how the teaching should be done must be answered with reference to this fundamental aim," Lee said.

> How far should we carry our English work on into the fields of literature, and thence to the drama, music and art, is one of our moot questions. And the same question presents itself with regard to the teaching of natural science, in the form which such teaching usually takes when it tries to be popular. These things are in demand. Considering the limitations of the time and energy at our disposal, ought we to regard them as essentials or as dispensable luxuries?[58]

For Lee, workers' education was valuable only insofar as it was immediately useful to the organization and social conscience of workers. Literature and science might be pleasurable pastimes, but they were of little value to an overextended labor movement.

For others involved in the formation of the Bureau, the primary usefulness of workers' education was conceived as a tool to tilt the worker's hand in collective bargaining. Workers' intelligence was not unlike a smart tie a negotiator could wear to impress the bosses, signifying that they were not dealing with the "common" element. In this respect, education was envisaged as a means to betray the "authentic" nature of the working class by dressing it up in the trappings of middle-class cultural capital. Though this definition of working-class intelligence effectively wrested control of working-class identity from the overdetermined bodies of the working class, the emphasis on gaining entrance into an old boys' network effectively displaced the women-centered labor movement of the ILGWU and competed with the ideals of the BMSS. Frank B. Metcalfe, secretary-treasurer of the Workers' College of Milwaukee, espoused such a view in a letter to Spencer Miller, director of the AFL-sponsored WEB, in 1922:

> The employer or his representative, usually educated, is willing enough to meet a dozen big, strong, ignorant working men, who for lack of education cannot express their thoughts and demands clearly and properly and are, therefore, easily *outtalked*, if not convinced, but they simply loathe to meet one small educated man, whom the union engages to represent it. In a battle of brains, intelligence only counts and the employers know it. To obtain enough education, so as to meet his employer on equal footing, is one of the many reasons why the workingman should seek better education.[59]

The precise ambition of education was thus to provide something of a middle-class mask, threatening the smug intellectual self-confidence that gave employers the upper hand in negotiations. Though this might be read as a capitulation to middle-class control over the politics of intelligence, the use of education as a weapon also represented an important point where workers upset the logic of a division of labor that disempowered the working class.

The more radical conception of education as a vehicle for empowerment threatened the very structure of labor organization, placing greater control in the hands of workers. The first pamphlet produced by the Bureau was a how-to manual for implementing workers' education courses, authored by Broadus Mitchell, associate professor in economics at Johns Hopkins University and instructor at Brookwood Labor College. Referring back to comments made by John Brophy, president of District 2 United Mine Workers of America, at the First National Conference on Workers Education in the United States, Mitchell advocated an intelligent working class. Workers education, according to Mitchell, ought to develop "thinking proletarians," who believe that "not force, not violence, but the Idea is power," and who are "convinced that education will win a better ordered industry and indirectly a better ordered society." Such groups will not only serve immediate demands by studying the social sciences, but will learn to want knowledge of literature, art and the natural sciences.[60]

Mitchell's pamphlet builds on the broad conceptualization of workers' education advocated by Fannia Cohn and promoted at Bryn Mawr's Summer School.

By contrast, Spencer Miller argued two years later that the "primary task of workers' education is to interpret modern industrial society to the worker that he may better understand his relationships to the industry in which he works and the society in which he lives." Still, Miller conceded that knowledge of labor history and economics were important tools for labor. "Collective bargaining does not exist, in fact, merely when an equal number of workingmen sit down with an equal number of employers to discuss problems of wages and hours," he said in an address to the Forty-Third Convention of the AFL. "An equality in numbers is not a real equality. Unless there is an equality or parity of intelligence and understanding of all the financial and industrial problems involved in a particular industry, there is no parity, in fact."[61] Yet overwhelmingly, the value of education remained tied in with promoting the goals of a craft union—and thus to accredit the rank and file as professionals. "Workers have a very special interest in education," he declared in 1924. He continued describing how "they see the world as craftsmen just as any other professional group, whether they be doctors, engineers, farmers, or the like."[62]

Under Miller's direction, the WEB defined the workers in workers' education as skilled and, for all intents and purposes, male. Intelligence was located in a male body and was valuable only insofar as it was a hallmark of union membership. "Constant progress is achieved through the increasing intelligence of the rank and file of the membership," a resolution of the AFL Educational Committee declared. "The worker must know the relation of the industry in which he works, not only to the labor movement, but also to the structure of our modern society." The courses and materials offered through the WEB programs were by necessity sympathetic to the goals and ideological underpinnings of the AFL. "We must face hard, unpleasant reality," wrote the WEB Committee on Curriculum in 1923. "The fact is that workers' schools today, particularly those under trade union control and management, are in no position to organize classes in the hundreds of subjects which may quite properly appeal to workers."[63] The shape of workers' education under the direction of the WEB, in sum, was brought into alignment with the politics of the AFL, and the fate of workers' education would rise and fall with that of the unions that controlled it.

*   *   *

Though there was little consensus within the workers' education movement of the 1920s about the specific goals it was promoting, the movement shifted the politics of brainpower in four critical ways throughout the 1920s. First, education was represented as a tool for militant action among the downtrodden. Just as Einstein introduced representations of intelligence as critically important to ordinary Americans, workers' education positioned educational institutions as sites of action for marginalized people, especially women and immigrants, who were disproportionately represented within the working class.

Second, brainpower was conceived as essential to overcoming the ignorance of many Americans about groups who seemed different. Many of those who attended workers' education classes saw their diverse student body as part of their education. Similarly, teachers and designers of workers' education programs envisioned intelligence as both a tool to overcome the tensions and conflicts of a pluralistic society and as a means to promote learning and respect for racial, ethnic, and national difference. Intelligence was represented as a tool to bring the working class together without foisting an assimilationist definition of working-class identity. As one student at the Wisconsin Summer School put it, "no one brilliant solution came, but out of that chaos I am getting something. Not one clearly defined path to the workers' goal, but a resultant of the thousand lines of force, which some day will accomplish our purpose."[64] This emphasis upon identity again suggested how brainpower was connected with progressive political programs that threatened conservative ideas about American identity.

Third, the workers' education movement represented intelligence as site of contest: the specific language invoked in calls for workers' education was recognized to be deeply ideological. The question of whether one was or was not intelligent was replaced with a new set of more complicated questions. Was intelligence something shared between classes, or was it a site of class conflict? Were some more entitled to education than others? Though those figures most active in the workers' education movement were not in total agreement about the answers to these questions, the fact that they were being posed reframed intelligence as a politicized ground and pushed the quest for brainpower to the center of discourse surrounding labor.

Finally, discussions about working-class brainpower incorporated questions about the relationship between intelligence and social change. Though more radical activists within the workers' education movement, such as Fannia Cohn, promoted a vision of working-class education that replicated the idea of a well-rounded intelligence, the fact that they encountered increased pressure to tie intelligence in with actual results (due largely to the fact that unions were funding these initiatives) forced them to increasingly moderate their defense of workers' intelligence to narrow its scope. In the context of the capitalist economy of the United States and the conservative demands of crafts unionism, intelligence was increasingly represented in terms of its value in adding to the number of union members. This framed intelligence as a set of skills as opposed to a set of available tools.

The workers' education movement introduced identity categories such as sex and ethnicity and extensive ideological debates into the discourse surrounding brainpower in American political, social, and cultural life. As these debates heated up, the Harlem Renaissance added an important set of new voices into these conversations. The next chapter studies the role of black cultural politics in shaping brainpower in the twentieth century. Just as the workers' education movement radicalized workers by centralizing their intelligence, the Harlem Renaissance's culture workers reframed brainpower to centralize black experiences and intelligence. The potential for brainpower to fundamentally change American society and the eagerness of ordinary women and men to lay claim to this important tool were critical components of the surge of black culture that took root in New York in the 1920s.

4

"The Negro Genius": Black Intellectual Workers
in the Harlem Renaissance

Without the New Knowledge the New Negro is no better than the
old. And this new knowledge will be found in the books.

—Hubert Harrison

In 1937, Benjamin Brawley, dean of Morehouse College, published an assessment of the recent literary movement known as the Harlem Renaissance. His book, *The Negro Genius*, attempted to account for the explosion of black literary and artistic accomplishment during the 1920s and into the 1930s. As he surveyed this vibrant cultural movement, spearheaded by black writers, artists, and performers, Brawley detected a particular form of intelligence—a rising black intellectualism—among African American culture workers, a feature that Brawley attributed to his title phenomenon. "Every race has its peculiar genius," Brawley declared in his introduction. "As far as we can at present judge, the Negro, with all his manual labor, is destined to reach his greatest heights in the field of the artistic."[1] For Brawley, the accomplishments of African Americans in the performing and literary arts derived from black culture's unique claim to artistic genius and offset associations of blackness with physicality. Though his analysis occasionally rehashed a familiar ideology of racial uplift whereby culturally accomplished African Americans were upheld as paragons of racial progress and others were expected to adhere to similar aspirations, Brawley departed from Booker T. Washington and other self-improvement advocates by arguing for an organic intelligence already found in every stratum of African American culture; within this narrative, the Harlem Renaissance was refigured as both sign and symptom of an intellect that needed greater recognition rather than further development.[2] Using textual evidence drawn from literature, music, and visual art, Brawley redefined genius by suggesting it derived from race and promoted the visibility of a New Negro, characterized by his adroit use of cultural tools to express himself and his racial identity. Through a rhetorical nod to African American history, Brawley distilled ongoing discussions about brainpower into a rising black nationalism centered on the intellectual contributions of his race.

Benjamin Brawley was faithful to the Harlem Renaissance focus on literary and artistic expression as major black contributions to American culture.[3] At the same time, he relegated the space for black brainpower to the cultural realm, effectively dismissing the possibilities for "Negro genius" in politics, science, mathematics, philosophy, and so forth.[4] His attempt to legitimize black genius excluded those forms of accomplishment that were most favored in uplift ideology, eschewing skills that had immediate, practical application. Brawley's aesthetic judgments, then, earnest though they might have been at aligning already recognized contributions by African Americans in a literary and cultural canon, slid into a complex argument about brainpower, in which the particular form of intelligence he celebrated explicitly racialized intelligence: genius, for Brawley, denoted a site of black experience and expertise.

The Negro Genius was part of a larger narrative about the New Negro that emerged in the early decades of the twentieth century. The *Cleveland Gazette* had defined the New Negro in 1895 as representative of an emerging "class" of African Americans characterized by "education, refinement, and money."[5] Intelligence was one defining trait of the New Negro, but so was class ascendance and "refinement"—the latter a gesture toward the discourse of civilization that, as Gail Bederman has persuasively argued, could not be disentangled from the shared language of gender and imperialism.[6] Benjamin Brawley's dissection of the Negro genius, appearing several decades after the New Negro's emergence, detached intelligence from its onerous association with white standards of cultural achievement, masculinity and manliness, bourgeois values, and wealth. Instead, "Negro genius" denoted an untapped reserve of social empowerment uniquely available to black women and men; as such, the building up of literary and cultural institutions to privilege African American contributions was uniquely poised to over-throw white supremacy within the United States.[7] The Negro genius posed a powerful threat to whiteness, ignorance, and assimilationist patterns in American liberalism.

The Harlem Renaissance staged a particularly vibrant scene in the developing drama around the New Negro in American culture. In novels, poems, and articles published in both mainstream and black periodicals, the political and aesthetic value of intelligence was debated and renegoti-ated, always with an eye toward liberating African Americans—too often narrowly defined as black men—from the repressive institutions in the United States.[8] Writers such as Claude McKay challenged definitions of in-telligence that assumed middle-class values. In novels, poems, and essays, conflict roiled around the relationship between intelligence and racial/sexual identities. The framing of intelligence within a racialized definition, and therefore as a destabilized and deeply politicized category, reinforced a growing conception of brainpower as potentially valuable for political change while also cautioning against the idea that intelligence was a uni-versalizing and deracinating tool. Intelligence further represented a cate-gory through which definitions of and demands for heteronormative masculinity among black workers, activists, and cultural producers could be productively challenged, posing a threat to the dominant racial and sexual order.[9]

Brainpower was inextricable from representations and expressions of the New Negro in the 1920s. Within these representations a paradox emerged: the New Negro was conceived as cultured and intelligent, but also as grounded in lived experience. While the Harlem Renaissance imagined black identity in a far more expansive form than had earlier cultural move-ments, it also presented an occasion for putting forward a trenchant critique of intellectual elitism and uplift ideology. Writers of the Harlem Renais-sance attempted to unify the impulse toward associating African American cultural practices with the body in the growing culturalism embedded in black political and social life. I begin this chapter by looking at the relation-ship between brainpower and the New Negro. I then examine the ways in which intelligence was represented through Harlem Renaissance literary aestheticism. I conclude by discussing the role of brainpower in Claude McKay's 1928 novel, *Home to Harlem*. Through his characters of Ray and Jake, McKay resisted the self-help form of racial uplift, which, in Kevin Gaines's words, "bore the stamp of evolutionary racial theories positing the civilization of elites against the moral degradation of the masses."[10] McKay resisted this stamp by highlighting the contradictions in black intelligence and attempted to resolve the dialectic between brain and body through his queer evocation of home.

Brainpower and the Politics of the New Negro

The malleability of the New Negro in the 1920s was one of the figure's most salient features. Depending upon who was writing, the New Negro could be defined as a figure of resistance against white supremacy; an urban, cosmopolitan character swinging to the latest jazz; an educated radical threatening the status quo with socialist (or worse) ideas; a returning soldier traversing the cultural landscape with a cocky Parisian and/or Pan-Africanist swagger; a newly liberated interracialist daringly cavorting in New York's famed black-and-tans; a race-conscious aesthete; or a combination of any of these. Among historians looking back at the Harlem Renaissance, disagreement about the term is similarly profound.[11] Yet even within these highly varied efforts to contain a cultural shift in a snappy alliterative category—or to release the subject from its denotative bonds—the New Negro's expansive definition has consistently implied for both contemporary and later critics a certain sharp intellect, an interest in the life of the mind, and a newly widespread concern with the possibilities and utility of brainpower for advancing black politics.

The interest in brainpower within African American culture had deep roots, but it was articulated perhaps most famously by Booker T. Washington and W. E. B. Du Bois. In 1901, as a new century dawned, Booker T. Washington published his influential autobiography, *Up from Slavery*, in which he narrated his life story and outlined his famous work with the Tuskegee Institute. Washington offered a passionate defense of the quest for citizenship his industrial college was set up to promote. Two years later, Du Bois published *The Souls of Black Folk*, an important literary, historical, sociological, and philosophical study read by some as a response to Washington's work, in which he articulated his profound exploration of double-consciousness, American race discrimination, and black culture. Though their approaches to combating the stubborn persistence of American racism differed in significant ways, Du Bois and Washington agreed on one fundamental point: the surest way to achieve racial equality was by promoting brainpower. For Washington, this was an inevitable conclusion to the march of racial progress; education was bound to expand the progress of freedom. "One might as well try to stop the progress of a mighty railroad train by throwing his body across the track," Washington wrote, "as to try to stop the growth of the world in the direction of giving mankind more intelligence, more culture, more skill, more liberty, and in the direction of extending more sympathy and more brotherly kindness." Du Bois, for his part, conceived brainpower as best promoted by his "talented tenth," the educated elite who, he famously argued, would "guide the Mass away from the contamination and death of the Worst, in their own and other races."[12]

Du Bois and Washington might have disagreed about the particular contours of brainpower, but both were outspoken advocates for the value of intelligence to achieve the goals of social justice, and each vigorously pursued a vocation dedicated to combating racism. "I sit with Shakespeare and he winces not," Du Bois wrote. "Across the color line I move arm in arm with Balzac and Dumas, where smiling men and welcoming women glide in gilded halls."[13] Washington and Du Bois's differing definitions of intelligence—one steeped in classical knowledge, the other in acquiring usable information—have too often masked their fundamental agreement that freedom begins in the mind and that building alliances begins with expanding access to brainpower.

By the 1920s the idea that intelligence was a fundamental feature of black life and was essential to social change was fully embedded in New Negro politics. One of the hallmarks of the New Negro was accomplishment in education. Though the New Negro had not necessarily advanced through higher educational institutions, most of which remained inaccessible to all but the most privileged African Americans, a fundamental shift had occurred in both the accessibility of education and the centrality of demands for education among black women and men. The trumpeting of black educational accomplishment functioned as a rebuttal to the lingering charges that African Americans were unworthy of education and would debase the educational potential of whites. Washington was especially adept at using white fears about educated black men to secure funding for educational programs that threatened racial hierarchies through uplift ideology; the New Negro animated parallel fears to entice black women and men to enter educational institutions. The Crisis (edited by Du Bois) published regular profiles of black college graduates; similar articles were commonly featured in many other black periodicals.

The New Negro challenged uplift ideology by highlighting the ways in which educational accomplishment gave lie to the false presumption that African Americans should be denied access to higher education; stressing how racial intelligence both uplifted the race *and* undermined uplift ideology. In his famous 1919 *Crisis* article, "Returning Soldiers," Du Bois attacked racist constructions of uneducable African Americans by pointing to a militant cadre armed with a healthy reserve of intelligence. "A dominant minority does not want Negroes educated," he declared. "It wants servants, dogs, whores, and monkeys. And when this land allows a reactionary group by its stolen political power to force as many black folk into these categories as it possibly can, it cries in contemptible hypocrisy: 'They threaten us with degeneracy; they cannot be educated.'" Against this mob Du Bois offered his trenchant rebuttal:

We *return.*
We *return from fighting.*
We *return fighting.*[14]

The experience of the returned soldier resonated not only in the militancy and spectre of revolutions that would resound throughout the violence of red summer, but it also pointed to the liberated Negro who was equipped with a new demand for recognition to challenge intellectual oppressors. George Schuyler, a leading figure in the Harlem Renaissance, echoed this construction in his discussion of the *newness* of the soldiering New Negro: "No longer ignorant, terrorized, or lacking confidence," he wrote, "he waits, and schemes, and plans." Schuyler's choice of terms the New Negro resisted—ignorance, lacking confidence—indicted the suppressed intelligence of prewar African Americans; the New Negro, in contrast, relied upon intelligence: he "waits, and schemes, and plans." Brainpower prevented white terror from taking hold; built up the self-confidence of black women and men; and provided a reserve of intelligence that would remind black subjects and the white folk clinging tenuously to their grip on the machines of power that "everywhere he is on the march, he cannot be stopped, and he knows it."[15]

It was not only these soldiers, these men, who were uniquely charged with accessing and spreading brainpower as a challenge to white supremacy. The intelligence of women threatened the organization of both racial and gender hierarchies in the United States.[16] In 1894 Fannie Barrier Williams, who achieved national visibility with a talk at the World's Columbian Exposition titled "The Intellectual Progress of the Colored Women of the United States Since the Emancipation Proclamation," proclaimed that "the great problems of social reform that are now so engaging the highest intelligence of American women will soon need for their solution the reinforcement of that new intelligence which our women are developing. In short, our women are ambitious to be contributors to all the great moral and intellectual forces that make for the greater weal of our common country."[17] The women of the Harlem Renaissance, including Nella Larsen, Jessie Redmon Fauset, and Zora Neale Hurston illustrated the central role women could play in leveling hierarchies of race, sex, and gender.

Though intelligence, as Benjamin Brawley demonstrated, was not identical with education, the 1920s saw a growing interest in representing educated African Americans. The increased number of black women and men who earned college and graduate degrees broadcast a variety of meanings: they represented the accomplishments of a people confronting the historical legacies and persistent obstacles of a racist past and present; a reaction against a religion that was ironically celebrated in mainstream white culture as a quaint, simple faith; and a rebuttal to Jim Crow stereotypes that were used to justify racial restrictions. In a *Crisis* article debunking the fallacious intelligence tests that attempted to legitimize through scientific discourse reigning myths about black intellectual inferiority, the distinguished professor Horace Mann Bond made the bold claim that attacks on black intelligence were frankly designed to "demonstrate that the Negro is intellectually and physically incapable of assuming the dignities, rights and duties which devolve upon him as a member of modern society."[18] Education was a marker of the newly emboldened New Negro who resisted such political aspersions and traded Christian doctrine for the intellectual liberation implied in new scientific works—many of them symptomatic of a radical impulse lying just below the surface of calls for brainpower. In contrast to the "Old Negro," for whom "improving his mind by reading good books and acquiring a knowledge of the history of his racial group, is . . . a real pain," J. A. Rogers wrote in a 1927 *Messenger* article, the New Negro "jettisons Matthew for Marx" and "David for Darwin." The New Negro was scientific, radical, and smart enough to refuse supine acceptance of the malicious labels of white society. Rogers sketched a "New Negro [who] is not afraid of such bogey labels as rebel, atheist, pagan, infidel, Socialist, Red, heathen, radical, realizing that what they really connote is 'thinker.'"[19] The recitation of unsavory signifiers attached to the educated African American was repositioned in the New Negro discourse as symptomatic of the racist demand that black women and men be denied both access to education and full inclusion in American life. Yet this threat offered the opportunity for the New Negro to disrupt the illogic of white supremacy by adopting the identity of a "thinker"; brain-power offset a series of labels that were used to keep racial hierarchies in place.

Hubert Harrison was an especially vocal advocate for putting the education of the New Negro in the interest of black nationalism. "We Ne-groes must take to reading, study, and the development of intelligence as we have never done before," Harrison wrote in a 1920 text that preserved over-tones of racial uplift.[20] Though Harrison often advocated political programs that positioned educated African Americans as pinnacles of the race, the nuances of Harrison's program, articulated most cogently in his classic 1920 work, *When Africa Awakes*, reveal how radicalism, race, and brainpower were intimately tied during the height of the New Negro movement.

Harrison remains one of the most complicated and controversial char-acters within African American culture of the 1920s.[21] Moving between identities as a socialist, Garveyite, and independent radical, Harrison's con-sistent tilt toward black nationalism kept him at the forefront of black po-litical life throughout the decade, and he held that education was a vital tool for the emancipation of his race. His Pan-African radicalism led him to envision brainpower as a critical component of the anticolonial, anti-racist, anti-imperialist project. "It is not with our teeth that we will tear the white man out of our ancestral land," he writes. "It isn't with our jaws that we can ring from his hard hands consideration and respect. It must be done by the upper and not by the lower part of our heads."[22] Harrison was insis-tent that brainpower could accomplish what physical threats never could, though he refused to deny that violence was also part of revolutionary (and especially anticolonial) struggle.

Harrison occasionally fell into a conciliatory mode, conceiving brain-power as offering a site of equality for white and black—a position that imagined racism as resulting in part from a misunderstanding about Afri-can American intellect. This framework corresponded with the uplift ideol-ogy that Harrison tried to resist with mixed success. "[N]ever until the Negro's knowledge of nitrates and engineering, of chemistry and agricul-ture, of history, science and business is on a level, at least, with that of whites," Harrison writes in *When Africa Awakes*, "will the Negro be able to measure arms successfully with them." In this striking passage, he rehearses the claim that brainpower would make up for Negro deficit, and promotes intelligence as an equalizer that demanded African Americans live up to the standards set by white culture. "We can not win from the white man unless we know as much as the white man knows," he writes. "For, after all, knowledge *is* power."[23]

Yet in spite of his occasional lapses into intellectual racial romanticism and uplift ideology, Harrison's frequent references to brainpower also accentuate the legitimate claim to intelligence that he detected was already present among the Negro masses. The New Negro leadership, Harrison argues, "will be based not upon the ignorance of the masses, but upon their intelligence." Furthermore, this intelligence drew upon a knowledge base outside the rarified institutional channels of the elite educational structure embedded in the discourse of American intellectual culture. "Today the masses include educated laymen who have studied science, theology, history, and economics, not, perhaps in college but, nevertheless, deeply and down to date." Harrison refuses to put faith in the earthy, organic knowledge of the masses, but similarly accords little favor to the talented tenth that boasts of their accreditation from the existing scholarly institutions. Instead, Harrison positions the autodidact, the armchair academic, directly alongside traditional intellectuals as being symptomatic of the new mass movement toward radical intelligence. *When Africa Awakes* includes a comprehensive reading list comprised of texts ranging from Charles Darwin's *Origin of the Species* to Gibbon's *Decline and Fall of the Roman Empire* and Franz Boas's *The Mind of Primitive Man*, which, if successfully read, would afford the humble reader "a better 'education' than is found in nine-tenths of the graduates of the average American college."[24]

That the bulk of Harrison's reading list relates to the science of society and human evolution reveals another important dimension to his specific positioning of intelligence in the New Negro movement: brainpower was accessible to the masses and directed their growing intelligence toward social critique. Harrison upheld the Russian Revolution as a model historical moment when brainpower changed the world. "As knowledge spread, enthusiasm was backed by brains," Harrison writes. "The Russian revolution began to be sure of itself. The workingmen of the cities studied the thing that they were 'up against,' gauged their own weakness and strength as well as their opponents.'"[25] The Russian Revolution could provide a script not only because of the interest in Bolshevism that had swept the United States in 1919, but also because it had succeeded in no small measure thanks to the premium placed on intellect.[26]

Finally, Harrison's appraisal of the New Negro recognized that theoretical knowledge represented a necessary component for liberation and emancipation, but that valuing brainpower required more than spreading intelligence around to the broadest group. The freedom he sought balanced education on essential subjects for self-determination and the ability to recognize social injustice with practical, applied knowledge. "What kind of knowledge is it that enables white men to rule black men's lands?" he asks. "It is the knowledge of explosives and deadly compounds: that is chemistry." Intelligence was necessary for constructing ordnance and outsmarting the enemy. It was also directly connected to lived experience. "For in this work-a-day world," Harrison allows, "people ask first, not 'Where were you educated?' but 'What do you know?'"[27]

If Harrison represented a singular figure in the effort to theorize the relationship between brainpower and black emancipation, his foil in the discursive formation of intelligence through the New Negro might arguably have been a man from a strikingly different social, political, and racial background: the dandified bohemian slummer and chronicler of Harlem as spectacle, Carl Van Vechten. Though Van Vechten, especially in his signature work of the Harlem Renaissance, the controversial bestseller, *Nigger Heaven*, did not explicitly theorize the relationship between brainpower and black emancipation, he shared with Harrison a fundamental understanding that the "lived experience" of African Americans was central to understanding the mind of the New Negro.[28] Yet rather than following Brawley or Harrison in seeing through lived experience the potential for harnessing brainpower to achieve self-determination, Van Vechten epitomized an intellectual gaze, whereby the meaning of the New Negro was determined by the intellectual observer whose assumed superiority was both raced through whiteness and depicted as a matter of critical distance accessible only by and through the bohemian intellectual. The white writer was thus positioned as uniquely qualified to describe the "scene" in Harlem not only because he was participating in the embodiment of black life, but also because he was able to process this through intellectual procedures that were uniquely qualified to observe it from a distance. If one, in the words of popular Harlem songwriter Andy Razaf, were to "like Van Vechten, start inspectin'," this entailed positioning African American life as an object for scrutiny, objectification, and pseudo-scientific inquiry.[29] "In the intellectual realm," Alain

Locke wrote in 1925, "the Negro is being carefully studied, not just talked about and discussed."[30]

Though *Nigger Heaven* followed a familiar formula for Harlem Renaissance depictions of (lumpen)proletarian black life as represented in, for example, McKay's *Home to Harlem* and Wallace Thurman's fictionalized treatment of "Niggeratti Manor" in *Infants of the Spring*, and treated as a writerly responsibility in Richard Wright's classic "Blueprint for Negro Writing" and the "slumming literature" popular in the early decades of the twentieth century, Van Vechten's novel occupied a uniquely vexed position in fiction of the 1920s.[31] Among Harlem Renaissance writers, Van Vechten's novel was met with both celebration (his book was a bestseller and praised by some luminaries among Harlem's literati, most famously by Langston Hughes, who provided Van Vechten with blues lyrics) and condemnation, the latter culminating in an especially damning review by Du Bois in *The Crisis* in which Du Bois charged Van Vechten with having produced an "affront to the hospitality of black folk and to the intelligence of white."[32] Literary historian David Levering Lewis contends that "it was considered bad form among Afro-Americans to be caught reading *Nigger Heaven*, and virtually everyone in Harlem discovered never-before-expressed misgivings about Carl Van Vechten or remembered some telltale incident of his racial insincerity."[33]

Sincere or not, Van Vechten made no effort to obscure the white audience for whom his book was intended: at the end of the book he included an extensive "Glossary of Negro Words and Phrases," a standard generic convention in slumming literatures. Though this lexicographical appendix might be seen as a mere supplement to the text, its inclusion serves as an important reminder that the anticipated readers of the book were not familiar with the Harlem slang peppered throughout Van Vechten's narrative. The terms he chooses to define are, tellingly, drawn from African American slang; it is not, then, the language of Van Vechten's own highbrow literary culture (or the stuff of ethnographic description) that he deems unfamiliar enough to require definition; instead it is the language used by characters in the novel to identify themselves. Van Vechten does not find it necessary to define all vernacular language: notably lacking amidst his catalogue of racial classifications (which include "jig," "dinge," "high yellow," and "spagingy-spagade") is the controversial title slur that precipitated so much heated debate about the novel. Van Vechten's work borrowed the vocabulary, gaze, and ethnographic sensibilities of the burgeoning Chicago School of sociology, and Van Vechten relied heavily upon the fascination among whites with all things black while profiting upon the assumption that such knowledge would protect those in the know from accusations of racism.

At the same time his glossary imagined an audience with a curious alchemy of racial knowledge and ignorance, Van Vechten's reliance upon naturalist depictions of black life constituted a bid to be accepted as a regular participant—rather than a meandering dilettante—in Harlem life. The act of slumming and the recording of one's travels into the underworld represented a signature gesture toward establishing a particular form of authority, treating the "foreign" and unfamiliar landscape within one's urban environment as an object for increasing both knowledge about oneself and the other. In the case of Van Vechten, slumming in Harlem offered a confirmation of both his and his reader's superior understanding, insofar as the distance from the subject, reinforced through the book's glossary, made visible the superior knowledge required to recognize and assess the world of black urban life. At the same time, reducing difference to a matter of producing and consuming knowledge offset the troubling distance between the white reader and black subject. A reader could learn the terms in Van Vechten's glossary while reading his novel to gain access to the putatively authentic world of the New Negro; to confirm one's bohemian credentials; to position oneself as a cosmopolitan citizen of the world. Learning was employed as a tool for accessing the authenticity accorded black urban life without undermining the privilege implied in a cross-racial readership.

Both Hubert Harrison and Carl Van Vechten reimagined brainpower in relation to the New Negro. For Harrison, building intelligence meant increasing both knowledge and access to education among African Americans. Brainpower was part of a program for emancipation, inclusion, and liberation. For Van Vechten, brainpower was also inherently racialized, and intelligence was found in cultural rather than political life. In contrast to Harrison, Van Vechten's deploying of brainpower both naturalized his hierarchy of white intelligence as superior to black lived experience and, at the same time, threatened the division between racialized forms of knowledge.

New Negro Aesthetics and the Representation of Brainpower

If the New Negro represented a characterization of the modern black radical, intellectual, and artist, Harlem epitomized the space and the scene where literary circles emerged to foster a robust community of artists, writers, performers, and musicians and to share the newness of the New Negro with the world. Within the texts produced during the Harlem Renaissance emerged representations of intelligence among the inhabitants of Harlem. Black writers featured intellectual figures within novels, poems, songs, and plays of the 1920s, and intelligence was represented as a facet of folk and modern culture; black and white representations; mass and high culture; and straight and queer sexual knowledge. The diverse and roiling cultural milieu in the Harlem Renaissance offered a site of negotiation within a discursive economy in which bodily pleasure was often enjoyed at the expense of intelligence.

In a symposium published over several issues of *The Crisis* from 1926, a variety of artists, writers, and intellectuals associated with the black literary world of the 1920s were invited to weigh in on the question of "The Negro in Art: How Shall He Be Portrayed." Along with several other questions, the editors posed this one: "Does the situation of the educated Negro, with its pathos, humiliation and tragedy call for artistic treatment at least as sincere and sympathetic as 'Porgy' received?"[34] The question itself was pointed: black writers were expected to be especially interested in treating subjects rich in "pathos, humiliation, and tragedy," as had DuBose Heyward in his wildly successful novel.[35] The framing of the question also equated education with intelligence; as we will see, writers such as Claude McKay resisted such constructions of both education and intelligence. Still, the writers' submitted responses represent a dynamic range of ideas about the role of intelligence in shaping Harlem Renaissance aesthetics and the centrality of black literature in articulating the politics of brainpower.

The timing of this query could be directly related to the growing, yet still disproportionately small, number of African Americans attending college and earning higher degrees. David Levering Lewis asserts that "there were 2,132 Afro-Americans in college in 1917. Ten years later, there were 13,580. . . . By 1927, 39 had won doctorates."[36] This sizeable increase in higher education opportunities and graduation rates signaled a potential site for disrupting racial hierarchies in education, but it also pointed to the continued disproportion of highly educated African Americans. A combination of infrastructural limitations, white resistance, segregationist policies, and simmering racial prejudice prevented African Americans from gaining admittance into many universities. Historically black colleges attempted to

redress discriminatory practices in higher education, but they could not accommodate every young person who sought entry. Still, the number of
black college students was growing, and this fact affected representations
of African Americans more generally.

Vachel Lindsay responded to the *Crisis* inquiry by ironically proposing
writers shop their wares in nations less familiar with the U.S. penchant for
romanticized depictions of beaten-down black characters. "The situation of
the educated Negro in America surely merits all possible sincere and artistic
treatment," he allowed. Yet "if such enterprises seem doomed to failure in
this country, they should be taken to Canada or England, or to the conti-
nental countries, and so finally reach the United States public with their
prestige already established."[37] Building this foundation, in Lindsay's esti-
mation, required thinking outside U.S. borders.

Mary White Ovington, a founder of the NAACP, replied by foregrounding ordinary women and men rather than within a rarified intellectual
class. "Publishers will take books dealing with the educated Negro," she
trenchantly declared, "if he can be written of without our continually seeing
his diploma sticking out of his pocket."[38] Ovington's devilish reply, slyly
critiquing the implicit assumption that intelligence would be the province
of males (who had greater access to education, if not intelligence), pointedly
targeted both the pretensions of educated elitists who believed intelligence
was a matter of degrees and the male bravado "sticking out of his pocket"
that characterized the talented tenth. Ovington advocated for representations of intelligence that would avoid reinscribing class privilege through
educational achievement and, implicitly, undo uplift ideology by rendering
the signs of scholarly achievement obscene; intelligence was, in short, best
represented without recourse to middle-class manliness.

Ovington continued on to demand that representations include the
banalities of black life to effectively resist the patronizing fascination of audiences who treated educated African Americans as curiosities and structurally different from the masses. "Just as soon as the writer can believe
that his reader knows there are educated Negroes, and doesn't have to be
told that they live in pleasant homes and don't eat with their knifes, he can
begin seriously to write about them."[39] Again, Ovington carefully signified
against the framing of the *Crisis* question by placing the representation of
intelligent black women and men in a broader social context: the opening
of access to education would render educated African Americans quotidian enough to be represented in naturalistic prose. Her invocation of the

primitivism used to marginalize black experience through reference to stereotypically "uncivilized" eating habits undermined the racist logic that rendered black intelligence exceptional. The question in *The Crisis* implied that aesthetic responsibility came before social practice and that writers produced the social conditions they described. Ovington instead placed the burden of responsibility for challenging limiting representations on readers, disrupting both the expectation that authors were solely accountable for the cultural politics shaping their output and the special responsibility placed on black writers. Education, Ovington suggested, was necessary for all Americans; her response, in sum, shifted the conversation from a limited question about representing educated African Americans to a broader intervention in the cultural politics of brainpower in the United States. Ovington's demand that educated women and men be recognized as ordinary displaced the question of representation by instead advancing a call for resisting a strategy that would position intelligence among blacks as anything other than typical.

Other responders to the question engaged in similar disavowals. Langston Hughes's short reply refused to distinguish between the value of representing educated or uneducated characters: "You write about the intelligent Negroes. Fisher about the unintelligent. Both of you are right." Walter White took this equalizing gesture further, suggesting that the question embedded a hidden racial assumption about intelligence. "Suppose we carry this objection to the utilization of experiences of educated Negroes to its logical conclusion. Would not the result be this: Negro writers should not write, the young Negro is told, of educated Negroes because their lives paralleling white lives are uninteresting."[40] For White, representations of intelligence had the potential to undo the logic of racial hierarchy: black writers were expected to revel in the lives of the uneducated in order that black lives not be confused with the lives of whites; subjecting educated black lives to representation would eliminate the distinction between black and white lives. White's response incorporated aspects of racial uplift ideology, but he reappropriated this language by framing his reply as a critique of the line of questioning rather than as a call for such representations. Rather than directly responding to *The Crisis*'s provocation, White carefully deconstructed the question by adjudicating between the pitfalls in either a wholehearted embrace of educated representations or its refusal, in the process suggesting the complicated racial politics of intelligence and the value of brainpower for upsetting racial hierarchies.

Though their responses to the question about the "educated Negro" were not in full agreement, the writers represented in the forum illustrate how central were discussions about brainpower within the Harlem Renaissance. Jessie Redmon Fauset's laconic response to the questionnaire—"I should say so," she replied curtly to the *Crisis* question about educated black characters[41]—might be taken as of particular interest insofar as her most significant literary work, *Plum Bun*, dealt with the subject of middle-class passing and refused the exuberant carnivalesque of many of her peers. Passing, or "going over," was a regular topic in black fiction of the early twentieth century. The role of intelligence in passing was widely acknowledged among writers on the subject in the 1920s. Louis Fremont Baldwin, in his 1929 study *From Negro to Caucasian*, echoed Walter White when he suggested that detection of passing was made difficult because "white people are not inclined to think of a Negro in terms of intelligence or equality."[42] Within passing novels, it was often the experience of being educated, usually in the context of a cultured and anonymous northern city, that presented an occasion for passing. The process of racial passing by way of education introduced a form of double-consciousness that often frustrated efforts at shaking off racial heritage enough that the protagonist's black subjectivity returned. Intelligence, then, was destabilized as a racial signifier as it was associated with bourgeois education.

Jessie Fauset's important 1929 passing novel *Plum Bun* follows the occasionally intersecting lives of two sisters, Angela and Virginia Murray, in New York before and after Angela decides to pass for white. Fauset was a key figure in the Renaissance both because of her well-regarded and influential works, especially *There Is Confusion* and *Plum Bun*, and because of her high-profile role as literary editor of *The Crisis* from 1919 to 1926. In *Plum Bun*, Angela Murray, a young African American woman from Philadelphia, after experiencing both the thrill of passing and the shaming effects of racism, moves to New York and becomes Angéle Mory, a white aspiring painter moving through the rarified and bohemian worlds of the city. One of the contradictions Angela is attentive to early in her life, which informs her decision both to become an artist and to pass for white, appears in her decision to choose a profession other than that of a schoolteacher: though teaching is one of the few occupations available to black women, Angela notices that "coloured children may be taught by white teachers, [but] white children must never receive knowledge at the hands of coloured instructors."[43] The paradox in this social reality lies in its racial illogic. Angela's friend Mary, for example, achieves the height of schoolyard popularity despite being "rather stupid in her work, in fact she shone in nothing but French and good manners"; Roger Fielding, the profoundly racist man Angéle pursues while passing, is profoundly ignorant about both race matters—he bumbles along through a series of humiliating episodes in racism—and the world around him.

Even in her early life as a child in Philadelphia, Angela envisions her intelligence as a means to move beyond her circumstances. "She possessed the instinct for self-appraisal which taught her that she had much to learn," Fauset writes, "and she was sure that the knowledge once gained would flower in her case to perfection."[44] Fauset particularly focuses on Angela's abilities in French, a form of knowledge that both provides a point of entry for her passing (her passing name mimics her birth name given a superficially French spelling and accent) and gestures toward a form of intelligence that is particularly reserved for women.[45] "Study for its own sake held no attractions for her," Fauset writes of Angela; "she did not care for any of her subjects really except Drawing and French."[46] As she becomes more enamored of the possibilities attendant to passing, Angela increasingly surrounds herself with people characterized by their intellect: her friends Walter and Elizabeth Sandburg, for example, are both brainworkers.

Angéle increasingly finds herself encountering women and men who are both black and intelligent, a coupling that she reads as a racial contradiction. These characters are female and male, poor and wealthy, educated and not; in each case, however, the definition of what black identity means in relation to whiteness is structured for Angéle by the characters' relationship to black New York's intelligentsia. Paulette, for example, is a black woman Angéle meets who "seemed bathed in intensity" and who possesses "restless, clever mental energy"; she offers an especially attractive threat to both patriarchy and racial hierarchies because she "took love and marriage as the sauce of existence and [her] intellectual interests as the main dish." Rachel Salting is a Jewish woman who "spoke . . . with a knowledge and zest which astounded Angela, whose training had been rather superficial." The bohemian circle surrounding Martha Burden and Ladislas Starr "were all possessed of a common ground of knowledge in which such subjects as Russia, Consumers' Leagues, and the coming presidential election figured most largely." Even Angela's sister, Virginia, "spent a good deal of time with a happy, intelligent, rather independent group of young coloured men and women; there was talk occasionally of the theatre, of a dance, of small clubs, of hikes, of classes at Columbia or at New York City College."[47]

It is this paradox for Angela—observing the scintillating intellectual world black women and men occupy even as she surrounds herself with ignorant whites including her young friend Mary Hastings, who is not bright, and Roger Fielding, who is both ignorant and had "black-balled Negroes in Harvard"—that leads her to question her passing. A significant turning point occurs for Angela when she attends a lecture by Van Meier, a "great coloured American, a littérateur, a fearless and dauntless apostle of the rights of man," and a thinly disguised Du Bois.[48] Meier is both proudly black and unquestionably brilliant, and Angela finds herself pulled between dismissive remarks made by Roger Fielding and her burgeoning racial pride. Van Meier produces a crisis of racial identity by fully embodying both intellect and race pride, an admixture that becomes for Angela a site of new possibility.

Recognizing the potential for intelligence to open doors otherwise closed to many African Americans initially spurs Angela to pass as Angéle, but observing the smart set with whom her sister socializes in Harlem provides a point of entry for Angela's awakening black racial pride and instigates a bold acknowledgment of her racial heritage. Within Fauset's novel, passing is made possible not only through the possession of a light complexion, but also by assuming intelligence. Yet the impossibility of passing—its limitations for developing a holistic sense of self that incorporates racial identity—functions as a critique of the use of brainpower to promote and legitimize white hegemony. Intelligence is ultimately shown to be most valuable when it is acknowledged to be always-already available within black communities, and the premium placed upon white intelligence is revealed as a raced construction that undermines brainpower's progressive potential.

Though Harlem Renaissance writers who wrote about passing sought to disavow the alignment of white privilege with intelligence—their works were, to put it mildly, critical of both the practice of passing and the notion that it was desirable—in the context of the deeply embedded structure of racism that existed in the United States in the 1920s, passing novels rebutted the idea that intelligence was a deracinated construction, that brainpower was automatically antiracist, or that it could be detached from the social structure within which it was articulated. Passing novels also commented on themes interlacing gender and sexuality. Literary historians have commented on the queerness of the Harlem Renaissance, both in terms of the writers and artists as well as the content of their work. Wallace Thurman's *Infants of the Spring* features characters that engage in intellectual conversation that foregrounds race and cultural topics and touches on queer intellectualism. "Their likes and dislikes in literature were sufficiently similar to give them similar philosophies about life, and sufficiently dissimilar to provide food for animated discussions," Thurman writes of the inhabitants of "Niggerati Manor." "It was only when their talk veered to Harlem that they found themselves sitting at opposite poles." This intellectual conversation provides a titillating glimpse of the queer subtext underlying Thurman's characters' literary tastes: the semi-autobiographical character Raymond, a sexual libertine and highbrow intellectual, proposes that "Thomas Mann and Andre Gide were the only living literary giants."[49] For Raymond, intellectual chatter both elevates the race and provides an occasion for queer canon building.

Perhaps the most influential argument for envisioning brainpower as a tool for overcoming discrimination appeared in Alain Locke's edited volume *The New Negro* in 1925. In defending his classification of the New Negro and the geography of Harlem, Locke repeatedly referred to the "mind" of black Americans. This racialized mind signified a community joined in struggle, but it also represented a brain in pursuit of intellectual stimulation. "No sane observer, however sympathetic to the new trend, would contend that the great masses are articulate as yet," Locke writes in his introductory essay, "but they stir, they move, they are more than physically restless." This "more than physical" restlessness marks the collective brainpower animated through efforts at producing a renewed racial identity. "The intelligent Negro of to-day," Locke continues later, "is trying to hold himself at par, neither inflated by sentimental allowances nor depreciated by current social discounts"; in fact, the "Negro renaissance" was uniquely poised as a social intervention because "the 'spite-wall' that the intellectuals built over the 'color-line' has happily been taken down." Moreover, "an intelligent realization of the great discrepancy between the American social creed and the American social practice forces upon the Negro the taking of the moral advantage that is his."[50]

Alain Locke stood out even among the culturalists who promoted the Harlem Renaissance as especially invested in promoting cultural achievements that would both embody and appeal to elitist values and definitions of art. Yet his selections for *The New Negro* reflect a growing consciousness among the most bourgeois black culturalists that the intelligence of the New Negro was becoming visible within the mass culture that was incorporated into literary works by writers ranging from William Stanley Braithwaite to Gwendolyn Bennett. It was the work of Claude McKay, however, that posed one of the most trenchant challenges both to the elitist definition of intelligence favored by Alain Locke and to the underlying rhetoric of racial uplift that many representations of intelligence in the Harlem Renaissance recapitulated.

The New Negro and Mind/Body Dualism
in Claude McKay's *Home to Harlem*

Claude McKay's 1928 novel *Home to Harlem*, which has been described by both critics and its author as a response to *Nigger Heaven*, in Deborah E. McDowell's words attempted to "strike a balance between portrayals of the black intelligentsia and the black underworld."[51] Rather than describing this polarity in terms of separate institutions, economies, geographies, or even social locations, however, McKay carefully places his two protagonists, Jake and Ray, in the same Harlem "home," setting his novel in interzones where conversation collapses the categories of intellectuals and non-intellectuals and privileges a distinctly black cultural space. As a response to Van Vechten-style "inspectin'," McKay's novel also does important work eliminating the distance found in ethnographic writing, opting instead to detail the intimate forms of knowledge that Jake and Ray share.[52]

Home to Harlem is as famous for having provoked the ire of the esteemed W. E. B. Du Bois as it is for throwing up the curtain on Harlem nightlife, intraracial hierarchies, violence, perversion, and sexual libertinism. In an oft-quoted *Crisis* review, Du Bois declared that the novel "nauseates me, and after the dirtier parts of its filth I feel distinctly like taking a bath."[53] It was McKay's fetishistic cataloguing of base behaviors—his prurient recitation of the pleasures of drink, sex, violence, and more sex—that received the most critical comment and scorn. Yet in contrast with the slumming literatures prevalent in the Harlem Renaissance, McKay's carefully crafted narrative affirms the liveliness, labor, and lust of his characters' minds as well as their bodies. Literary scholar Shane Vogel has pointed to *Home to Harlem*'s "affective resonance" to differentiate between the spectacular fetishization in Van Vechten's work and the intimacy found in the novels of McKay.[54] McKay's attention to humor, frustration, and self-conscious dissection—his characters talk incessantly about *everything*—offers an expansive repertoire for his black characters which in turn suggests the spirited intelligence of the masses. McKay's refusal to split brain from body comprises a powerful response to the primitivism that critics have detected in much white pa-tronage of the Harlem Renaissance—and even within some of the renais-sance's most celebrated work. For critic Michael B. Stoff, McKay's work fails to resolve the unsettling contradiction in the way McKay "pursued a primi-tive life-style as he struggled with the special problems of the black intellec-tual."[55] I argue instead for rereading McKay's work as a special form of resolution to the artificial division of mind and body in modern black fiction.

McKay begins *Home to Harlem* with a corporeal description that grounds Jake's brain in his self-consciously laboring body: "All that Jake knew about the freighter on which he stoked was that it stank between sea and sky."[56] McKay provocatively suggests to readers that Jake's reflexive body graphs a knowledge that constructs his unique claim to brainpower, further suggest-ing that the physical sensations of work represent a form of intelligence that points to McKay's particular investment in affirming the black working class. As a black Marxist writer who was both a celebrated member of the intellectual class and a tireless advocate for the proletariat, McKay articu-lated a decidedly dialectical defense of the black worker's brainpower.[57] As his narrative proceeds, especially through the introduction of Ray, a savvy radical train waiter who attended a black college, McKay layers multiple forms of intellectual labor. *Home to Harlem* launches with an evocation of the laboring body and the pungent stink of the sea, resolved through Jake's knowing brain. Jake's base-level intelligence refuses the dualism that struc-tures intelligence in a capitalist context (worker as body, manager as brain), but it also challenges the debasement of labor by asserting work as demand-ing intelligence: Jake's recognition constitutes a cognition that might be posi-tioned as utopian. This construction of the proletarian intellectual anticipates a significant trope that reemerged in the radical fiction of the 1930s.

At times *Home to Harlem* reads like a catalog of everything Jake knows: the plot meanders through episodes that highlight his learning on race, geography, sex, cabaret, liquor, blues song, dialect, and transnational black politics. The resolution to the conflicted mind/body dualism that is grafted onto Jake emerges through his strong sense of home: it is in Harlem where Jake is most expert and most efficient at navigating social, geographical, sexual, racial, and class boundaries: he "gained access to buffet flats and private rendezvous apartments that were called 'nifty'"—no small feat for a black longshoreman. Home is also a mess of sexual and raced identities: "Dandies and pansies, chocolate, chestnut, coffee, ebony, cream, yellow, everybody was teased up to the high point of excitement." Harlem represents, then, a space between sea and sky where black intelligence is uniquely rewarded, highly visible, and distinctly democratic: a significant benefit of going home to Harlem is that one finds a locus for the "Negro genius." The education of Jake takes place on the streets and in Harlem nightclubs. In the Congo, a Harlem cabaret, Jake absorbs a newly cosmopolitan and transnational vocabulary: "Ever since the night at the Congo when he heard the fighting West Indian girl cry, 'I'll slap you bumbole,'" McKay writes, "he had always used the word."[58]

Neither is Jake's education limited to vernacular wisdom he acquires within the neighborhood. Ray, the Haitian waiter on a train where Jake works as a cook, schools him about historical subjects such as Toussaint L'Ouverture by way of a Wordsworth recitation.[59] Some critics have read the relation between Jake and Ray as representing two sides—mind and body—of the same character. Wayne Cooper, in his authoritative biography of McKay, conceives these characters through this lens, asserting that Ray "possessed powers of conceptualization and analysis that Jake lacked, but he also lacked Jake's spontaneity and confidence."[60] Yet throughout his career, McKay insisted on undoing such Cartesian dualism, not least by wedding his political action with his literary production. McKay's narrative ramblings in *Home to Harlem* acknowledge the intelligence and embodiment of both Jake and Ray, and his narrative discounts knowledge that detaches itself too fully from bodily pleasures or work. Jake, as we have seen, is introduced to readers as a storehouse of knowledge. Ray, for his part, is no stranger to pleasure or pain: he left Howard University because his father was arrested and his brother killed.

McKay depicts the relationship between Jake and Ray as something beyond friends. As *Home to Harlem* progresses, these two characters begin to meld into one another. "A big friendship had sprung up between them," McKay writes, and "the other cooks and waiters called Ray 'Professor.' Jake had never called him that. Nor did he call him 'buddy,' as he did Zeddy and his longshoremen friends. He called him 'chappie' in a genial, semi-paternal way."[61] Jake's term of endearment, signifying on the "big friendship" he and Ray share, characterizes their relationship as a queer form of affection. This unusual closeness reinforces the mutually shared investment each has in the other: claims over the brain or the body belong to neither, and McKay's depiction of their relationship highlights the boundedness of intelligence within black experiences of embodiment.

One feature that does distinguish Ray's intelligence from Jake's is his acute awareness of double consciousness and racial oppression. Though this wins him the scorn of some characters—the mean chef on the railroad detests "that theah professor and his nonsense"—it also challenges the degradation experienced by black workers: "Ray felt that as he was conscious of being black and impotent, so correspondingly, each marine down in Hayti must be conscious of being white and powerful." Ray's intelligence spurs him to align with the working class, even as his racing thoughts—"what would become of that great mass of black swine, hunted and cornered by slavering white canaille!"—keep him awake at night. Yet his intelligence represents a respite from the world of intellectual elitism Ray found in the university. "Howard University," McKay reminds his readers, "was a prison with white warders."[62] On the other hand, it is in the realm of action—upsetting the quiet repression of anger that keeps the mean chef onboard the train, for example—where Ray is equally useful. At the start of a riot on the train where he works Ray is found quietly reading *Crime and Punishment*; by the time of the riot's conclusion he has become an active participant and instigator as much as his fellow workers.

Ultimately, it is the symbiotic nature of Ray and Jake's relationship that both disrupts the either/or narrative of brain versus body and excites a racial consciousness that challenges the hierarchy of whiteness (and lightness) in the United States. In the narrative of *Home to Harlem*, intelligence represents both the natural outgrowth of having a home in Harlem and the best route to find a home of one's own. Self-conscious reflection represents an important site for the beginnings of political action, but it begins through the experience of being black; intelligence is conceived, in McKay's construction, as an outgrowth of lived experience, and life can only be experienced as an accumulation of knowledge. McKay's novel refuses to distinguish between brain and body, intelligence and ignorance, and cognition and affect. His version of brainpower refuses primitivism, slumming, and uplift, instead imagining a radical redefinition of home that centralizes black intellectual experience and prioritizes queer affection.

*   *   *

Representations of New Negro intelligence in the Harlem Renaissance precipitated both an important redefinition of black politics of the mid-twentieth century and a reconsideration of race in relation to brainpower.

By putting black identity at the center of cultural representation, Harlem Renaissance writers and artists highlighted the potential for brainpower to enact radical political meanings. Though this sometimes aligned with the dominant racial uplift ideology, culture workers such as Claude McKay attempted to supplant uplift with a renewed politics of home—an important stage in the development of black nationalism that also departed from definitions of "Negro genius" that partitioned the range of activities that constituted black contributions to American intellectual life. In contrast with the idea that education would provide a foundation for black accomplishment, representations of intelligence during the Harlem Renaissance were connected to the notion that African Americans possessed the requisite moral and intellectual authority to advance true democracy, and the experience of being subjected to and resisting racial discrimination shaped an organic intellectual tradition in African American literature of the 1920s.

With the onset of the Great Depression, some of the burning questions about brainpower, education, and intelligence that had been contemplated within the Harlem Renaissance were taken up within broader cultural representations. The experience of being marginalized within mainstream definitions of American identity and attempting to survive under a political system that was unsympathetic to the plight of economically and socially disenfranchised women and men extended to many Americans who had previously believed their cultural power to be unassailable. Representations of intelligence during the Great Depression built upon the organic intellectual tradition carved out during the first several decades of the twentieth century and further connected brainpower with progressive political cultures in the United States.

5

"We Have Only Words Against": Brainworkers
and Books in the 1930s

The criticism which future generations will level at us will
doubtless be not that we employed brains, but that we employed
so few.

—*Collier's*, 1934

On October 29, 1929, following a decade of wild growth and unfathomable profits, the New York Stock Exchange took a nosedive and crashed, sparking an American economic crisis of unprecedented magnitude that defined American life for the next decade and beyond. The effects of this crisis threw into doubt any optimistic predictions about the future of American capitalism and shattered faith in the nation's economic, cultural, and political foundations. A new set of national problems demanded bold, creative solutions, and an experimental political climate in the United States emerged during the Great Depression that gave permission for even the most patriotic Americans to reconsider basic and cherished ideas about the nation they had long taken for granted.[1] Emerging from the crisis depended upon the availability of new, sometimes radical, ideas and the brainworkers who produced them.

The Depression fundamentally altered the character of intelligence in American cultural representations and brought discussions about brainpower to the forefront of mainstream political conversation. Within literature, art, and politics, intelligence was broadly represented as a crucial tool for dismantling and reconceptualizing American society, economic life, and government. Ideas were proposed to fix the problems confronting the nation as well as to question the underlying structure of society. Perhaps even more significantly, radical ideas were explicitly promoted as pragmatic, necessary, and desirable for responding to the moment of crisis. Intellectuals were embraced as they suggested solutions to the massive economic problems affecting ordinary Americans and theories concerning the Depression, and the intelligence of ordinary women and men was similarly promoted within government programs and cultural representations. Two books were published in the 1930s with the title *Intelligence in Politics*, each suggesting new opportunities to use smarts as a vital tool for political action.[2] Whereas brainpower in the 1920s had been advanced through new institutions and discourse that challenged America's existing intellectual hierarchies, 1930s representations were inflected with hope that intelligence could rescue the nation's citizens from their current crisis and rebuild American society upon more democratic, for some even revolutionary, principles. For some, this salvation took the shape of liberal reform, as Franklin D. Roosevelt's New Deal offered social programs while affirming the basic structure of democracy and capitalism. For others, intelligence could only move the country toward revolution, as in the program of the Communist Party USA (CPUSA) or the ideology of the New York Intellectuals' Trotsky-inspired leftism.[3] On either side, brainpower was understood to be an important tool for emerging from the Depression.

The changed indexing of Depression-era intelligence allowed ordinary women and men to imagine a world in which creative solutions to social problems would cultivate a more humane future for all. Though fears persisted concerning the potential for concentrated brainpower to create division between smart and ordinary Americans or to set up an intellectual class that disavowed the putatively populist foundation for American democratic praxis, this potential conflict was increasingly depicted as a small price to pay for emerging from the Depression as quickly as possible. Additionally, the social, economic, and political crises of the 1930s were used as an occasion to advance principles of brainpower that had been brewing for decades among feminist, labor, black, and working-class activists. Cultural producers in the 1930s crafted representations of intelligence that inaugurated a new commitment to experimental politics. The burgeoning conversation about the politics of brainpower gained significant traction over the course of a decade, characterized by a passionate belief that intelligence could act as a social equalizer to achieve democratic ideals.

Though some radicals lamented, as did one of the *Intelligence in Politics* authors, that "the medium of violence proves to be much more expedient than investigation through the medium of intelligence," it was this latter category that was arguably most influential throughout the 1930s.[4] The promised revolution, despite some visible direct actions, wildcat strikes, and spirited antifascist campaigns, was played out primarily through ideas rather than in military coups, in large part because the decade was largely defined by a remarkably visible and seemingly more respectable Communist Party that entered into mainstream political culture through its post-1935 Popular Front strategy. John Dos Passos articulated the position of those who sought to use intelligence to effect radical political, economic, social, and cultural change with a forceful aphorism: "we have only words against."[5] Rather than a dispirited lament, Dos Passos expressed confidence that words were more than up to the challenge of renewing American society. The notion that language, the pure product of brainwork, could solve crises, and that intelligence could pose a threat to the dominant forces in U.S. society, found a receptive audience within the mainstream political discourse at this critical juncture in American history.[6]

Of course not everyone who advocated for the use of intelligence to solve the Depression was aligned with the radical ideologies advocated by leftist figures such as Dos Passos and his proletarian-literature scribbling cohort. Many Americans recognized that even liberal reforms required an expansion of brainpower to achieve success in a period of crisis. During the 1930s new departments of government, agencies created to address specific social concerns, and experts whose guidance was solicited from all sides offered an opportunity for politicians to experiment with the basic principles of American government.[7] Communism appeared as a constant foil to the perceived foolishness of a successful democracy brought to its knees by its own economic, political, and cultural excess.[8] The need for a solution to the national crisis quelled the notion that expertise was antidemocratic and resolved some of the tension between intellectuals and ordinary women and men. The emergence of the brain trust and the proletarian cognoscenti introduced new representations of brainy, politically active Americans who were conceived as both upstanding individuals and acutely intelligent. The Depression-era emphasis upon the power of ideas allowed ordinary Americans to conceive themselves as having access to full citizenship regardless of their social location or how much money they had in the bank; by simply visiting a library or taking a class, anyone could access the brainpower necessary for citizenship. The crisis in the American economy opened a space for radicalism in everyday political conversations.

The charged setting of cultural conflict brought on by the Depression in the 1930s offered an opportunity for various cultural producers, political actors, and social activists to reframe and foreground the political opportunities brainpower afforded in American life. Conceptualized alternately as a weapon of class war and a homogenizing agent, intelligence in the 1930s was represented as a critical cultural force that remained available for addressing Depression-era concerns from a variety of ideological positions. There remained much debate in American society about how to harness brainpower to move the United States forward, but whether advancing a radical, populist, or liberal perspective, brainpower was increasingly recognized to be a legitimate political tool and was a veritable constant in national conversations about America's past, present, and future.

Creating Roosevelt's Brain Trust

By the time Roosevelt entered the White House his commitment to and faith in American brainpower was already making headlines.[9] "For not the first time in history, but for the first in our age," declared a writer in the *Saturday Review of Literature* in 1933, "disinterested experts, whose studies have been theoretical, with regard for the truth, but no need of immediate success impelling them, have been given an opportunity to experiment on a vast scale—the only kind of an experiment which ever proves much in the field of economics."[10] Roosevelt's decision to employ a group of professors—Columbia professors Rexford G. Tugwell, Raymond Moley, and Adolf J. Berle among them—to help him craft policies and introduce expansive initiatives represented an experiment that quickly received media attention. The catchy phrase "brain trust" soon appeared in newspapers to describe Roosevelt's crackerjack team of educated experts, and the snappy appellation quickly turned into a popular culture phenomenon.[11]

"Words like 'brain trust,' 'intellectual radicalism,' 'lost generation' and such become popular for a time," wrote a 1936 author, "glow in the headlines of newspapers and journals, are colored by derogatory or eulogistic qualifications, then gradually wear out."[12] The term "brains trust" first appeared in the *New York Times* in September 1932, the creation of a reporter, James Kieran, who was covering the Roosevelt presidential campaign from its headquarters in Hyde Park, New York.[13] In an earlier article describing the professors who assisted Roosevelt, Kieran had mentioned "the 'brains department,' which aids the Executive in gathering data for speeches."[14] Referring to the professors as a "department" designated their specific space within the campaign and made connections with their academic origins. Yet within a week of that article, Kieran had changed his designation for the experts to "brains trust."[15] In his 1952 memoir recounting his Roosevelt years, Sam Rosenman recalled the term as having emerged among those closely associated with Roosevelt.[16] Regardless of the phrase's originator, Roosevelt's brain trust—the plural "brains" gave way to its singular form in most usages—was quickly accepted as the term of choice for this professorial crew.[17]

Roosevelt's brain trust represented brainpower in the form of a collective.[18] The specter of treason that would attach to intellectual associations in the McCarthy era was seen in a germinal stage here, announced by the shadowy collective spirit of Roosevelt's brainy advisors. The term "trust" encouraged associations with nefarious capitalist and elitist interests: the nineteenth-century trusts had been held responsible, in part, for the Depressions of 1893 and 1907, and parallels between gilded-age excess and the unsustainable prosperity of the 1920s were hardly in short supply.[19] The brain trust's appearance at a time of crisis in capitalism might have suggested the expert's culpability for the crisis; paralleling robber barons and trusts with intellectual experts suggested their undesirability as problem-solvers. Yet the trust was also a reserve that was available in case of an emergency; the brain trust could just as likely step in to solve the terrible problems brought on by the Depression.

The brain trusters quickly became pop culture celebrities, inflecting intelligence with a glint of glamour. Books written by the various members of the brain trust became desirable commodities among both politicians and ordinary women and men. "Bookstores are selling [brain trust professors'] books like hot cakes," one journalist wrote in 1933. "Their works are not available at the Library of Congress."[20] The rush to capitalize upon the sensational celebration of intelligence was accompanied by journalistic fervor to report on every move of the brain trust. "All Washington is going to school to the professors," wrote Arthur Sears Henning in the Chicago *Tribune*, "learning all about political science and economics. Debutantes hang on their exposition of the quantitative theory of money, the law of diminishing returns, and the intricacies of foreign exchange."[21] The popularity and visibility of the brain trust offered Americans a unique opportunity to gauge their relationship with experts, their understanding of intelligence and its relation to labor, and their own relationship to government and intelligence. It also imbued brainpower with evident sex appeal, suggesting that intelligence was still tied to masculinity.

The popularity of the brain trust forced Americans to rethink their occasional dismissal of intellectuals based solely upon their accumulated cultural capital. The Depression era advanced the incorporation of traditionally academic intellectuals into ongoing discussions about intelligence among ordinary women and men. "Just as not all Scotchmen are so absurdly thrifty as the endless stories in the funny column would indicate," proclaimed *Saturday Evening Post*'s Albert Atwood in a 1933 feature, "so not all professors are so absurdly absent-minded or impractical or theoretical or generally unworldly as the funny columns suggest."[22] *The Absent-Minded Professor* was a popular comic strip that specialized in ironic scenarios in which a professor could not succeed at the most basic tasks. The appearance of the brain trust threatened to disrupt such representations by depicting intellectuals in a decidedly favorable light.

As though to underscore this point, magazines were packed with advertisements featuring the endorsement of scientists and other educated experts who emphasized the smartness of both producers and consumers. Borrowing from the fad for associating smarts with sophistication that had swept across mass culture in the early decades of the twentieth century and culminated in the appearance of the magazine *Smart Set* in 1900 and its editorship under H. L. Mencken in 1911, Depression-era popular culture furthered widespread associations of intelligence with urbane consumption.[23] An advertisement in the *Saturday Evening Post* featured a scientist endorsing Mennen Brushless by affirming that it was a "real" cream. Though it was not uncommon for doctors to endorse the health benefits of various products in ads accompanied by images featuring physicians in white coats interacting with patients, this advertisement instead boasted that "we made thousands of experiments" and depicted a chemist "looking at micro-photographs of Brushless Shaves."[24] A 1933 ad for the De Soto described the car, the car's designers, and American consumers as smart. "De Soto has that thing called smartness!" the copy proclaimed. "It's a *smart car* for *smart people*. And that's true of every interior detail!" The ad continued, "Here's comfort. Here's smoothness. And that spells smartness."[25] Of course, that did not actually spell smartness at all; it spelled luxury. Yet with the brain trust popularizing intelligence for Depression-era audiences, smartness once again provided a catchall term for the seductive desirability of this car for 1930s audiences yearning for access to any luxuries. Early twentieth-century faddish smartness had tended to appeal to middle-class consumers who sought to affirm intelligence as a means to legitimize their social power and enhance their already assured social standing. By the 1930s, with scarcity defining Americans' experiences across the economic spectrum, both middle-class and working-class consumers were hungrily grasping for the cultural capital brainpower implied. That intelligence was so readily incorporated into the growing language of consumer culture speaks to the power of brainpower to accommodate the vernacular of the left and the right, and though the Depression era marked a moment of brainpower's radicalization, it also heralded a moment in which intelligence was transformed into a commodity.

The popular cultural interest in that tiny group of men who comprised the brain trust was clearly out of proportion to their actual numbers. One author, no doubt emboldened by the recent repeal of the Volstead Act, noted cleverly "the percentage of Brain Trusters in Washington, or anywhere else, is hardly more than the amount of alcohol in prohibition near-beer. Enough to prevent spoiling but not enough to produce a kick."[26] Still, though they may have lacked the numbers to constitute a metaphorically satisfying high alcohol proof, the brain trust was hardly incidental. Their significance within American politics was typically characterized in a *Cincinnati Enquirer* article as the "intellectual leaven in the bread of political power."[27] They were small but essential, and the fashion for smarts made intelligence appealing regardless of its actual utility for empowerment.

Several representations of the brain trust treated them as important cultural ambassadors, assessing their aptness for exporting American culture abroad and looking to international reaction to determine whether the group was worthy of their celebrity. European responses to the brain trust were used to alternately sustain and challenge the authority of intelligence in the United States. "The fertility of their minds," wrote Arthur Krock in a *New York Times* article, "has particularly astounded the French visitors to the international conversation."[28] Americans' enterprising promotion of experts to solve the problems of the Depression was set up as a worthy foil to the backwardness of European nations; the international appeal of the brain trust was treated as an occasion for proclaiming American superiority on a global scale—ironically, of course, since many of the initiatives being faddishly celebrated in the United States borrowed liberally from solutions that had already demonstrated positive results in Europe.[29] Despite the reality of transatlantic political exchange during the Depression, representations of the brain trust insisted upon exceptionalist readings of their ingenuity. The brain trust "has surprised the British and concerned the French," Krock continued, "neither of whom is much inclined to go to the colleges for statesmanship."

In 1934, Dr. William A. Wirt, a well-known midwestern educator, publicly accused the brain trust of comprising the center of a nefarious communist plot to take over the United States.[30] Red scares were common in periods of American crisis, but during the early years of the Great Depression and the Roosevelt presidency red baiting was less in vogue than were flirtations with the left.[31] The 1934 incident began with accusations leveled by Wirt, who was at the time superintendent of the Gary, Indiana, school system and founder of the Gary Method of education, an educational philosophy that applied the principles of scientific management to public schooling.[32] Wirt charged that the brain trust constituted a "plot to overthrow our form of government and set up a Communist state."[33] Framed in the standard hysterical rhetoric of red scares past, Wirt stated that his incriminating information came directly from the brain trusters themselves. Wirt wrote an official letter to James H. Rand, Jr., the chairman of the Committee for the Nation, an anti-New Deal group, detailing the plot, which Rand then made public.

Accusations of subversive intent leveled by political enemies were not uncommon in the twentieth-century United States.[34] What is most striking about this particular episode of anticommunism is how easily the media and public dismissed the charges against the brain trust. History has shown that American media has often been complicit in the panic associated with anticommunism. In this case, however, journalists' responses came swiftly and decisively: Wirt's charges were not to be taken seriously. "It took a Hoosier schoolmaster no less eminent than the inventor of the Gary system—the work-play-study plan," wrote an author in the *Literary Digest*, "to give Washington its biggest laugh since the advent of the hard-working Roosevelt Administration."[35] Though the writer made no effort to hide his political sympathies with the Roosevelt Democrats, his sardonic tone of bemused laughter was hardly unusual. Oswald Garrison Villard, former editor of *The Nation*, echoed that response in a stinging editorial for his periodical:

> I cannot remember when I have laughed more over a news item
> than I did over the dispatch from Washington announcing that on
> behalf of the Committee for the Nation (the title is surely an in-
> fringement of the copyright of *The Nation*) James H. Rand, Jr., its
> chairman, offered in evidence a letter from Dr. William A. Wirt,
> head of the school system of Gary, Indiana. . . . I have known some
> of these Brain Trust professors for some time and I cannot see why if
> they were going to reveal their hands so completely they chose the
> mere head of the Gary school system instead of the well known ex-
> editor of *The Nation*.[36]

Villard's sarcasm and smarmy dismissal of Wirt's charges suggested an unwillingness to characterize intelligence as an attribute of alien ideology. In fact, Villard went so far as to suggest he himself might be more legitimately targeted as a red, implying that the brain trust was freer of ideological communism than even liberal journalists. Such an easy disregard for Wirt's and Rand's red-baiting further suggests that associations of brainpower with subversion were not, at this time, thoroughly implanted in American discourse. The strong associations of intelligence with New Deal liberalism along with a greater willingness to embrace radical positions in the 1930s prevented Wirt's reactionary anti-intellectualism from taking hold during the Depression years.

This is not to suggest that the brain trust was wholeheartedly embraced across the board. The *New York Herald Tribune* in 1933 editorialized against the Pure Food Law, a standard progressive reform act endorsed by the brain trust, by simply averring that "the professors" were behind its proposal.[37] Yet such suspicion was met with swift retribution in the *New Republic*, which countered, "professors disagree among themselves just as vehemently as the members of any other professional group."[38] The *New Republic* rebuttal suggested that intelligence did not produce classes of people as much as it presented particular opportunities to articulate a variety of political and ideological positions. The need for problem-solving created a climate where brainpower was embraced as a necessary tool for emerging from the Depression; the production of a professional class was a mere by-product.

The brain trust was held up through the Depression as a timely, yet short-term, presence in American politics that infused government with an extra shot of intellectual heft. This measure was conceived as necessary during a time of crisis. Representations of Roosevelt's brain trust demonstrated how brainpower—even when it was concentrated and associated with prestigious university education—could benefit all Americans. Though they were useful for finding solutions to problems during the Depression, the brain trust was aligned with a liberal understanding of brainpower's function that cracked open the door for radical representations of intelligence to enter mainstream political discourse but stopped short of embracing the left.

Brains and Bodies

Intellectual labor continued to meet with particular resistance from working-class women and men who had been engaged in redefining intelligence to privilege their interests rather than upholding the status of management and aligning themselves with elites. In keeping with long-standing efforts to undermine the pervasive belief that intellectual labor was not authentic work and that some work did not require intelligence, Depression-era representations of intelligence within mass culture reflected a producerist ideology that suggested brains could be trusted precisely because they were inextricable from material production.[39] Here the craze for braininess was incorporated into the iconographic shorthand foregrounding the laboring bodies of model citizens. The fetishization of male workers' bodies reached a fevered pitch in a decade that saw many desiring work and placing their hope in the promise of workers as ideal citizens. Representations of intelligence attempted to connect intellectual types with laborers, reinforcing the worker's body as the site of citizenship during the Depression, but also opening the definition of labor to include those who were not performing the labor of over-determined masculinity.[40] Such representations placed the brainworker in the same category as the industrial worker.[41] Rather than opposing the ideal body of workers with the disembodied brain, this Depression-era representational strategy foregrounded brainworkers as fully integrated citizens whose bodies signified their brains rather than contradicting them.

The idea that brainwork and muscle work were organically connected—and that the muscular body might be complemented by rather than contrasted with the intelligent brain—shifted during the 1930s. An article appearing in a 1930 issue of the *Literary Digest*, provocatively titled "Brain Workers Need Little Food," had claimed that a "maid dusting in a professor's desk for five minutes would do more actual work as measured by heat production, than her employer would in an hour of intense mental effort."[42] This scenario articulated the difference between a brainworker and a laborer not only in terms of their intelligence, but also by presenting an immediately recognizable and unequal class dynamic. The contrast between the maid and the professor drew attention to the injustices of capitalism by invoking the absurdity of a society where a brainworker was rewarded—presumably both in terms of salary and cultural respect—for doing less work. The professor was represented as producing less "heat" than the maid. In this article, production was measured in terms of calories expended, figuring the value of these workers' labor as measured exclusively by their bodily exertion.

This typical representation of embodied work—emphatic in its opposition between the real labor of the maid and the artificial, nonproductive labor of the professor—was replaced during the Depression years with a defensive set of claims that positioned the brainworker as a laborer whose body suffered the same wear and tear as any worker's might. A *Commonweal* article from 1933 described the bodily fatigue that connected brain with body:

> One of the perennial disadvantages under which labor those who are so-called brain workers, is the idea that their work is not fatiguing. Wives of such are prone to say, for instance, "Oh shucks, you've been sitting down all day; you're just lazy and sluggish, you're not really tired." Usually the so-called brain worker is shamed into believing this because it doesn't seem right that he should be tired after sitting so long. He goes out feeling like an empty shell and is easily buffeted and bruised on the tides of energy of, say, some bouncing brokers who have gone through a few relatively repetitious mental operations during the day and a good deal more of kinetic thrashing around, and feel pretty good.[43]

This author's defense of the brainworker summoned physical exhaustion as evidence for the brainworker's status as a legitimate worker and, by extension, a worthy 1930s citizen.[44] The author's opposing mental and kinetic movement retained the binary of brain and body, but the article also broke down that opposition by offering an explanation for the tiredness of the brainworker. The therapeutic language used to describe the brainworker emphasized his "bruised" feelings and sense of shame, underscoring the author's conceit that it was not intellectual labor itself that was emasculating, but rather society's disapproval of it.

In part because of the cultural emphasis during the Depression on physical labor, much of the discussion of intellectual labor, brains, and bodies within mass culture marginalized women's work. The connection between brainwork and male embodiment received perhaps its most bizarre treatment in a proposition offered by famous adman and Betty Crocker creator, Bruce Barton, at the 1936 convention of paper tradesmen. In his address, Barton postulated that there exists "an unexplained and undefined, but nevertheless definite connection between shaving and brain activity—thinking."[45] That this connection excluded women is not incidental; for Barton, intelligence was uniquely available to men, whose rugged masculinity he had already famously praised in his masculinist retelling of the story of Jesus, the 1925 bestseller *The Man Nobody Knows.*[46] Intellectual labor was being embraced within working-class and middle-class communities, but it was also being linked with masculinity.

Women did not passively accept this growing tendency toward masculinization of brainpower. Many instead endeavored to offset negative representations of female brainpower by exposing and politicizing the exclusion of women from intellectual professions. In a song titled "Chain Store Daisy" from Harold Rome's *Pins and Needles,* a 1937 musical revue produced by the International Ladies' Garment Workers' Union, a character played by brassiere operator Ruth Rubinstein laments how her college degree and connection to the intellectual elite (the Vassar "daisy chain") fails to find meaningful employment that makes use of her formidable intelligence.[47] "They told me my fine education would help improve my situation," she complains upon realizing her college degree and book learning did not translate into job opportunities. After being subjected to a variety of humiliating measurements of her bust and other bodily features, Rubinstein laments, "they tested my IQ, and asked what I'd like to do, and when that exam was through, what there was to know, Macy's knew."[48] Drawing attention to the marginalization of women's intelligence was posed as an important political challenge to both class and gender hierarchies.

The WPA Iconography of Intelligence

FDR's New Deal administration engaged in a series of concerted efforts during the Great Depression to imagine intelligence as a commonly available tool for achieving democratic goals, redressing economic inequality, and steeling up the defenses of the American working class. Intelligence was promoted as both a tool for liberal reform and a bulwark against radical ideologies. New Deal policies and initiatives advanced brainpower as a key component to solving to the national crisis in three primary ways. First, the federal government promoted the accessibility of public institutions such as libraries to illustrate the similarly public nature of intelligence.[49] Second, the government became more involved in advocating workers' education programs and thus legitimized efforts at harnessing working-class intelligence that had begun with women workers' education while also advancing the centralization that defused its most radical potential.[50] Third, boosting intelligence was recast as a means of solving the challenges posed by a pluralist society: programs that rewarded intelligence moved ordinary women and men toward a common goal that was not subjected to the derision of identity and inured government programs against charges of overlooking important minority communities.[51] Within these programs visual culture was a particularly effective tool for extending the promotion of brainpower to ordinary women and men. Debates about brainpower were distilled into legible shorthand that condensed complex messages into their bare essentials.

The Works Progress Administration (WPA) produced posters through the Federal Art Project (FAP), an initiative of FDR's second hundred days. Federal Project Number One was a section of the Division of Professional Service within the WPA, and it included the Federal Theatre Project (FTP), the Federal Writers' Project (FWP), the Federal Music Project, and the Federal Art Project. The FAP was one of four New Deal art initiatives, and it was one of only two that gave work to unemployed artists without competition as a form of relief. Under the directorship of Holger Cahill, the FAP lasted from 1935 to 1943, sometimes thriving, at other times struggling for survival.[52] The posters discussed in this section appeared on buses, in schools, and in other public spaces. They promoted FTP productions, FWP books, art exhibitions, libraries, and tourism as forms of civic engagement.[53] Intelligence was connected with citizenship, but also with an expanding liberal state.

A 1940 print produced by the WPA illustrates some of the significant features attached to intelligence in FAP posters (Figure 8). The poster features a black and white print with a blue zigzag pattern resembling a roadway or a river running down the center. Four iconic figures are featured in a staggered layout, each of which is labeled: doctor, lawyer, merchant, or chief, in reference to the traditional children's rhyme (conveniently omitted career path: thief). This intentionally wide-ranging list of characters reinforces

Figure 8. WPA poster promoting reading in Chicago. Library of Congress Work Projects Administration Poster Collection, reproduction number LC-USZC2-5188 DLC.

the broad range of types bridged by the unifying text: "Agree . . . these books are too good to miss!" The modernist blue streak serves to both highlight the characters' difference and underscore their commonality as purveyors of intelligence. Rather than exclusively foregrounding diversity, the poster also positions its subjects as citizen readers bonded through their literary taste. The connection between national unity, professional development, and reading suggests the value of intelligence within narratives of national citizenship. That these books were widely available in public libraries suggests how investing in brainpower advanced the goals of an expanded state and a unified citizenry.

WPA posters celebrated public libraries for their potential to advance intellectual equality and as evidence for American striving toward democracy. A 1937 poster features four characters—presumably representing a family—laid out in ascending height, walking in linear formation (Figure 9). The repetition of the design calls to mind the repetitive modernism of artists such as Orozco, just as it also indexes a hierarchy of knowledge commonly found in charts of human evolution.[54] As was the case in "Agreed," the poster's figures are printed without distinguishable physiognomic features, rendering their racial or ethnic identities ambiguous. The text for the poster emphasizes again the diversity and varied identities of the subjects: "Young and old visit the library on the parkway." It is unclear whether the sentence should be read as declarative or imperative. Still, the emphasis upon accentuating the difference of the subjects sharing in the pursuit of knowledge and mutual use of a civic institution recasts diversity as unified citizenship, in this case signified through a nuclear family, and building intelligence is conceived as forging national unity.

Many FAP posters sidestepped identity by depicting mere suggestions of human form, expanding the range of those for whom brainpower could be made accessible while separating brains from the bodies of these subjects. A 1941 poster for Ohio's adult education classes (Figure 10) depicts a subject standing proudly in snappy grey flannel suit. The text next to the figure, "Get A-Head," draws attention to the gaping hole where the figure's head should be. The lack of a head universalizes the subject: any viewer of the poster could imagine their head on the character. The men's suit donned by the decapitated body still delimits the characteristics of those who might get ahead by suggesting a male professional subject.

A 1941 poster advocating library use (Figure 11) features a drawing of a globe onto which is mapped a crude cartography that erases every land

Figure 9. WPA poster promoting libraries in Pennsylvania. Library of Congress
Works Progress Administration Poster Collection, reproduction number
LC-USZC2-1886 DLC.

mass other than the Americas (seen also in Figure 12). The earth is represented as a pan-American map that flagrantly erases national borders
while deleting all other continents. Yet the disappearance of five continents
marks only one erasure in the graphic: the globe-as-head also lacks a body.
The poster anthropomorphizes the globe by adorning it in professor's cap
and spectacles, signifying intelligence through reference to educational

Figure 10. WPA poster encouraging adults to attend adult education classes in Ohio. Library of Congress Works Progress Administration Poster Collection 1, reproduction number LC-USZC2-5400 DLC.

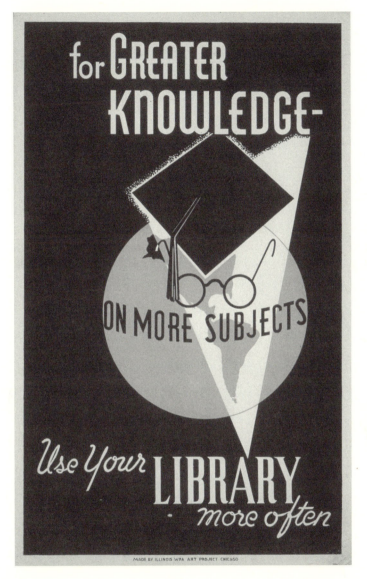

for GREATER KNOWLEDGE-

ON MORE SUBJECTS

Use Your LIBRARY
more often

MADE BY ILLINOIS WPA ART PROJECT CHICAGO

Figure 11. WPA poster showing a mortarboard and a pair of glasses superimposed over a globe, promoting use of libraries, in Illinois. Library of Congress Works Progress Administration Poster Collection, reproduction number LC-USZC2-5183 DLC.

Figure 12. WPA poster promoting Chicago Library Week. Library of Congress Works Progress Administration Poster Collection, reproduction number LC-USZC2-5238 DLC.

achievement while also locating intelligence outside the body. This professorial head hangs suspended in the ether, its missing body ignored, its corporeal absence naturalized. The professor provides an archetype for intelligence, a modality privileging intelligence that was restricted to a narrow subgroup within American society: those who could afford—and were permitted access to the institutions of—higher education.[55] Such representations stand in contrast to other FAP representations that diminished educational achievement in favor of the experiences of ordinary readers. Still, the globe's truncated geography and association with a global intelligence suggests that the whole world might have access to the power knowledge could provide simply by making use of public and democratic institutions such as the library; the social distance between professors and ordinary women and men was simultaneously made as short as a jaunt to the closest library branch. This perspective was recapitulated in a poster promoting foreign languages that depicts a book perched atop a globe. Their juxtaposition and the collapse of scale in the illustration suggesting knowledge might bring the world together, albeit through professional choices within the United States (Figure 13).

Historian Daniel Rodgers has shown how the Depression era was marked by a spirit of transatlanticism in American politics. Politicians looked beyond the shores of the United States to study the ways their European counterparts treated their own economic crises, creating a transatlantic exchange of ideas.[56] This crossing and erasing of borders was visible in a 1941 poster promoting the month of March as "reading month" (Figure 14). The poster depicts a woman being blown by a breeze of international cooperation, the woman cast in a modernist, angular international style as several books in red, white, and blue toss about her. The visual style of the poster borrows liberally from Russian constructivism both in its layout and the design of the woman's functional dress.[57] The chaotic force of the wind that scatters the woman's books is tempered by their organized march: the books blow fortuitously into an alignment that renders their authors' names legible as they neatly encircle the woman. Only one book has fallen open; the others are contained in their closed covers and orderly composition. The authors' names suggest the self-conscious transatlanticism of New Deal brainpower: Dickens, Austen, Eliot, and Thackeray are English authors; Scott is Scottish; Dumas is French, Tolstoy Russian; and Clemens and Hawthorne are American. The woman at the center appears surprised, though not especially agitated, by the storm engulfing her. The significance of the cold wind is central; the

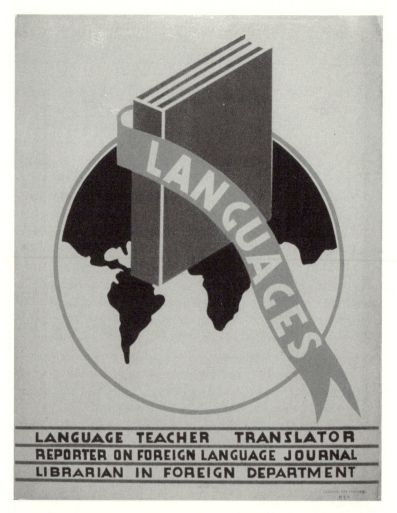

Figure 13. WPA poster promoting occupations in the field of languages. Library of Congress Works Progress Administration Poster Collection, reproduction No. LC-USZC2-5663 DLC.

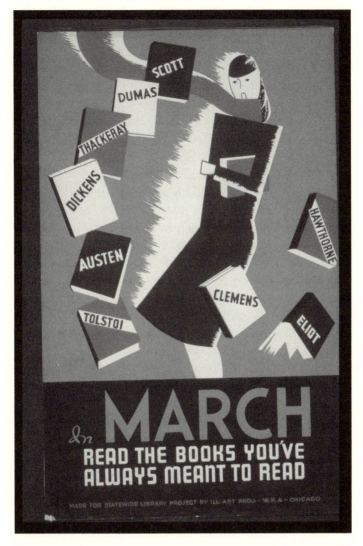

Figure 14. A WPA poster for a statewide library project in Illinois. Library of Congress Works Progress Administration Poster Collection, reproduction number LC-USZC2-5175 DLC.

storm signifies both the capriciousness of March weather and the Depression's unpredictability. The month of March represents a transition between the cold, bitter winter and the warm spring, just as brainpower endeavors to inaugurate a transition from a period of crisis to an era of stability.

Though posters promoting brainpower often placed women at the center, the vestiges of indicatively male citizenship persisted. Even in the Reading Month poster, the books flying about the woman in the red, white, and blue image were mostly written by Anglo-European and American men.[58] The poster illustrates global citizenship and a woman-centered vision of brainpower, yet it positions women primarily as readers rather than writers. Posters advocating intelligence expanded the iconography of citizenship beyond the burly male body, but unlike the vision for brainpower advocated through early efforts such as Christine Frederick's scientific management or Fannia Cohn's women workers' education initiatives, WPA posters most often depicted men as workers to legitimize the pursuit of civic nationalism. A 1941 poster promoting library use featured a figure based upon Rodin's famous thinker (Figure 15).[59] The angle of the figure, along with the rough-sketch style of the image, accentuates both the heavy, masculine brow of the thinker and his bulging musculature. Just as the poster celebrates the power and accessibility of intelligence—the bold text urges "greater knowledge on more subjects"—this liberatory potential is circumscribed by the thinker's over-determined masculinity and his fetishized body. The poster presents its subject as definitively masculine, emphasizing a perceived connection between the thinker's intelligence and his embodiment, attaching intelligence to male bodies while challenging representations of weak-bodied intellectuals. Brainpower was connected to social power through visual reference to manly embodiment.

Though the contingencies of identity were often ignored in efforts to promote brainpower as unifying, WPA posters also advocated African American participation in American civic life through library usage. African Americans mobilized during the Depression to control their destinies, challenge American racism, explore their diasporic and pan-African connections, and organize against capitalism.[60] Activists used every tool at their disposal from militant protest to cultural production to address persisting American racism. Membership swelled in organizations such as the NAACP, and art exhibitions were launched in New York with names such as "Struggle for Negro Rights" and "An Art Commentary on Lynching."[61] Vibrant new black cultural institutions appeared in cities such as Detroit and Chicago.

Figure 15. WPA poster promoting library use, showing a man in a pose based on Rodin's "Thinker." Library of Congress Works Progress Administration Poster Collection, reproduction number LC-USZC2-5223 DLC.

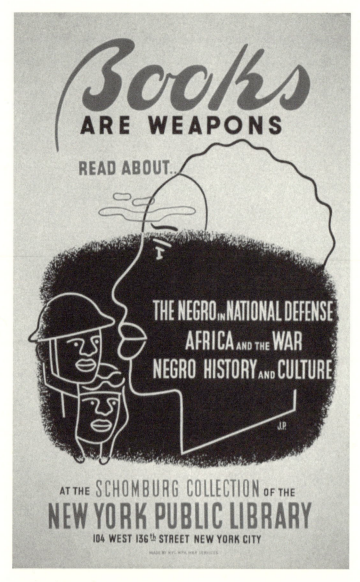

Figure 16. WPA poster encouraging citizens to use the Schomburg Collection of the New York Public Library to learn more about African and African American history and culture. Library of Congress Works Progress Administration Poster Collection, reproduction number LC-USZC2-1124 DLC.

WPA posters promoted brainpower within black communities as a means to social empowerment, racial pride, and cultural citizenship. African American-centered posters registered cultural difference far more explicitly than other New Deal posters, reflecting the growing influence of a Popular Front vision of racial difference in the 1930s.[62] A World War II-era poster promoting the Schomburg Collection of the New York Public Library illustrates the progressive notions of black identity that connected African American history with brainpower (Figure 16). This poster features simplified, modernist line drawings of black faces. The figures in this poster appear to be male, and they represent multiple social locations, including civilian and military. A stylized blue cloud representing intelligence transects the head of the largest figure. The text accompanying and overlapping the image is bold and uncompromising: "Books Are Weapons." In the midst of war, the immediacy of weapons in people's minds might have swayed viewers to draw parallels between the war abroad and the fight against racism at home.[63] The poster also posits the enlistment and admirable performance of black GIs as evidence for model citizenship.[64]

By encouraging Americans to visit the Schomburg Collection in Harlem, arguably the cultural center of 1930s black America, and read books about African American involvement in war and American culture, as well as the role of Africa in the war, this poster anticipated a vision of black politics that was advanced by increasing Americans' knowledge of black history.[65] Brainpower here underscored the necessity of building up knowledge of one's own race—or the race of another—rather than overlooking difference through a deracinated version of knowledge.[66] This racialized vision of brainpower's reach proposed intelligence as the basis of democratic practice, thereby rendering an intimate knowledge of black history essential to proper U.S. citizenship. A similar vision of brainpower appeared in a poster advertising the Illinois Writers Project's volume, *Cavalcade of the American Negro*, featuring a black man holding a broken chain in an upraised fist (Figure 17). Again, education about black history was positioned as a tool for empowerment and citizenship.

Finally, WPA artists designed posters depicting machinery rather than human figures, deftly circumventing representations denoting specific subjectivities. In these posters the modernist poster designs were employed to signify the technical innovation of American machinery and, by extension, industry. Mechanical gears also pointed to the modernist aesthetics in the posters themselves, aligning social and technological innovation with new

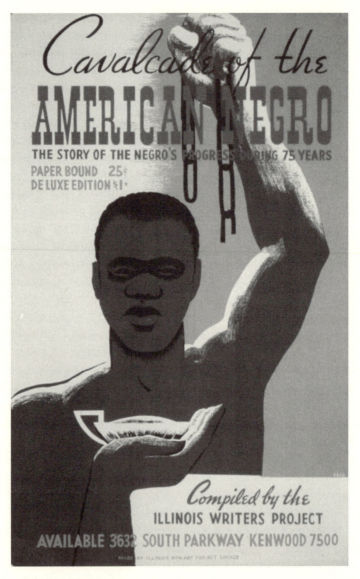

Figure 17. WPA poster for a book about African American history. Library of Congress Works Progress Administration Poster Collection, reproduction number LC-USZC2-1180 DLC.

aesthetic ideas. A veritable staple of modern design, the cog or component of a machine was often used to signify the dialectic between optimistic associations of technology as progress and the terrifying fear of dehumanization of both labor and identity through mechanization.[67] The machine promised a future without work, but its grinding bowels also threatened to swallow humankind in its unforgiving gears.[68] Charlie Chaplin's descent into the machine in his 1936 film *Modern Times* reflected the tremendous anxiety that could be triggered through the gears of industrial machinery.[69] Still, the machine also offered a vision of a future without work, a future that the Little Tramp would likely have been content to inhabit.

Taking into account the cultural context of a modern society experiencing a crisis of economics, politics, and identity due in no small part to the processes of modernization, the emphasis upon machine iconography within WPA posters appears odd, if not outright counterintuitive. But depictions of machinery served an important purpose by collapsing working-class identity into modernist design. Posters depicting mechanized components suggested that intelligence could extend even to that group seemingly most immune to its pull: the industrial working class. The twentieth-century industrial worker was commonly associated with total alienation from brainwork. Representations of machinery in posters effectively challenged the seemingly naturalized contest between brainworkers and laborers, or management and workers. New Deal posters recast workers in the center of civic life by aligning modern machinery with the pursuit of intelligence. Rather than presenting images of machines as juxtaposed with images of brains, WPA posters deployed signifiers of machinery to articulate the pursuit of intelligence among the working class. Posters such as "Know the World You Live In" and "Register Now—Informal Study Groups" incorporated books and intelligence into the machinery of industry— literally in the latter case—as part of their promoting working-class brain-power (Figures 18 and 19). The machine was just another cog in the gears of nationhood and citizenship.

WPA posters promoting library use, workers' education, and reading offered brainpower as a means to full citizenship. Rather than situating a particular definition of American at its ideological center, New Deal efforts to advance brainpower encouraged difference by promoting knowledge while also incorporating all Americans into a progressive vision of engaged democratic practice. This was accomplished alternately by erasing ethnic, racial, and gender differences and by accentuating them. For radical cultural

Figure 18. WPA poster announcing informal study groups for workers in New York City. Library of Congress Works Progress Administration Poster Collection, reproduction number LC-USZC2-954.

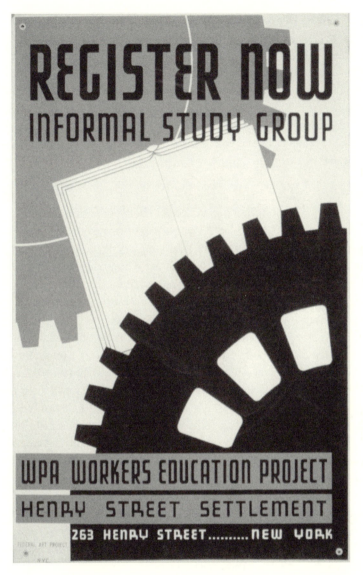

Figure 19. WPA poster announcing formation of educational study groups for workers at the Henry Street Settlement in New York City. Library of Congress Work Projects Administration Poster Collection, reproduction number LC-USZC2-951 DLC.

workers in the Depression, incorporating multiple American identities did not go far enough toward empowering democratic practice. Writers on the left located intelligence within working-class culture and posed a significant challenge to the principles of New Deal liberalism by positioning proletarian cognoscenti in contrast to the conservative academic intellectuals and stupid bosses.[70] Rather than opposing brain-trust intellectuality and New Deal liberalism with anti-intellectualism, however, proletarian novelists imagined a revolutionary political program that rewarded working-class intelligence.

Proletarian Cognoscenti in Radical Fiction

In Ernest Hemingway's 1926 novel *The Sun Also Rises*, a group of loquacious men assemble in various Spanish cafes, bars, hotels, and bullfighting stadiums to talk, drink, and heartily engage with a lusty world. As they navigate their way through a variety of social engagements with an abundance of booze and conversation, the characters give voice to a bereft spiritual age. "I can't stand it," one character moans in the early pages of the novel, "to think my life is going so fast and I'm not really living it." "Nobody ever lives their life all the way," his friend sagaciously replies, "except bullfighters."[71]

Although much of their time is spent in speech, the repetitively hollow conversation among Hemingway's characters betrays their limited potential for liberation, personal or political. As they pursue their heady, inebriated leisure in the bullfighting capital of Pamplona, Jake Barnes, Robert Cohn, and other characters' words stack up and collide, ultimately failing to reach any apogee of enlightenment or liberation. The "terrible honesty" characteristic of Hemingway's men is predicated upon a narrative of tough masculinity that assumes a casual—if passionate—relationship between language and life.[72]

By the onset of the 1930s, disempowering representations of the potential of words to effect change were conceived by many partisan writers as wearyingly decadent, suggestive of a luxuriously listless life ill-afforded in a time of crisis. James T. Farrell complained in 1931 that Hemingway "depicts, with gusto, the meanderings of a class whose main difficulty is that they have nothing to do."[73] With the onset of the Great Depression and the rise of the fascist threat in Europe, few Americans possessed the resources to cavalierly run around the world in the pursuit of leisure, and fewer still believed their alienation was best expressed through idle chatter. The pressing need for Americans to address the problems of the Depression forced writers into a new form of labor: that which might bring about social change. The casual speech that idealized objective language seemed suddenly detached from the stark reality of problems that could be too easily contained in words like poverty, unemployment, and capitalism.[74] Novelists of the 1930s insistently represented characters whose words took on the yoke of a culture confronting an immediate crisis that could only be solved through major social change and even violent political upheaval.[75] In the midst of this revolutionary ferment, even Hemingway relocated his characters from the heady pleasure grounds of Pamplona to the bloody and politicized earth of the Spanish Civil War.[76] Yet it was particularly in the reams of proletarian fiction produced throughout the 1930s that writers emphasized the intellectual capacity of a radicalized working class.[77]

Representations of working-class intelligence abounded in novels such as Dos Passos's *U.S.A.* trilogy and Jack Conroy's *The Disinherited*, and within historical accounts of revolution such as Edmund Wilson's *To the Finland Station*.[78] Images of the proletarian intellectual, the worker and/or radical poring over books by Karl Marx and other tough texts, loomed large over the decade's literature, representing in unequivocal terms the explosive potential of the common thinker to liberate workers from their common fate. Radical brainpower, leftist novelists suggested, could be advanced by representing a working class defined by its intelligence. Such representations both detached intelligence from association with elite intellectuals and empowered workers to adopt new ideas that could overthrow the state. "And today you are talking about smashing with your hands instead of fighting with your brains," wrote Fielding Burke damningly in her novel, *Call Home the Heart*.[79] The proletarian intellectual found ways to smash with her brains, and the prominent placement of this character within many of the leftist novels of the decade is instructive for understanding how radical brainpower was represented as against the universalizing model of New Deal liberalism.

In the opening scenes of Robert Cantwell's 1934 novel, *The Land of Plenty*, several characters attempt to navigate their way through a northwest lumber mill that has lost power and lies in darkness. As a description of American society during the Great Depression, the power outage offers a bleak metaphor. "Suddenly the lights went out," Cantwell's novel begins. "There was no warning fading or flickering of the bulbs; there was only a swift blotting out of the visible world." Cantwell's opening scenes describe an industrial environment in which managers and bosses, figures who were typically rewarded for their intelligence and assumed to have climbed the social ladder due to their intellectual abilities, are exposed as ignorant at the precise moment unskilled laborers reveal their essential knowledge. Harking back to the rhetoric of scientific management as the book begins, Carl, the mill's "efficiency engineer," finds himself pinned against a pile of lumber following a power outage. As he lies immobile, Carl reflects on his knowledge even as he is paralyzed by his ignorance. He is pinned by the leg of the suit he wears underneath his overalls, the suit a stubborn reminder that his industrial drag is but a disguise. As he lies trapped, Carl reflects on the knowledge he had assumed would protect him. He "knew what to do in case of a fire, and he had learned what men to give the cutting orders to when the shift started and where to check up when the stock seemed to be running short." And if all this thinking were not enough to accentuate the tragic irony of Carl's paralysis, Carl whiles away the time as he awaits his rescue calculating the profits being lost through the wasted time: "Three hundred and fifty men at sixty cents an hour, cent a minute, three dollars and fifty cents a minute."[80] He is a prisoner inside his scientific mind.

By contrast, the workers in the plant move with swiftness and agility even without light to guide them. Carl's thoughts are interrupted when he hears "a dim shuffle as the men moved casually through the dark, sure of their footing, knowing the floor around their machines as they knew their own houses even when the lights were out." As the scene continues, more light is shed upon the framework of knowledge that underscores the entire machinations of the plant, whose workers "became aware of minute differences that no one else could detect, and learned to recognize the fine shadings, the nuances of sounds that were only confused or terrifying to anyone who came in for the first time."[81] It becomes evident that the intelligence of the workers represents the only hope for Carl to be extracted from his circumstances. One worker in particular, Hagen, is explicitly contrasted with Carl as Cantwell retells the story of the power outage from Hagen's perspective, replacing the critical hostility of Carl's self-important ruminations with Hagen's own adroit and skilled action.

The power outage in *The Land of Plenty* staged a dramatic scene that contrasted the ironic ignorance of an efficiency expert who lacked the knowledge to navigate a plant in crisis with the brainpower of an intelligent worker who possessed all the knowledge he needed but ordinarily was not given an opportunity to use it. Through representations of proletarian cognoscenti, the Depression-era working class—like Cantwell's millworkers—could finally exploit their historical moment to create new opportunities for political change by capitalizing upon their brainpower. The insistence of radical writers of the 1930s upon representing an intelligent working class reframed discussions of brainpower to privilege working-class brains as more authentically intelligent than those of the educated middle class.

Tess Slesinger's popular 1935 novel, *The Unpossessed*, explored the contradictions and complications that met writers trying to comment on Depression-era brainpower from a radical perspective. Slesinger was herself a New York-based journalist whose only published novel was this smartly funny, lightly fictionalized sketch of her relationship with her husband, Herbert Solow, and their involvement with the *Menorah Journal* and its radical collection of editors.[82] Slesinger offered an ironic, self-conscious dissection of the relationship between literati and leftist politics in her depiction of a motley group struggling to create a radical publication, referred to with tremendous self-importance as "the Magazine."

Paula Rabinowitz has written of *The Unpossessed* that Slesinger "retains the form of the proletarian novel without its content, [twisting] the gender conventions of the genre into a dystopian vision of literary radicalism." Rabinowitz conceives Slesinger's novel as a document of failure, since "the failure of language to convey meaning or effect change deconstructs the female intellectual subject."[83] The characterizations of proletarian intellectuals in the "golden age" of radical literature served to challenge the premise of intellectuals as a category easily distinguished from workers, a challenge that tied intellectual revolt in with all other forms of class struggle and was premised upon a radical definition of brainpower that had been expanding in preceding decades. In other words, proletarian cognoscenti drew on representational strategies developed throughout twentieth-century mass culture that had affirmed the intelligence of ordinary women and men, shifting these representations only slightly to privilege a leftist perspective.

The Unpossessed profiles an unlikely assortment of proletarian cognoscenti, most of them representing conventional intellectuals as a type, but each of them confronting scenarios in which their status is dislocated. Slesinger describes a group of professors, wealthy patrons, and a circle of radical students as they venture to transform their radical thought into a program of political action by creating a leftist magazine. The central cast of editors and writers is comprised of present and past members of the "Black

Sheep," a loose grouping of politically outspoken academics who are frustrated with the conservatism of contemporary politics. At the head of this group is the tragicomic figure of Bruno Leonard, a professor at the school where he was once valedictorian, whose dream of starting up the magazine represents his quixotic desire to use his intelligence to effect political change in spite of his remaining perpetually incapable of translating even his most banal ideas into action. The novel begins with Bruno sitting blankly in his office where his thoughts are interrupted by the abrupt delivery of a filing cabinet. For Bruno, the filing cabinet represents what he most fears: the reification of his ideas into practical reality, a process that causes him much anxiety throughout the novel:

> As he saw his Idea tampered with, taken up, exposed, Filing Cabinets ordered to put it into action, it became less clear, less dear to him. Build it up, concretize it—and one must compromise; face a public; recognize a policy and in thus limiting the horizon deal only with a portion of life instead of perceiving the whole illuminated by the Idea; and finally admit that no matter how lofty the hopes, how valid the Idea, reality must consist in dealing mediocre articles to mediocre readers.[84]

Bruno's tortured meditation upon the filing cabinet introduces many of the themes that appear repeatedly throughout Slesinger's novel: the dialectic of thought and action; the troubling constriction of reality upon the life of the mind; the endemic unwillingness of intellectuals to embrace a real-world program for political change and to entertain—ironic for a social revolution—the public. Bruno struggles in the novel to reconcile his radicalism with his status as a member of the American intellectual elite.

In the pages of *The Unpossessed*, Bruno Leonard—like Tess Slesinger—confronts not only a crisis in individual engagement as an intellectual with the world, but also a crisis in negotiating social hierarchies that relegate intellectual radicalism to the academy and detach academics from politics in the street. Throughout the novel characters confront the world armed with their intelligence and attempt to incorporate it into their lived (and worked) experiences; the quotidian nature of this struggle makes for a variety of comic episodes, particularly in the sexual affairs between the characters. Unsurprisingly, Slesinger's novel teems with sex and sexuality, and it is this relationship that stands in for the tension between brains and bodies (or spirit and matter) that the proletarian intellectual resolves in 1930s radical fiction. There are love triangles and squares; affairs and consummated marriages; homosexual and heterosexual liaisons; bodies kissing and lusting on virtually every page of *The Unpossessed*. The title itself is a clever bit of wordplay that intentionally confuses spiritual, capitalist, and sexual ownership at the same time, as it imagines no possessions. On a structural level, then, Slesinger introduces over-determined, highly sexualized bodies that are equally intelligent.

One of the most explicitly sexual scenes in *The Unpossessed* occurs as Jeffrey, one of the founders of the Magazine, seduces Margaret, who is married to another editor, Miles, in her kitchen. As they nervously make love against a door while Margaret's husband converses with Jeffrey's wife on the other side, Margaret decides that "the kitchen door itself was ludicrous; that Miles was talking Marxian determinism on its other side was the final crowning idiocy." And yet the ostensible antagonism between Margaret's bodily pleasure and Miles's self-important brainwork is not total: Jeffrey himself discusses theory as he makes love to Margaret. "He continued his impassioned speech," Slesinger writes, "punctuated it with kisses oddly lacking in sensual intelligence."[85] Jeffrey is comical here precisely because his sensuality is divorced from his intelligence, a rupture that signifies his alienation from the proletarian masses he aims to liberate. His disembodied intellect renders him clownish. If radical discussions of brainpower were to celebrate the role of intelligence in advancing a leftist political program, they could only do so by envisioning a working-class militancy that was equally at home marching in the streets and rolling in the sheets. Slesinger's characters fail to acknowledge that their brainpower is misplaced when detached from working-class bodies and the vernacular of labor.

Slesinger introduces another specter into representations of intelligence in *The Unpossessed*: the specter of a homosexuality that transgresses gender expectations and breaks down the brain-body divide. It is through an intensely homoerotic male-male relationship that Slesinger articulates the moment of Bruno's becoming fully radicalized. One of the central relationships explored in the novel occurs between Bruno and one of the most prominent members of his Black Sheep: the stuttering, effeminate Emmett Middleton. Emmett's mother is a wealthy patron Bruno solicits to support the journal; his father is unsympathetically capitalist. Bruno's sycophantic need for Emmett's mother's approval mirrors Emmett's own attachment;

their shared interest in her upsets the predictably hierarchical relationship between teacher and student, mother and son, man and woman. Even more fundamentally, however, Emmett is clearly marked as a homosexual, and Bruno is torn between his bodily impulses toward his ex-lover, Elizabeth, and the weepy advances of the highly vulnerable Emmett, whose young body offers a notable foil to his female paramour yet is the link to the realization of Bruno's intellectual goals.

The consummation of Bruno's relationship with Emmett occurs when the two become extremely drunk together and Bruno's resistance is worn down by Emmett's seductive vulnerability. As Bruno puts Emmett's intoxicated body to bed, he muses on the paradox between his desire to possess Emmett and his longing to destroy him, a dialectic of passion and violence. "His head was so close, so vulnerable; as easy to crush it as to caress it." Yet Bruno finally makes his first real decision in the book: "He put out his hand and rested it gently on Emmett's head." Bruno's decision to follow his fleshly impulses represents a challenge to the positioning of a separate intellectual class, even as it supports ambivalence about the possibility for a truthful sexuality that does not deviate from social norms. This is the first point in Slesinger's novel where Bruno's ideas align with his action, and as such it is a liberating moment for both himself and for Emmett. It might be contrasted, for example, with an earlier moment in the book when Bruno and Norah sit together, yet "so intellectualized was he, he thought and sighed, that he could no longer feel even sensation unless it were accompanied by a smile or wink to show the stimulus aware."[86] In bed with Emmett, intoxicated and semi-conscious, Bruno at last needs no stimulus as he responds to the male body offered up to him. His homoerotic relationship with Emmett effectively melds the impulse toward ideas with the desire for the body. Through the queer union of Bruno and Emmett, brain and body are merged, and the intellectual is rendered indistinguishable from the libertine.

The association between homosexuality and intelligence explored in Slesinger's novel was by no means unique. A glossary of slang produced within the homosexual community in the 1930s and 1940s included a revealing definition of the term cognoscenti: "all persons in the fraternity of homosexuality, including homosexuals, their prostitutes and friends[,] and others who understand the argot, are acquainted with the current popular meeting places, and share the homosexuals' fear and detestation of the police."[87] In keeping with this definition, H. T. Tsiang's 1935 novel, *The Hanging in Union Square*, includes a variety of queer proletarian cognoscenti, including one character who appears on page 69 of the novel ("I wish your tastes would be like mine / we could just be sixty-nine"), and another named, not incidentally, Mr. Professor. This latter character first appears when Mr. Nut, Tsiang's protagonist, is looking for a place to sleep. Mr. Professor offers his home and his bed to a desperate and unsuspecting Mr. Nut. But Mr. Nut is awoken when he "felt something uncomfortable touching the lower part of his back. It was not the old man's hand. Nor was it the old man's finger. Of course, Mr. Nut knew what it was."[88] As an excuse for his unwanted advances, Mr. Professor offers a line that ties his reading habits with his homosexuality and the fall of Western civilization:

> I review books. They paid me little before. Now there is a Depression, so there are fewer books and they pay me only with review copies. Tell me how I can help getting excited, when I read those sexy, hot novels. And how can I get the money to buy women and to cool myself? I tried to help myself sometimes. Jesus! That was so meaningless. Then I took whatever I could and it got to be a habit. Oh Jesus! The Decline of the West![89]

Mr. Professor's brainwork leads him into a web of same-sex desire. Given the amount of scholarship detailing the overt homoeroticism of representations of labor in the 1930s, it is unsurprising that the homosexual character would belong to a working class.[90] Yet Tsiang's portrayal of homosexuality situates it specifically within the context of intellectual labor, particularly in its low wages and solitary working habits. Though Mr. Professor bemoans his desire as decadence on the lines of the fall of Rome, this representation queers the proletarian intellectual by underscoring the relationship between brainwork and sexual desire. The proletarian intellectual was described as sexually deviant, but he was also finally permitted a working sexual outlet.

The specter of homosexuality—and its potential to offer a seductive alternative to the brain/body divide—was countered occasionally in radical fiction by proletarian cognoscenti whose bodies were presented as hypermasculine and aggressively heterosexual. Max Eastman, an author whose mother encouraged his bohemian lifestyle, populated his unintentionally homoerotic writings with robust paragons of straight masculinity. In his coming-of-age novel, *Venture*, Eastman describes in roughly equal measure the social, political, and sexual awakenings of its central characters, particularly emphasizing his protagonist Jo Hancock's masculine body. "Jo Hancock was healthy. He was the strongest man in his class in college, and would have been a Varsity football player, if his eye-sight had been as good as his build. He was sensitive, but like many other sensitive people, fond of a fight."[91] Eastman's description of Jo Hancock (whose androgynous name also incorporates a male vulgarity) equally emphasizes the polarities of his character: brain and body, sensitivity and pugnacity. Masculinity is accentuated to disrupt the possibility of the proletarian intellectual being read as explicitly homosexual, but there is something a little queer about proletarian cognoscenti that Eastman cannot quite evade.

Though 1930s radical fiction writers most often depicted the proletarian intellectual as a character who was both intelligent and radical, writers also expressed, as we have seen in Slesinger's novel, frustration with intellectuals as a class. The proletarian intellectual was frequently represented as a character who retained the bodily signifiers of work and labor yet also managed to think, a characterization that was contrasted with depictions of an intellectual class at a far remove from the tedious realities of manual labor. In one telling descriptive detail, the proletarian intellectual was often portrayed as a thinker who did not wear glasses, an accessory deployed to signify thinkers who were not outfitted for work. Reactionary intellectuals, on the other hand, were often hidden behind their spectacles. "What book, what professor, what strange idea," muses one character in *The Unpossessed*, "had taught him to hide behind his glasses?"[92] One of the most damning criticisms of disembodied intellectuals as figured through glasses was represented through the allegorical character, Mr. Wiseguy, in *The Hanging on Union Square*:

> The using of his eye-glasses was scientifically studied. Sometimes he had his glasses placed low at the bridge of his nose. When his eyes were lifted up above the glasses, he had the air of a learned professor. Sometimes he put on a monocle over a not deep-set eye and with his body leaning back and head stretched to one side, he gave you a grand impersonation of ex-Police Commissioner Grover Whalen.[93]

Mr. Wiseguy performs intelligence as an affect both to separate himself from common folk and to align himself with the powerful, but his glasses also prevent him from doing the sort of work that operated as metonym for labor in the 1930s: physical work.

One of the most curious—and most complex—of the proletarian cognoscenti represented in radical fiction was Bigger Thomas, the central character in Richard Wright's *Native Son*.[94] Though Wright's novel is frequently read as didactic, with the lengthy exposition of Boris Max, Bigger's lawyer, routinely offered as evidence, such a reading requires one to ignore much of the novel, particularly those sections probing the complex thought process of Bigger Thomas. Though Bigger lacks education, his obsessive thoughts dominate the novel. He thinks about the context of every decision he makes, constantly frustrated that his actions are restricted by the limited options for action available to him. In a famous essay on the writing of *Native Son*, Wright refers to a common feeling among African Americans that he depicted through Bigger: "this intolerable sense of feeling and understanding so much, and yet living on a plane of social reality where the look of a world which one did not make or own struck one with a blinding objectivity and tangibility, that made me grasp the revolutionary impulse in my life and the lives of those about me and far away."[95] The character of Bigger Thomas represents one who both understands and acts, a signature feature of the proletarian intellectual who broke down the opposition between ideas and action. In this light, rather than contrasting Max with Bigger, Boris Max might be better understood as a less distasteful, more socially acceptable vehicle for Bigger's brainpower. Yet the brutality of Bigger's horrifying acts of violence against women underscores the need for revolutionary upheaval to allow for brainpower to be used to fulfill its potential for productive social action. Rather than celebrating black intelligence as had Harlem Renaissance writers, Wright complicates the narrative of black intellectuals by suggesting how a society that offers no outlet for expressing their ideas pushes proletarian intellectuals into criminal behaviors. Bigger may be understood as political only insofar as his emancipatory gesture is found in his thought as opposed to his action. Otherwise, his actions are limited by, as Wright noted, "his own lack of inner organization which American oppression has fostered in him."[96] Though critics such as Irving Howe have argued that Bigger was "no admirable intellectual or formidable proletarian," Wright suggests he is a decidedly more complicated alchemy of both.[97]

The relationship between Bigger Thomas and Boris Max has been discussed by many literary critics who conceive Max as Thomas's mouthpiece.[98] These critics have often accused Wright of using Max to voice his social critique.[99] Yet such charges ignore the fact that Max essentially replicates the exact thought process and social explanation Bigger himself articulates in the first half of the novel.[100] The contrast between Max and Bigger is not in their thoughts, but rather in their social location. Wright's revisiting of the Bigger's thoughts and actions through Max functions as a whitewashing of black intellect. Wright both challenges the idea that African Americans are not cognizant of their own thoughts and, perhaps most radically, suggests that white radicalism can at best offer a retelling of black ideas. In other words, Max does not speak for Bigger, but rather Bigger speaks *through* Max. The scenes of Max's exposition serve to reveal Bigger's intelligence, rather than to negate it. As literary scholar John M. Reilly notes, *Native Son* represents an articulation of "the right of a black to tell a black story. . . . Wright makes Bigger's voice the emblem of his novel signifying that through the brilliant complex of linguistic acts we know as *Native Son* freedom also comes to black writers."[101] By recognizing and illuminating the parallels between the thought of Max and Bigger, Wright presents to readers a passionate defense of intelligence as a political tool. Wright's demand for recognition of black intelligence resonates with the politics of proletarian cognoscenti in the cultural front.

Bigger Thomas reveals several critical points about representations of intelligence in American culture. First, the reemergence of the African American proletarian intellectual in 1930s radical fiction reinforces the point that intelligence was often used as a political tool among Americans who might otherwise be marginalized. Second, the character of Bigger Thomas necessitated a renegotiation of definitions of intelligence. By refusing to present an educated, genteel black man as the proletarian intellectual of his novel, Wright demanded that audiences consider intelligence as situated within racial discourse and to recognize that its definition was contingent upon one's social position. Third, by juxtaposing Bigger Thomas with a more typical intellectual in the figure of Boris Max, Wright offset dominant signifiers for intelligence. By presenting contrasting images of intelligence Wright challenged the dominant iconography of intelligence as the provenance of educated professionals. His representation of Bigger Thomas also challenged the idea that liberation represented the inevitable outcome of black brainpower by revealing how in a racist society brainpower could just as easily result in unfathomable violence.

John Dos Passos's massive *U.S.A.* trilogy features some of the widest variety of Depression-era proletarian cognoscenti. *U.S.A.* could be classified as what literary critic Barbara Foley refers to as the "proletarian bildungsroman," a form that lends itself particularly easily to efforts at representing intelligence as a weapon in the class war.[102] In *U.S.A.*, Dos Passos both used the model of the bildungsroman and also challenged its structure, opting ultimately to reimagine the novel itself as a site for proletarian expression and resistance.[103] For Dos Passos, the form of the novel was too constricting and bourgeois.[104] By situating readers as workers who had to labor to navigate the unfamiliar form of the novel, he did not merely advance the bourgeois goals of the avant-garde. He depicted readers and workers as united in the project of bringing about the goals of the radical left. Dos Passos confronted the words and language that gave birth to capitalism itself.

The claim that "we have only words against" referred to three intertwined ideas in Dos Passos's attack on capitalism in the 1930s. First, it suggested the limited tools of the proletarian. Second, it proposed that language was always born out of conflict. To speak in the voice of the proletariat was always-already to speak against. Third and lastly, it suggested that words were a strong enough tool—we do not need more than we already have. This complex interweaving of ideas about language and social change informs the narrative structure of *U.S.A.*

The biography sections of Dos Passos's novel describe a number of well-known Americans by centralizing their intellectual labor. Each of these biographies places the figure within a social milieu that promotes brainpower. The range of figures Dos Passos catalogues includes politicians, scientists, inventors, writers, cultural figures, and businesspeople. The primary feature that unites these figures is their fame and success. Dos Passos mines their biographies to find they are also unified through their vernacular intelligence. Thomas Edison, for example, is celebrated because in "Detroit there was a public library and he read it. / He rigged up a laboratory on the train and whenever he read about anything he tried it out." Luther Burbank is praised because "he went home and sat by the stove and read Darwin / Struggle for Existence Origin of Species Natural."[105] Veblen is noteworthy because "he fought the boys all right, pedantry, routine, timeservers at office desks, trustees, collegepresidents."[106]

Significantly, Dos Passos matches his embrace of ordinary intelligence with a markedly unsympathetic treatment of intellectuals as a class. In John Reed's biography, Dos Passos notes with disdain that "Harvard stood for the broad *a* and those contacts so useful in later life and good English prose," lamenting how "at the Harvard Club they're all in the Intelligence Service making the world safe for the Morgan-Baker-Stillman combination of banks."[107] Rather than using their intelligence to make the world safe for democracy, Dos Passos suggests that Harvard's graduates instead give over to the Intelligence Service and use their brainpower to preserve privilege globally. Dos Passos's *U.S.A.* biographies position his heroes' intelligence as inversely proportional to the bourgeois version of intellect valued within elite institutions.

Dos Passos's skepticism about intellectuals is repeated in several sections of "The Camera Eye" that employ Joycean stream-of-conscious writing. Describing his undergraduate career at Harvard, Dos Passos unhappily describes how he lacked "the nerve to break out of the bellglass / four years under the ethercone breathe deep gently now that's the way to be a good boy one to three four five six get A's in some courses but don't be a grind be interested in literature but remain a gentleman don't be seen with Jews or socialists."[108] Intelligence at this elite college is connected with whiteness and political moderation. In contrast to the realities of his own educated biography, Dos Passos's memories are framed as typical of a proletarian intellectual; he endeavors to draft "pencil scrawls in my notebook the scraps of recollection the broken halfphrases the effort to intersect word with word to dovetail clause with clause to rebuild out of mangled memories unshakably (Oh Pontius Pilate) the truth."[109]

Dos Passos's fictional characters are also represented as heroes of the proletarian cognoscenti. Fainy, a socialist character, bemoans the fact that the "interests own all the press and keep knowledge and education from the workin' men," suggesting his own refusal to submit to intellectual hierarchies through his desire to read Marx. Another character, Janey, "used to get books like *The Inside of the Cup, The Battle of the Strong, The Winning of Barbara Worth* out of the library," and also imagined "she was the heroine." J. Ward Moorehouse "graduated from highschool as head of the debating team, class orator and winner of the prize essay contest with an essay entitled 'Roosevelt, the Man of the Hour.'" Eleanor Stoddard "lay down on the bed and read *Romola*. She was reading through the complete works of George Eliot that were in the Moody House library."[110] Throughout *U.S.A.* Dos Passos represents his characters as both workers and thinkers, emphasizing the books they have read as foundational to their character and political commitments.

Of course, Dos Passos's characters do not all end up as revolutionaries. As did Richard Wright, Dos Passos acknowledged that the thinking worker could use her intellectual capital for good or for ill. Radical brainpower could just as easily devolve into reactionary intellectualism; words against might quickly become words used against the proletariat itself. J. Ward

Moorehouse, for example, becomes a fierce capitalist who resents the working class for not using their brains. Still, Dos Passos's insistent representations of the working class as a thinking class through both the structure of his novel and his foregrounding of the proletarian intellectual illustrates the centrality of intelligence among representations of workers in 1930s radical fiction. Depictions of proletarian cognoscenti built on existing associations between brainpower and working-class identity in twentieth-century American culture while moving these representations inexorably to the left.

*   *   *

The emergence of proletarian cognoscenti in Depression-era fiction reveals how leftist cultural producers represented intelligence as a weapon in the class struggle and promoted progressive ideas about the potential for brainpower to produce radical social change. These representations built upon and expanded the existing vocabulary for articulating the politics of intelligence in the 1930s United States. Popular depictions of the New Deal brain trust, ordinary women and men's quest for knowledge, and proletarian intellectuals represented strategies for mapping intelligence across a broad political spectrum. The shifting representations of brainpower during this decade capitalized on the unique circumstances in this moment to bring together a wide variety of ordinary Americans by appealing to their intelligence as a tool for advancing political positions ranging from New Deal liberalism to American communism. Brainpower continued to be invoked within cultural representations to advance democratic ideals, but in the 1930s the complicated discourse about intelligence revealed how easily these discussions could plot opposing political positions in a moment of crisis.

Though paradoxical ideas about brainpower persisted into the thirties, the economic crisis confronting Americans reshaped discussions about intelligence and a consensus emerged that intelligence was necessary to bring about economic, social, and political recovery. Ultimately four conclusions may be drawn about representations of intelligence and the politics of brainpower in the 1930s. First, anti-intellectualism was at best a marginal force during the decade. The Depression forced Americans to reassess their relationship with experts in an effort to correct the economy, and the value of intellectuals in confronting the challenges plaguing the United States was assumed. Second, the oppositional relationship between brainpower and embodiment was complicated during the decade. Many efforts were made to blur the line between brains and bodies. Yet representations of working bodies complicated the notion of intelligent bodies by joining the iconographies of work and intelligence. It was in radical novels where efforts to resolve the contradiction between brains and bodies were most successful. Third, brainpower was put at the center of political concerns. No longer merely a topic of entertainment or criticism, intelligence became an explicitly political subject. Fourth, and related to the last point, intelligence became widely associated with ideology. It was impossible to conceive intelligence without considering the politics of class, sexual, racial, and other identities. Brainpower was incontrovertibly associated with mass social movements.

The so-called "red decade" was, perhaps more fundamentally, the brainy decade; and though the centrality of brainpower in cultural life was sometimes represented as a flashpoint for criticism, it was more often recognized as a useful and positive development. It was during this decade that intellectualism shed many of its associations with embourgeoisment and elitism and instead began to be associated with liberal and radical politics. Depression-era representations built upon earlier models of radical brainpower and attempted to harness intelligence to advance progressive social and political reforms. Representations of intelligence in the 1930s mobilized ordinary Americans to conceive themselves as intelligent enough to challenge social and political institutions. Though the Depression years represented a signature moment in the expansion of brainpower to a wider swath of the American population, these representations of intelligence were recapitulated in later years to discredit those who had been most vocal in challenging American inequality.

6

Dangerous Minds: Spectacles of Science
in the Postwar Atomic City

You can't expect a high-powered scientific joe to sleep with ants.
—U.S. army lieutenant, 1945

In 1945, following the dropping of several terrifying bombs powerful
enough to level whole cities and cultural centers in Japan with unfathomable cataclysmic force, the United States government revealed that massive research facilities had been built in three recently spawned U.S. cities
seemingly without arousing a whisper of suspicion about what was going on
within their gates. The dangerous force of the just-unleashed atomic bomb
might have been the reserve of military personnel who delivered the deadly
ordnance to Hiroshima and Nagasaki, but the technical know-how that
made it possible was firmly located in the minds of domestic geniuses who
designed and built the deadly device—in many cases without ever knowing
the whole of which they were a part. The burst of information about America's destructive new technology of war was quickly met with public fascination over the spaces where scientists had participated in the mammoth
Manhattan Project.

"The War Department revealed today," reported the *New York Times*
on August 7, "how three 'hidden cities' with a total population of 100,000
inhabitants sprang into being as a result of the $2,000,000,000 atomic bomb
project, how they did their work without knowing what it was all about,
and how they kept the biggest secret of the war."[1] The implications of this
"big secret" were paralyzing: not only did the work of these genius scientists

produce the most devastating weapon in the history of humanity, but the revelations of three secret atomic cities also pointed to the explosive potential of compressed intellectual energy for the democratic process. Many of the anxieties that greeted Einstein's emergence in American popular culture—fears about extreme intelligence, apprehensiveness about the relationship between intelligence and revolution, concern that brainpower could be dangerous—were dusted off on hearing of these hidden cities. This time, however, the implications of this new and incomprehensible science were tangible rather than theoretical, and the cast of smart characters was too great, invisible, and diffuse to be represented as disarming.[2]

Much of the cultural concern surrounding the revelations of the Manhattan Project was focused on the all-American city of Oak Ridge, Tennessee, the site of the uranium enrichment facilities that bore a town name evoking folksy rurality and an appealing naturalness seemingly designed to throw neighbors off the scent of scientific labor's technical rationality. This city had arisen, almost literally, overnight, and was populated primarily by those who had perfected the bomb and their brighter-than-average families. Oak Ridge was insistently represented in postwar media as a "normal" town, inhabited by "normal" Americans. In Oak Ridge, the smarter-than-average citizen was not an academic type living in an ivory tower, an over-educated D.C. politico, or a rogue expert. The brainy citizen was an ordinary family man or woman (though most often man), cunningly piercing the most sacred of American institutions and threatening the very basis of citizenship.[3] As the secrets of Oak Ridge were revealed, representations of its residents pointed out the dangerous potential of intelligence for ordinary women and men colluding in secret. Yet the cultural fascination with the Oak Ridge lifestyle also belied a more complicated engagement with brainpower, where highly technical, classified scientific research was paradoxically represented as indicatively American and potentially devastating. In contrast to the intelligent brain trusts occupying a central, visible position in the New Deal government, Oak Ridge's residents required the protection of a complicated state apparatus to prevent these brainworkers from threatening the American way of life. Brainpower had never more critical to national security, but neither had it ever been conceived as so markedly dangerous.

This chapter studies representations of scientists working at Oak Ridge's uranium enrichment facilities to unpack the complicated negotiations of region, family, education, science, and intelligence in the aftermath of the atomic blasts at Hiroshima and Nagasaki and revelation of the Manhattan Project. Representations of Oak Ridge's residents reflected anxiety about the meaning of brainpower in a world where intelligence was both highly sensitive and potentially destructive. Before turning to Oak Ridge, however, it is necessary to unpack some of the significant changes impacting the politics of brainpower that had taken shape during the war.

Brainpower and the State in World War II

The context of World War II dramatically impacted the meanings ascribed to brainpower in the United States in the postwar years. The connection between intelligence and state power in American life that crystallized during the Depression continued during World War II through new representations of intelligence as a weapon in the war. "Fighting with learning is the slogan of victory," declared U.S. Commissioner of Education John Studebaker as he proposed a program for Education and National Defense. Within the Federal Security Agency publications concerning wartime educational efforts, brainpower was repeatedly invoked as vital to winning the war, a critical tool to "enable the people to make intelligent decisions on war and post-war issues."[4] Whereas brainpower had been seen in the Depression years as a tool for promoting radicalism and a means for equalizing the American population, it was here reframed as an essential weapon for victory in World War II, and Americans were encouraged to smarten up to win the war. This was not a matter of simply imparting knowledge but also entailed positioning U.S. citizens as intelligent to achieve political and military goals. Government publications demanded that Americans conceive themselves as intelligent and learn about and understand other cultures as part of an effort to hasten victory by promoting alliances where there was division.

The demand that education include an intercultural component was motivated in part by the patriotic frenzy that swept over the United States during World War II. In order to both justify American involvement in the war and to rally Americans into a united front behind the war effort, many government agencies were highly invested in presenting evidence for U.S. superiority on a global stage. Among those attributes offered as evidence for American exceptionalism was the inclination of most Americans to learn more about their neighbors. Such a national quest for intelligence was represented as a natural by-product of American democracy. "In any effort to achieve national unity or strengthen national morale," wrote Commissioner Studebaker, "we must be mindful that one of the priceless values of the American way of life is that of intellectual and spiritual freedom."[5] Efforts at building up the intelligence of ordinary women and men were conceived as part of the American search for freedom, the linchpin of democratic character.

At the same time, the unique threat of fascism was also used to legitimize the quest for intelligence in the United States. Popular understanding of fascism tended to depict smart, crafty leaders who led dumbstruck masses to their own demise. The first line of defense against fascism, then, was intelligence. "Education for democracy," Studebaker wrote, "is, therefore, a very large order. It must be sufficiently comprehensive to enable young people and adults to meet the trained dogmatic disciples of the new political religions of totalitarianism with convictions soundly based on broad understandings."[6] Intelligent Americans were less likely to be seduced by fascism, and brainpower was positioned as critical to a broader antifascist project. "The program of national defense," a Federal Security Agency pamphlet urged, "calls for men and women who are mentally well adjusted and physically fit to endure, whether in the field, in the factory, in the office, in the home, or in the armed forces."[7] Brainpower not only brought Americans from all walks of life together to form a united front; it also provided a sound deterrent against the threat of foreign governments.

Finally, brainpower was invoked to prevent interethnic alliances from falling apart in light of the simmering prejudices and incivility that boiled over in the United States during wartimes.[8] "In a time of emergency," one pamphlet announced, "the alien is always suspect."[9] As "a safeguard against possible disintegration," one government pamphlet urged, "we rely upon [an] essential characteristic of democratic procedure, namely, 'faith in human intelligence.'"[10] The educational programs introduced by the U.S. Office of Education during World War II particularly emphasized hemispheric education. These initiatives built on education programs that had been introduced in the preceding decades by figures such as Dr. Stephen Dugan, whose Institute of International Education was formed in the wake of World War I to foster international student and professional exchanges, primarily by transporting people between the United States and Latin America.[11] Similarly, Rachel Davis DuBois, founder of the Service Bureau for Intercultural Education, challenged U.S. exceptionalism by creating programs for intercultural education. In a 1939 article, "Peace and Intercultural Education," Davis DuBois called on educators to develop curricula devoted to promoting understanding among American ethnic and racial groups and their close neighbors.[12]

The association of brainpower with government programs advancing citizenship and national security goals was extended after World War II through liberal state-sponsored educational initiatives, none more influential than the Servicemen's Readjustment Act, popularly known as the GI Bill. Signed into law by President Roosevelt on June 22, 1944, the GI Bill aimed to make education affordable to working- and middle-class veterans who completed military service; the bill was a significant influence in connecting education with economic citizenship.[13] The GI Bill was designed to provide college education to veterans in order to encourage their civic participation after the end of their military service. Though it embodied an important set of educational goals that were critical to the expanding of university education in the postwar period, its chief objectives were to stimulate the economy, expand occupational opportunities for returning veterans, and promote active citizenship by both producing model citizen soldiers and making the choice to enter into military service more attractive.[14] "The G.I. Bill bore less resemblance to New Deal legislation—which tended to target citizens as workers—than to an older American tradition of social provision geared for citizen soldiers," historian Suzanne Mettler writes.[15]

Though it was an important program for extending education to many Americans, working-class men especially, the GI Bill contracted the range of Americans who had access to brainpower's social, economic, and political rewards even as it expanded the university's reach. The GI Bill continued to marginalize women's intelligence and pitted worthy beneficiaries of brainpower's benefits against the masses that either refused or were ineligible for military service. Women were especially excluded from the GI Bill's benefits; they comprised 2 percent of the World War II armed forces, and Mettler argues "the exclusion of the vast majority of women from the program, given that they were civilians, widened the gender divide in educational attainment."[16] Historian Margot Canaday further notes that many homosexuals were also excluded from the benefits.[17] Though the GI Bill was a significant factor in extending educational opportunities to returning veterans, it was arguably more instrumental in constructing soldiers as ideal citizens than in redefining brainpower for ordinary women and men.

Yet in spite of its limitations the bill successfully pushed against conceptualizations of brainpower that attempted to restrict access to a small coterie of privileged Americans.[18] Harvard University president James B. Conant lamented that the Bill refused "to distinguish between those who can profit most by advanced education and those who cannot," further noting that "we may find the least capable" of American veterans "flooding the facilities for advanced education."[19] The GI Bill did flood universities with freshmen and fundamentally changed their composition to include working-class students who otherwise might have been excluded. Though it was not singularly instrumental in reframing the meanings attached to brainpower across populations, the bill's expansion of university populations to a greater number of working-class men undoubtedly shaped the relationship between intelligence and civic engagement in the postwar period.

The associations of intelligence with social, political, and economic power during and after the war advanced liberal conceptualizations of brainpower in relation to the state and provided a counterpoint to representations of the scientist as an alternate version of state-sponsored brainpower in the postwar years. The meanings attached to intelligence during the war and the expanded opportunities for higher education extended to veterans returning from service firmly implanted the state and national security in popular culture. Though these government-sponsored efforts suggested the positive impact the government could have in broadening access to brainpower and positioning intelligence as a critical tool for U.S. global expansion, the impact of the atomic bomb reverberated in popular culture to an extent that would be hard to overestimate. The recognition that American scientists were guarding their intelligence even as educational opportunities were being extended to more Americans than ever before created a rift between the smart and the ordinary, and popular representations of atomic cities reflected a society in which brainpower was in flux.

Revealing the Atomic Secret

On March 14, 1949, Oak Ridge celebrated the opening of its gates to the public. After years of having been fenced out of this 59,000-acre section of a small southern town—"no motion picture could provide a more dramatic entrance," one author wrote of the security gate—neighbors, tourists, and onlookers were invited to a public ceremony that included much pageantry and festivity.[20] Elza Gate, one of the secure entrances to the district, was literally exploded before the anxious eyes of those itching to finally gain access to the secret town. Oak Ridge had been built at a frenetic pace beginning in 1942, displacing the few local residents who had made their homes in this muddy community and denying entrance to those few who remained in the area outside the compound. The public opening was heralded with an explosion incinerating the gate, triggered by an atomic pile located at a fifteen-mile remove from Elza. The secret of Oak Ridge had been revealed through the blasts at Hiroshima and Nagasaki, and the opening of the gated community was made into a public spectacle that incorporated the danger, allure, and curiosity of the city itself.[21]

In spite of all the opening fanfare, this same public was still prohibited from entering the laboratories and manufacturing facilities where atomic scientists had worked around the clock to enrich uranium for the bomb. Instead, visitors were "free to explore the community." Though there was a tremendous interest in the development, implementation, and scientific knowhow behind the atomic bomb, much of the media attention given Oak Ridge focused on everyday life in the "atomic cities" that had housed the Manhattan Project.[22] The "open gates" of Oak Ridge did not allow access to the specialized world of atomic science; rather, the public were encouraged to indulge their fascination with the ordinary lives of extremely intelligent Americans. Communities such as Oak Ridge, Tennessee, were interesting to the public because they contained intelligence within a "normal" suburban community—and within dominant narratives of family life—but they also made the lives of the overly intelligent into a spectacle, transforming scientists and their families into fascinating objects.[23] The gates of Oak Ridge were made permeable to people from the world outside whose gaze penetrated the town's perimeter, and the public sought to contain the abnormal brainpower within Oak Ridge's perimeters by exoticizing and sensationalizing its residents.

The public fascination with Oak Ridge began with its alarmingly rapid development. The city seemed to materialize overnight, much like the many suburban housing developments—especially the Levittowns in Pennsylvania and New York—that also began appearing after the conclusion of World War II.[24] The town was planned and managed by a New York based subsidiary, the Roane-Anderson Company, that had been created out of a corporation with a history of involvement in massive construction projects. Because Oak Ridge adhered to the Jim Crow laws outside its gates, the town was also demarcated along racial lines that perpetuated racial segregation, created hierarchies of living standards according to race, and spurred further marginalization of African Americans in housing and public accomoda-tions.[25] Oak Ridge thus anticipated a number of shifts in postwar domestic patterns ranging from racial restrictions to pre-fabricated housing that would be shared by many Americans in the postwar era.

Yet Oak Ridge was an exceptional case of planned housing develop-ments: the sheer scale of its construction boggled the mind. "What had to be built in this race against time," wrote a 1945 *Architectural Record* author,

> included, besides the plant itself, some 10,000 family units, 13,000 dormitory spaces, 16,000 hutments and barracks units. By June 1945 (the site was acquired in 1942) there were 11,000 pupils and 317 teachers in the schools; the school buildings throughout the District cost some $3,700,000. There is also a 300-bed hospital, costing $1,000,000; and a separate dental service building, $92,000.[26]

These statistics served to render the project nearly incomprehensible. Oak Ridge was in some respects just another suburb, but it was also a smarter, faster, more sophisticated version of the suburban developments emerging across the nation. "The bus drivers were constantly getting lost and asking passengers the way," complained one bemused resident, "not because they were new at the job, but because the roads were being changed so fast. A worker lost his road-sprinkling truck and spent three days cruising around in an automobile looking for it."[27] Oak Ridge was conceived as an arche-typal new American town, but its was an extreme version of the normalcy found in other places. The city was depicted as booming in the midst of a country emerging from the Depression, dewy-eyed and a little dazed by the alacrity of its creation.[28] Oak Ridge was paradoxically populated with pro-foundly intelligent people but also hopelessly lost and confused by its own construction.

Though fascination with Oak Ridge began with the speed with which the town was created, the unique attributes of its residents were similarly made into a spectacle. The population represented "quite a concentration of Ph.D.s, as well as other educated folk," wrote Daniel Lang in the *New Yorker*, "who in their off hours play chamber music, study foreign languages, and sit around their B-Houses discussing the more technical aspects of nuclear energy."[29] Oak Ridge was a "typical" suburb, but its residents were of a particularly brilliant pedigree, both exotic and yet eerily familiar. One article discussed at length the usage and holdings of the town's library, noting that a startling "121,230 people have visited the Main Library Reading Room during these fourteen months."[30] Such discussions cast Oak Ridge's inhabitants and practices in familiar terms: the intelligence of Oak Ridge was within the grasp of any community that had a library (and used it). Yet other representations treated the intelligent Oak Ridge residents as spoiled, exceptional, and demanding of special treatment. "You can't expect a high-powered scientific joe," declared an Army lieutenant stationed at Oak Ridge, "to sleep with ants."[31] The tastes of Oak Ridge's residents at times came across as elitist and privileged.

One designation commonly used to describe the residents of Oak Ridge was "long-hairs," a term that has deep roots in the history of American intellectuals. One local worker explained his own ignorance about what was going on in the laboratories and plants by stating that he would "leave it to them long-hairs to think things out."[32] The intelligent folk at Oak Ridge were thus conceived at a distinct remove from everyday ordinary Americans. The term "long-hair" also suggested, in the context of a postwar style marked by short-regular haircuts for men, a conspicuous gender inversion: intelligent men were conceived as being feminine in nature.[33] Perhaps due to their association with the military-industrial complex, however, the scientists at Oak Ridge were just as often described as rugged frontiersman, working on the vanguard of the world of science, military, and manufacture.[34] "Adjectives applied to the whole project," wrote one magazine writer in an article titled "Birthplace of the Atomic Bomb," "include: mighty, staggering, solid, permanent, vast, utilitarian."[35] They might have been long-hairs, but the scientists at Oak Ridge were also manly pioneers.

Atomic scientists seemed to represent something new and different insofar as their research was represented as brash, bold, and ambitious. Yet the fact that they were largely involved in brainwork introduced a complex paradox in these representations: though these scientists were bold frontiersmen, they were also associated with labor that required little bodily exertion and had the potential to serve nefarious ends. A *New York Times* article described the city of Oak Ridge as bifurcated, using the pioneer myth to represent Oak Ridge's polarized identities:

On one side of a certain highway there are tall stacks to dissipate the radio-active fumes from one process of atomic splitting. On the

other side is a plain log cabin, chinked with clay and whitewashed—
and lived in less than three years ago. The centuries jostle each
other. A visitor may well wonder if the splitting of atoms in Happy
Valley has done humanity as much good as the older-fashioned art of
splitting logs.[36]

The log cabin, stalwart symbol of American democracy, rife with associations with Abraham Lincoln and lighting out for the territory, stood in
Oak Ridge as a symbol of older, more egalitarian forms of knowledge. The
Manhattan Project split Tennessee physically and ideologically as remarkably as the splitting of the atom itself. Oak Ridge was made to stand in for
the questions, conflicts, and paradoxes confronting Americans living in the
atomic age. The status of smarter-than-average citizens was fundamentally
reshaped by the revelations of the localized Manhattan Project, and representations of Oak Ridge shattered conventional notions of family, community, democracy, and scientific knowledge and revealed the truly explosive
danger lurking beneath the most benevolent mask of intelligence. Whereas
brainpower had been optimistically represented during the Depression as
producing an expansion of democracy that might fulfill American dreams,
the atomic city demonstrated how it could just as easily be used to mask the
truly threatening, insidious work of dangerous minds.

Strategies of Containment at Oak Ridge

One of the most striking features about Oak Ridge that was discussed in
nearly every media story concerning the town was its security, which was
represented physically with fences and structurally through containment of
knowledge.[37] Henry J. Taylor, host of the popular radio show "Your Land
and Mine," invited his audience to imagine the feeling of entering into such
a tightly monitored and controlled city. "Come with me," Taylor coaxed,
"through the guarded gate, deep in the Tennessee hills. An armored car,
manned by security police, stands at the gate; it is connected by radio-
telephone with central security headquarters and with every nerve center of
the isolated areas."[38] The fence surrounding Oak Ridge appeared especially
ominous in this otherwise ordinary-looking suburban community, and the
town was made into a metaphorical body with "nerve centers" connecting
its furthest limbs with its brain. "I saw gates within gates and barbed wire

fences and signs warning of 'Prohibited Zones' and 'Restricted Areas,'" wrote Louis Falstein in a *New Republic* profile of Oak Ridge. "And posters in dormitories, offices and stores: 'Protect Project Information...'"[39] These gates and signs contained brainpower within Oak Ridge, which was comforting during a time when the power of intelligence to unleash unfathomable violence weighed heavily on American minds. At the same time, the gates prevented ordinary women and men outside from accessing the most powerful brains in the nation.

The Oak Ridge fence served not only to contain the nuclear facilities and atomic scientists; it also served to physically differentiate Oak Ridge from other suburban communities. "Take away that forbidding high fence," wrote an author in *Newsweek*, and "Oak Ridge, Tenn., would look much like most any small American city."[40] The fence kept insiders in and outsiders out, but it also reinforced the boundaries between ordinary American towns and the domestic communities of the highly intelligent. The insistent representation of security in media discussions about Oak Ridge reinforced the notion that brainpower threatened the outside world. "At the entrance gate," wrote one author, "guards searched us, checked the auto's pockets, and even lifted the hood, looking for weapons."[41] Yet this performance was amateur theater compared with the efforts to keep Oak Ridge's intelligence contained within the city. "Mammoth red-and-black signs scream out excerpts from the Espionage Act which you signed," recalled a former resident of the town. "Another reminds that the penalty is stiff."[42] The demand for secrecy and security permeated every aspect of daily life in the Atomic City.

By far the most prevalent form of security at Oak Ridge regulated the circulation of knowledge about the atomic bomb and uranium's role in its production. "Since its construction during the war by Uncle Sam," one author wrote, "the atom city has been surrounded by secrecy."[43] The most insidious form of secrecy was that preventing workers from themselves knowing what they were producing. "We knew it couldn't be very big," a Y-12 uranium enrichment plant worker recalled, "and we were also pretty sure it wasn't mouse traps."[44] Ignorance about the scope of the project among some of America's most intelligent citizens represented a cognitive dissonance that was discussed extensively in magazines and newspapers. Even less aware were those working in staff positions ranking below the brainworkers, an intertwining hierarchy of prestige, compensation, and knowledge that bespoke a structure of intellectual inequality. "Workers... had no idea what terrific violence they were compounding," wrote a former employee. "A girl at a coded dial might control thousands of horsepower, and never know why."[45] This secrecy and enforced ignorance, compounded by the explicit gendering of the "girl" working the dial, rendered the city something dystopian, a vision of the consequences of intelligence so enormous it became alienating. "The whole atmosphere of the project today is as bewildering and misty as the setting in Franz Kafka's *The Trial*," wrote a *New Republic* author,

> with one important difference. In the novel, Joseph K— didn't know why he was accused or who was accusing him, but his inquisitors evidently did. At Oak Ridge even the interrogators apparently are ignorant of the investigation's actual sources and motivations; somebody higher up may know who is saying damaging things about the scientists, but in most cases the Security men here say that they don't.[46]

Oak Ridge, in other words, was *more* terrifying than Kafka! Both the knowledge of those creating the bomb and the intelligence of those monitoring workers were clouded by ignorance, intrigue, and alienation. The secrecy demanded of workers at Oak Ridge contained intelligence in the bodies of individuals and under the control of the state.[47] Outside these bodies, ignorance ruled. Intelligence was represented as more threatening to national security than ignorance, as it had to be contained, monitored, and controlled; brainpower was made a critical component of the military-industrial complex.

The secrecy that characterized life at Oak Ridge entered into popular representation at the same time that the world's most devastating weapon became public knowledge. "When America heard the news that a single atomic bomb had virtually wiped out a whole Japanese city," one article's author reported, "it was also disclosed that it had created a 'secret city' in this country, a city of 75,000 people busily working on they knew not what."[48] This evocative recounting of the revelation about Oak Ridge reveals the profound anxiety precipitated by the appearance of a destructive new weapon that was incomprehensible both in terms of its powerful force and the confusing theoretical formula that made it work. The framework for understanding cause and effect in military weaponry (explosive substances react to a catalyst) was replaced with a far more complicated and difficult chain reaction.[49] Yet anxiety about the incomprehensibility of the science behind the atomic bomb was also met with a new terror: just as the atomic bomb defied the ordinary characterization of explosions (it was no longer clear what was being exploded or how), so also the bomb's development and production were veiled in a process that was far more elegant and confusing than ordinary munitions manufacture. The production facilities for the atomic bomb were shrouded in a secrecy that was represented as nefarious and portended a new age in which transparency and openness in American life were replaced with paranoia and suspicion.[50] The A-bomb's catastrophic force decimated Hiroshima and Nagasaki, and its cultural impact reverberated in Oak Ridge, and, by extension, the entire United States. There was an equality of scale implied here: the atomic city was imagined to be the symbol of the new age, its threat conceived as inextricable from the terrifying blast that leveled two Japanese cities.

Representations of Oak Ridge ironically depicted a town in which everyone knew too much, but nobody knew anything. The residents were treated as postmodern citizens who were alienated by their own intelligence. "Even now," wrote Daniel Lang in a *New Yorker* profile of Oak Ridge, "a stranger in town like myself, casually mentioning U-235 or plutonium or any of the other obnoxious terms I never heard of until this summer, is likely to receive a stare fit for an Axis agent."[51] Lang reveled in the ambiguity of intelligence, knowledge, and paranoia that characterized postwar representations of Oak Ridge. His pursuit of knowledge was mistaken for possession of dangerous information, and his intelligence was rendered suspicious within a town that was ironically populated entirely by intelligent people. At the same time that Oak Ridge appeared as a town dominated by intelligence, it was also represented as a community governed by secrecy and isolation.[52] What was to become of brainpower in a world where intelligence signified alienation and separation? "Scientists still bit their tongues in mid-sentence," *Time* magazine revealed, "lest a secret pop out."[53]

The unique coupling of intelligence with secrecy that seemed inevitable in atomic cities had implications for representations of Oak Ridge families that were especially significant in a Cold War moment when, as historian Elaine Tyler May has noted, strategies of containment emerging within foreign policy often extended to the home. In her influential book *Homeward Bound*, May describes how the Cold War created a cultural context where it "was not just nuclear energy that had to be contained, but the social and sexual fallout of the atomic age itself."[54] Representations of Oak Ridge offered no shortage of descriptions of a family-centered community; the intelligence of Oak Ridge was contained within a domestic two-parent family structure. Public debate about nuclear power, disclosure of experiments relating to nuclear weaponry, and American responsibility to the global scientific community were all channeled through representations of families living in Oak Ridge. Depicting the typicality of Oak Ridge families defused suspicion about a classified government project working to introduce the world to a new age of paranoia, danger, and shared responsibility, and the families were represented as gatekeepers for the atomic age. Articles in magazines and newspapers obsessively detailed their ordinary lives. "People started having children, many children. 'Pretty much all there was to do in those days,' a father said."[55] Oak Ridge seemed to make families more secure while also transforming "ordinary" families into potentially dangerous weapons.

Oak Ridge rendered the family nuclear as well: the family collectively guarded the knowledge necessary to produce an atomic blast and had to be contained in Oak Ridge to prevent its brainpower from radiating beyond the town limits.[56] "Young people abound in [Oak Ridge,]" a *Saturday Evening Post* author delightedly reported. "In June, the 2,500th baby was born in Oak Ridge hospital, and the public school system has a capacity of more than 10,000 students."[57] The youthful vibrancy and comfortably secure families of Oak Ridge were offered up as evidence for its normality, confirmation of its security, and affirmation of its robust productivity (babies were the only objects observers could verify that Oak Ridge was actually producing). These representations of growing families served to both set up Oak Ridge as a community like any other—their intelligent citizens were not just idly theorizing, they were also making babies and creating families—while affirming the nuclear family as the standard by which American loyalty could be judged. Participation in the nuclear family narrative thus aligned ordinary Americans with their best and brightest.

Yet the secrecy required of workers at Oak Ridge was also depicted as a catalyst for the breakdown of family within the community. "There was a time, coming home from the lab, when I couldn't talk to my wife at all," one scientist complained. "I pretty well knew what the Project was making, but I couldn't tell her. We'd sit around the dinner table and the strain was terrible. A man could bust. Then we started quarreling. Over nothing, really. So we decided to have a baby."[58] In his deeply conflicted recounting of the atomic secret, this scientist imagined family as both obstacle and opportunity. Oak Ridge secrecy prevented the scientist from properly behaving as a "family man," yet it also provided the occasion for becoming more invested in the American family narrative through spontaneous procreation. In Oak Ridge, among America's most brilliant scientists, it was exceedingly difficult to balance one's intelligence and traditional family values, as an anecdote recounted by Louis Falstein illustrated:

> At home, evenings, they stared at their wives silently. They could report neither their near-successes nor failures. The wives learned not to ask questions. "So we played Chinese checkers," one physicist said, "till we got sick of it."
>
> "Once I found myself doodling on a piece of paper after dinner. My wife came up to where I was sitting. She didn't say anything. We'd gotten into the habit of not talking. But she looked at the paper on which I was drawing aimlessly and her eyes seemed to ask the question, 'What are you doing?' And what was I doing? Drawing a chain reaction on paper unconsciously. I tore up the paper and threw it in the fireplace. Then we went to bed."[59]

Falstein's informant resolved the tension precipitated by spousal secrecy through a retreat to the marital bed, a parallel site of secrecy and knowledge. The containment of knowledge within the individual represented a site of conflict. The family was reinforced as a solution to this enforced individuality, especially in its reproductive capacity, but also remained threatened by the demands of secret intelligence.

The narrative of the nuclear family emerged in a similarly paradoxical form when Oak Ridge became the site of a public debate about the proper uses of nuclear energy. In 1946 students at Oak Ridge High organized the Youth Council on the Atomic Crisis and wrote an editorial called "Atomic Peace" that was published in newspapers throughout the country.[60] In order to publish the piece, "the boys and girls have had to overcome the feeling among parents that 'children should be seen and not heard.'"[61] These same students also published an editorial in their school newspaper, the innocuously named *Oak Leaf*. "Our fathers," they wrote, "have told us that the atom bomb can wreck the world, and we believe them."[62] Their knowledge about nuclear devastation was predicated upon both the intelligence of male scientists and the authority of their fathers. Wives and mother also formed organizations to pressure the government for world control of the atomic bomb, a narrative that was repeatedly framed as a family story.[63]

The containment of Oak Ridge's families was furthered through architectural and geographical metaphors of suburbanization. As many historians have noted, the suburbanization of the United States was particularly accelerated in the postwar years, especially through the development of "planned" suburban communities such as Levittown. Historians Stephanie Coontz, Lisa McGirr, and Elaine Tyler May have noted how the push for suburban development dovetailed with both the demand for normative family values and the rhetoric of Cold War containment in the postwar years.[64] This suburbanization also neatly paralleled the models for containment of brainpower housed in wartime communities such as Oak Ridge. Representations of the town emphatically depicted its order; its functionality; its efficiency; its ideal conditions for expanding families; its safety, security, and social order; along with many other characteristics that would come to be prized in postwar suburban communities. "Considering that it is the home of the most explosive and most dangerous force known to man," wrote a *Newsweek* writer, "Oak Ridge is nevertheless a peculiarly calm and relaxed place in these final weeks of Year One of the Atomic Age."[65] Similarly, the "little boxes" of Oak Ridge's homes were prescient models for the prefab suburban architecture that exploded in popularity during the Cold War, especially the homes constructed quickly and cheaply of so-called "Cemesto Board," an inexpensive mixture of cement and asbestos:

> There are six types of Cemesto homes—"A-House," "B-House," and so on. "F-House," the largest of the models, has six rooms and rents for seventy-three dollars a month. Many people live in prefabricated plywood houses (they're called "A-1," "B-1," and so on), and even more live in trailers which the Army scrounged from the T.V.A., the Federal Public Housing Authority, and other government agencies.[66]

These homes originated as part of the wartime military-industrial complex, though their connection to liberal New Deal programs was clearly marked through reference to the Tennessee Valley Authority. "Makers of the most destructive weapon ever known, the people of Oak Ridge, Tenn., live more safely on their streets than any community of comparable size in the nation," wrote an author in *Business Week*. "With more than 300 miles of streets and highways, the atomic city in mid-July passed its 100th day without a traffic fatality."[67] Though Oak Ridge was a community planned to contain intelligence, such planning had the side effect of creating an ordered, conformist community; the scientist's city translated into a model American town.[68]

Insistent representations of Oak Ridge as an archetypal American community encouraged a boosterish mentality that framed the brainpower of its residents as emblematic of American national identity, and Oak Ridge's scientists were depicted peaceably producing chain reactions alongside ordinary Americans. In his 1950 book *The Oak Ridge Story*, George O. Robinson, Jr., described how the town, even in its early days, included "the famous Fuller Brush 'man,' his wares prominently displayed, with an appropriate sign, in front of a 'hut' in the midst of the thriving new business section."[69] Even as they emphasized the dangerous minds of Oak Ridge's atomic scientists, journalists continued to represent atomic science as connected with American ingenuity, the scientists easily coexisting with the Fuller Brush salesman. Henry J. Taylor offered precisely such an argument about the legacy of American intelligence at Oak Ridge on his radio show in 1948:

> Over and above the tremendous scientific achievement, the secret of Oak Ridge depended on two particularly American free-enterprise talents—process engineering and mass production.... Without the super-scientific kind of process-design resulting from competition in America's oil, electrical and chemical industries, in the machine tool, watch, rotary pump, radio, telephone and thousands of other branches of enterprise, and without the mass-production techniques developed through years of competition in the automotive industry, Oak Ridge could never have been designed or built.[70]

Just as representations of Einstein had defused the dangerous potential of his intelligence by foregrounding American ingenuity, Taylor emphasized American invention in a bid to depict the intelligence of Oak Ridge scientists as an American attribute.

Brainworkers, Labor, and Leisure at Oak Ridge

While representations of Oak Ridge families vacillated between treating them as odd and as ordinary, depictions of work and leisure in the atomic city seemed more inclined to accentuate the town's strangeness. A parade of writers described the uranium enrichment plants as anomalous for their cleanliness, quiet, and lack of productivity. If American industry was predicated upon the manufacture of goods, Oak Ridge was made to seem bizarre because it apparently produced nothing. "Among the low, brown hills of eastern Tennessee," wrote a *Time* writer, setting up the contrast between the ordinariness of the landscape and the weird specter of Oak Ridge, "stands a factory whose total product for 1949 weighed less than 1/10,000th of an ounce. The weight of its average shipment is less than that of the graphite in a penciled signature; the container usually weighs a billion times more."[71] Such descriptions invoked the recognizable images of a Tennessee landscape and a flourishing factory, a folksy image offset by the factory's freakishly microscopic output. Brainwork was treated as fascinating and more than a little disturbing; the factories of Oak Ridge were somehow ineffectual compared with the polluting smokestacks and high-yield assembly lines generally connected with American industry.

Equally unsettling in these representations was the cleanliness of the plants. "It's really a pretty quiet place. No big compressors stomping anything. Nice and clean, too. No grease to speak of," reported a straight-shooting informant in the *New Yorker*.[72] The fussiness associated with scientists was transposed onto the plants themselves: just as the longhairs were feminine, prettied-up versions of masculine laborers, so the Oak Ridge plants were oddly clean variations on the American factory. "The plants where U-235 is extracted from uranium ore are silent as they work and even austere in the warm Tennessee sunshine," explained *Newsweek*'s writers. "There are no smoke-belching chimneys, no animated movement, indeed hardly any external sign of the world-shaking activities going on behind their brick and concrete walls."[73] Instead, the *New Yorker* described "the mystifying manufacture of a mystifying product."[74] The work associated with American industrial life demanded representations that were dirty, polluting, and loud. Oak Ridge's curious cleanliness and conspicuous silence were interpreted as symptomatic of the strange world of brainwork, contrasted with the growing manufacturing economy elsewhere in the South. The Oak Ridge plant was strangely inauthentic for a work environment: it lacked the noise, dirt, and productivity associated with American labor.

Discussion of the successful plant that failed to produce seemed to mirror the descriptions of a mystical future world found in science fiction. Sidney Shalett's article on Oak Ridge's scientist for the *Saturday Evening Post* intentionally blurred the real scientific work going on in the laboratories with the sorts of cockamamie schemes being cooked up in comic books.

"Once a radioactive rat, lost from the laboratory, was traced down with a meter," Shalett reported, "the same device with which Batman, comic-strip character, overcame an unwholesome fellow named Professor Radium. The Scientists wonder whether they or Batman thought of it first."[75] This was no mere chicken-or-egg question; the blurring of science and science fiction at Oak Ridge was symptomatic of the perplexing paradoxes marking the advent of the atomic scientist: he was both vital in the modern world and potentially dangerous for the machination of democratic practice. The exciting recounting of the radioactive rat in the *Saturday Evening Post* was unusual; more often the dull labs at Oak Ridge were depicted as disappointingly banal.

The failure of Oak Ridge to live up to readers' expectations regarding workplace productivity or sci-fi futurity led a group of particularly plucky atomic scientists to exact their revenge on bored journalists by giving a group of reporters exactly what they sought:

> When nearly 100 reporters assembled here for the first sale of radioactive isotopes, the scientists were depressed about the unglamorous appearances of their machinery—nothing at Oak Ridge matches the bubbling caldrons and crackling death machines of a horror movie. So the scientists rigged up a "control board' "straight out of Karloff. When an excited girl reporter was told to push a button as radioactivated material was ready to come out of the uranium oven, the results were stupendous. Bells clanged, buzzers buzzed, colored lights flashed; the panel did everything but come up with three cherries.[76]

Representations of sci-fi genius were so powerful that the actual scientists at Oak Ridge had to prove they were appropriately oddball in their profession by constructing a cinematic set piece on which to stage their Hollywood-ready performance.[77] The reality of Oak Ridge was conceived as so mundane in contrast to the mythologizing around the bizarre work going on inside its walls that the truth had to be exaggerated to meet the expectations of an exoticizing public. Technical wizardry was also gendered here through the journalistic juxtaposition of the mystifyingly technical work of scientists and the stupefied eagerness of the masses, the latter embodied in the form of an "excited girl reporter."[78]

The fascinated gaze that rendered Oak Ridge scientists endlessly intriguing precipitated a paradox within representations: the scientists were both fully immersed in a narrative of normality and treated as spectacular exceptions. It was this contradictory impulse toward ordinary and extraordinary representation that rendered the Oak Ridge scientist an object of fascination and a latent threat to the social order. Louis Falstein's description of a scientist's engagement with popular culture—the funnies in a daily newspaper—offers a typical example of this tension. "I was introduced to my first long-hair in the lobby of the Oak Ridge Guest House," Falstein writes, treating the category as though it were self-explanatory. "He was a tall young man of about twenty-five, and was absorbed in the funnies when I came up. 'I like the funnies very much,' he said, 'but Orphan Annie's politics make me mad.'"[79] Falstein's scientist was invested in the pursuit of American ordinariness, but he was too smart to neatly assimilate to American values. That he read the funnies made this scientist ordinary; that he read them for their political content rendered him subversive. What could be more ordinary than reading *Annie*? What could be more absurdly un-American than contesting her politics?

Similar depictions of Oak Ridge citizens as too smart were easily read as snobbishness, but also as dangerous eccentricity. Louis Falstein recounted a suggestive anecdote about a scientist's bizarre performance of a typical encounter gone weird:

> In the evening I met another long-hair. He, too, was in his twenties. His wife looked like a girl recently out of college. "And this is my dog, Pluto," the young scientist said, "named after plutonium. A very intelligent dog." He turned to the dog and said, "Pluto, would you rather work for duPont or be a dead dog?" Pluto rolled over on his back and played dead. The owner tossed him a biscuit.[80]

Just as with the scientist overanalyzing an Annie cartoon, this scientist performed the mundane dramatics of a typical suburban existence by marrying young and playing with his pup. Yet his strangeness prevented him from becoming wholly normal. Both the Annie incident and the dog's trick were explicitly politicized: Annie became a comment on contemporary politics, and the dog's rolling over articulated a site of conflict between government energy programs and private industry. DuPont was one of the most significant companies shaping American industry in the mid-twentieth century. Pluto would not be caught dead working for crass business interests. Pluto was not even named after the tiny planet or the adorable Disney character, but rather after a rare element essential to the atomic age. A typical strategy for representing Oak Ridge scientists exploited this tension between scientists' mass appeal and their overweening need to complicate and politicize everything.

At times the intelligence of Oak Ridge's scientists compounded with their inability to assimilate to American mass culture was depicted as symptomatic of the elitism one often found among the intellectual class. An area of Oak Ridge that exclusively housed the town's most prestigious scientists was known to locals as "Snob Hill."[81] Yet this elitism was more often offered up as evidence for Oak Ridge's urbanity. "The city, for all its newness," wrote Daniel Lang, "is fairly cosmopolitan in character."[82] That Lang, a New York-based writer, offered such an imprimatur reinforced the notion that Oak Ridge was anomalous within its southern rural surroundings. The conflation of a government town with the glitz and glamour of New York also introduced the possibility that brainpower could render one's identity either as an individual or a community inauthentic.

Brainpower and Life Outside Oak Ridge

Oak Ridge was frequently represented in magazines and newspapers as though it were a social experiment in contrast to the traditional, ordinary community immediately outside its perimeter. The strangeness of Oak Ridge reinforced the ordinariness of southern life in surrounding Tennessee. When high-profile *New Yorker* reporter Daniel Lang was shown around town by a local southern woman, she drew a revealing connection between Oak Ridge and the native New York of her interlocutor. "Several hundred lights suddenly and inexplicably illuminated a corner of the building that I hadn't noticed was dark," Lang recounted. "The girl chauffeur ah'd at that. 'Bright lights,' she said in her slow southern voice. 'Tennessee's got the bright lights now, just like Broadway.'"[83] Lang's description of this performance hinged upon the legibility of the "girl chauffeur's" efforts to draw parallels between the brightly illuminated atomic plants and the shining marquees and glittering advertisements of Forty-Second Street, a comparison that was likely triggered by the dubious naming of the Manhattan Project. Yet Lang's description also implicitly described a failure: just as the scientists could not assimilate to local culture, Lang's chauffeur came off as dull-witted, utopian, and hopelessly starry-eyed in her wistful analogy, accentuated by her "slow" drawl.[84] The community of Oak Ridge was oddly situated within an overdetermined rural southern landscape, and the brainpower of its residents exposed the naïve unintelligence of ordinary women and men. Louis Falstein faithfully transcribed another southern girl's plea that he represent her accurately in his article for the *New Republic*. "'I want you-all to write a good story about Oak Ridge,' she said warningly. 'There's been many of you writers from the North, but I ain't seen a good story yet. You fellas don't seem to git the sperit of this place.'"[85]

The transplanted cosmopolitanism of Oak Ridge was assumed to be one of its peculiarities, and it was only through contrasting representations of local residents outside the city that the specific contours of a genius town were made visible. Just as representations of Oak Ridge exaggerated the intelligence and strangeness of the scientists conducting experiments in their spotless government-sponsored laboratories, so the folksy simplicity of the southern Tennessee residents outside Elza gate was offered up as evidence for both the alien nature of Oak Ridge and the lack of intelligence among other southern residents. Such a construction of southern earthiness was implied even in the name of the atomic city, which was carefully crafted to drape the town in so much southern charm. The A-bomb was developed in a city, *The American City* reported, given "the disarming name of Oak Ridge for the distinct purpose of keeping its important identity secure."[86] George Robinson, in his book about Oak Ridge, confirmed that the U.S. government hoped that "its rural connotation held outside curiosity to a minimum."[87] Disarming as it may have been, Oak Ridge failed to assimilate to the expectations of southern life.

Though the military may have dictated the name of the town, the resistance of southern locals to its incursion was framed in media representations through reference to the quaintly religious narrative of Tennessee plain folk. "The natives of this Bible Belt country," Daniel Lang wrote, "maintain that God is responsible for the picking of this particular spot as the setting for the Army's diabolical factories."[88] Lang's description of a belief that transformed the will of God into a means of advancing the work of the devil dismissed southern Christian beliefs as symptomatic of regional ignorance. This representational strategy assumed a conflict between scientific intelligence and the religious faith found proliferating in Tennessee communities outside Oak Ridge. "To Oak Ridgers the scientists are known as 'long-hairs,'" Louis Falstein confidently reported. "To mountaineer Southerners on the Project the long hairs are a peculiar lot who were at one time in favor of interdenominational services, 'all praying in one church and at the same time,' I heard said with obvious disapproval."[89] Ecumenicalism was identified with the intellectual lot who made Oak Ridge their new and unwelcome home.

Lang portrayed southerners in conflict with scientists who were depicted as northern and urban. "Villages disappeared to make way for Oak Ridge," Lang wrote. "Scarboro, Wheat, and Robertsville are the names of vanished places where the hill folk of this region went in for what amounted to non-profit farming—some tobacco planting, a couple of hogs, some poultry, perhaps a head or two of cattle, and a little moonshine-making."[90] Lang's drift into Erskine Caldwell-like description of the bucolic South exoticized Oak Ridge's Tennessee locale and suggested a linear narrative where agriculture was mindless, quaint, and headed for extinction. The work of the displaced locals was represented as a relic of a premodern economy that was destined to be supplanted by the smarter work at Oak Ridge in a process conceived as a natural progression. The simplicity of Lang's southern life offered a stark contrast with the mathematical precision demanded at Oak Ridge: the "couple of hogs" and "head or two of cattle" conveyed an apparent lack of interest among southerners with business as tricky as numbers. "People elsewhere in the South are also talking about Oak Ridge, seeing it as a cornerstone in the industrialization of their homeland," wrote one optimistic writer for *Business Week* in 1946. "They are increasingly confident that the Oak Ridge payroll, one of the largest in the region and offering higher individual wages than the average, will stabilize at a level that will provide a healthy economic contribution for a much larger area than Oak Ridge itself."[91] Scientific work was connected with economic advancement and at a far remove from Tennessee's rural agricultural economies.

Representations of Oak Ridgers' conflict with their native neighbors also allowed readers to indulge fantasies about awkward interactions between transplants and indigenous locals. The tensions between residents of Oak Ridge and its surrounding community came to stand in for conflicted ideas about intelligence and folk wisdom. Oak Ridge's intelligence was inauthentic and dangerous, but it was also contrasted with the equally distasteful "backwardness" of the South, particularly as figured through the figuration of the "hillbilly." Theodore Rockwell's graphic description of Oak Ridge for the *Saturday Evening Post* positions readers as outsiders observing the fascinating foment in this unexpected corner of southern conflict:

Like the mud, one thing that is always with you is the hillbilly-furriner feud. Hillbillies are good people, but, like the rest of us, provide their share of the laughs for those of us who are unused to their ways. You see signs warning, "Do not urinate in this building," and "Do not spit in this corner," and "Do not stand on the seat." They are admittedly indelicate, but apparently necessary. To the sign reading, "Do not throw cigarette butts into bowl," a wag has added the explanation, "It makes them soggy and hard to light." You see women nursing their babies at a bus stop; you hear twelve-year-olds bragging that they have given up smoking; you meet grandmothers in their early thirties; and all of this blended in with the British physicists, New York merchants and Texas construction engineers.[92]

The hillbilly represented everything Oak Ridge did not, and rural ignorance was imagined as un-ironic and simple. Particularly significant in this passage is Rockwell's apparent refusal to acknowledge the smartly ironic resistance implicit in the "wag's" proviso to the note about flushing cigarette butts. As J. W. Williamson has described in his study of southern rural stereotypes in American culture, the hillbilly

drinks hard liquor—and not at cocktail parties. He's theatrically lazy but remains virile. He nearly always possesses the wherewithal for physical violence—especially involving dogs and guns. He's gullible when skepticism would be wiser, and he's stupid when smart would be safer. He reminds us symbolically of filth, of disgusting bodily functions. Why else is he so frequently pictured with outhouses?[93]

Even as American industry was moving to the South, representations of intelligence within the South were opposed to southern ignorance, premodern industry, and uncivilized behavior.

Local schools, which drew from both non-project and Oak Ridge children, were a hot zone of tension around education, class, and intelligence. One longtime Tennessee resident complained about Oak Ridge residents in a magazine article, grousing that "their children in school are forever clamoring for more student representation on the council."[94] Daniel Lang confirmed the demand for a voice in their education among Oak Ridge's intelligent youth, noting how "the children from rural districts blink with bewilderment when precocious metropolitan brats, fresh from progressive education, agitate for more student control over this or that and tell their teachers, "That's not the way we learned long division at Dalton.'"[95] As this latter example also illustrates, the dichotomy between North and South, urban and rural, was inflected by class. Public education was forced to resemble the elite private education found in the actual Manhattan's Dalton School. Though at some points the identities of Oak Ridge and surrounding-area children blurred—"as the hidden city of Oak Ridge sprang out of the mud," one article's opening teased, "the girls went to dances in hip boots, and famous scientists lived like hillbillies"[96]—they were mostly conceived as at endless odds with one another. Intelligent scientists and ignorant southerners were depicted as wholly incompatible and at opposite poles on the intellectual spectrum.

Though tension was widespread, racial segregation represented perhaps the most significant dimension of southern life that was shared both inside and outside Oak Ridge. Because Elza Gate failed to prevent Jim Crow laws from entering the community, black workers held mostly low-paying positions in the town and were depicted at odds with the white scientists.[97] Representations of Oak Ridge tended to frame this disparity through reference to everyday living—rather than working—conditions; that scientists were white was apparently assumed. *Newsweek* reported on "the miserable Jim Crow hutments in which the Negro workers, now numbering about 1,500, dwell with an absolute minimum of living facilities." [98] The housing reserved for African Americans, Louis Falstein noted, "looks like an Emergency Housing Slum Area."[99] He described conditions for African Americans in stark contrast to those available to white scientists, particularly the

> "Colored Hutments," where living facilities are primitive, to say the least, though comparable to some of the housing for white workmen. Negro children are not permitted to go to school with whites; they journey to nearby Clinton for their education. And for that reason many Negroes did not bring their children to Oak Ridge. Plans are now being made to provide school facilities for the Negroes as soon as a sufficient number of children are enrolled to justify it. They have one recreation hall, the Atom Club, and one movie house, which is located 12 miles from their hutments, in the K-25 area.[100]

There are hints in Falstein's account that Oak Ridge residents experienced conflict around segregation, most notably in his detail that some African American parents chose to leave their children behind rather than force them into segregated schools. Yet his depiction resolves this tension by highlighting local efforts to adapt to segregation through their building of new schools specifically constructed "for the Negroes." Interestingly, Falstein notes that the poor living environment in the black section of the town was similar to the residences of other "white workmen," who were themselves similarly cut off from the relatively luxurious Cemesto accommodations available to scientific joes; brainpower was thus conceived as connected to both racial and class hierarachies. Still, Jim Crow represented a particularly conspicuous contact zone between Oak Ridge and its southern surroundings, and the imposition of segregationist restrictions and unequal housing for African Americans highlighted a point of conflict between scientists and ordinary residents even as it resolved some dissension between Oak Ridgers and their dispossessed neighbors. Though brainpower was conceived as threatening and dangerous at Oak Ridge, the shared investment in racist practices served as a bridge between ordinary and scientific Americans within and outside its gates.

Brainpower and Radicalism at Oak Ridge

Perhaps one of the starkest sites of conflict between local residents and the scientific community at Oak Ridge pivoted on the incidental radicalism at Oak Ridge. The association between radicalism and intellect was made solid as a Cemesto wall when the local government's collectivist values were reported in newspapers and magazine articles. "The Army may not know it," Daniel Lang wrote, "but it is operating Oak Ridge on a downright radical principle."[101] The Army may have been unknowing, but Daniel Lang certainly noticed Oak Ridge's radicalism—and the displaced Tennessee locals seemed to have detected this tilt toward the radical as well. The fact that the city was planned and run by a centralized (and secretive) government lent an air of the state-controlled bureaucracy to the city, and depictions of Oak Ridge indulged endless speculation about the impact of such experimentation. Connections between the scientific experiments being conducted in the Oak Ridge laboratories and the social experiments being conducted in the larger community were made visible through representations that conceived containment of intelligence as both dangerous and essential.

Following the revelations of the Manhattan Project, Oak Ridge struggled to convert its government from a military-run community to a democratically governed American town. "Oak Ridge's tax problem is entangled with the unique problem of converting a socialistic community into a traditional American, free-enterprise, self-governing city," wrote one author in 1953 in response to the city's complicated conversion.[102] Though this article did not openly favor one system over the other, the very notion that Oak Ridge was a community confronting this "unique problem" reinforced the widespread belief that it was an exceptional site of radical politics. Another author noted that the atomic cities "have private enterprise flourishing in the midst of socialism."[103]

Depictions of Oak Ridge's radicalism usually began with discussion of the town's state control. "The residents of Oak Ridge have no voting say about how their town is run," noted Daniel Lang. "The Army runs it."[104] "There are no election headaches," Louis Falstein concurred, "since the councilmen act only in an advisory capacity to the District Engineer, who is both an army officer and the mayor."[105] Though military control invited parallels with army life, the centralized bureaucracy of Oak Ridge was more often connected with socialist states. An author in *Business Week* called Oak Ridge "somewhat Utopian" because government "[kept] out excessive competition," and charged rent "based on the amount of business a particular store [was] expected to do."[106] Lang described a city in which "there are no panhandlers. Everybody has enough money to invest in a group medical plan, and it is excellently managed."[107] Oak Ridge was represented, then, as profoundly anticapitalist.

Though this radical bent was in part explained away as a symptom of government control, it was also attributed to the braininess of its residents. In particular, the solidarity among residents of Oak Ridge and their unique ability to take care of their own was conceived as an outcropping of the scientist's cerebral experimentalism. "From the beginning of the work here," wrote one author, "there has been no school library supervisor; rather, there are regular workshop meetings before, after, and during the school year to which all the librarians come with their problems and ideas."[108] The lack of conflict between those in power and those on the ground was represented as a by-product of the intelligence wielded by the community's citizens. "You learn to enjoy the feeling of youth and adventure that permeates the area; you like being able to call the big shots by their first names and share the watery Tennessee beer with them on week ends," recalled one resident in the *Saturday Evening Post*. "And above all, you know that all of them, including the Army officers, are top-flight scientists, and are worthy of your respect and support."[109] Oak Ridge seemed to totally dispense with social distinction. The town also appeared to be moving in the direction of eliminating social classes. "Some of the people around here who are up on their Lenin," wrote Lang,

> say that Oak Ridge is one of the better tries at a classless society. Both extreme wealth and poverty are non-existent. A number of construction workers live in crowded trailer camps, but the issue is blurred because a good many of these workers are among the highest-paid men on the reservation. Certain members of the community have private incomes and are therefore better-heeled than others, but money can't buy much here.[110]

For Lang, the absence of social conflict, limited value of money, and relative lack of inequality at Oak Ridge was symptomatic of "Leninist" social experiments. Lang quoted many residents confirming the peculiarity of social organization at Oak Ridge. "This is the first place I've taught," one teacher remarked, "where I haven't had to handle relief cases. . . . Conditions here make teaching a little easier."[111] The radical social experiments at Oak Ridge made welfare unnecessary, a situation that echoed Soviet-style redistribution of wealth.

Another Oak Ridge innovation, group health insurance, further distanced the community from its free-enterprising neighbors. "One of the town's most interesting institutions is the Oak Ridge Hospital," wrote Louis Falstein. "It is an experiment in what its brilliant young director, a lieutenant colonel, says 'has absolutely no relationship with socialized medicine.' He calls it 'The Group Insurance Plan.' Nevertheless, I advise Dr. Fishbein not to be lulled by the colonel's reassurances."[112] Not only were health-care issues resolved, unemployment, too, was eliminated as a problem at Oak Ridge. Daniel Lang proudly reported that "Oak Ridge is possibly the one American city in which there is full employment, a situation that ought to bring Senator Taft charging down here with an investigating committee,"[113] a claim confirmed by Louis Falstein, who reported that "this is the only city in the United States which has no unemployment and no reconversion problem."[114] Lang further noted that the "Oak Ridge crime rate is one of the lowest in the country."[115] Though analogies with socialism or Leninism suggest parallels were being drawn between Oak Ridge's government and Soviet-style communism—connections that were especially salient because of the

Russian Revolution's association with radical intellectuals—most journalists simply reported on the ideal social conditions at Oak Ridge, leaving it up to readers to determine how radical such a community might have been.

The tensions resulting from the combination of cutting-edge scientific work and progressive social communities at Oak Ridge were defused through representations of Oak Ridge as a "new frontier." George Robinson's 1950 exposé about Oak Ridge, *The Oak Ridge Story*, included several pages of excerpts from a letter written by a town official offered as evidence for "the frontier atmosphere of Oak Ridge's early days."[116] Associations of Oak Ridge with westward expansion and frontier living suggested that brainworkers could invite comparisons with stalwart American pioneers. Intelligence engendered an expansionist spirit that lighted out for the territory, and brainpower implied American ingenuity, individuality, and strength. "Somehow there is a touch of the Klondike about the place and the people," wrote Theodore Rockwell, III, in his *Saturday Evening Post* article given the unsubtle title "Frontier Life Among the Atom Splitters.[117] Louis Falstein noted of the residents how "they worked with such fervor and pioneering zeal" to create their community.[118] Even at its most dangerous, intelligence was boldly associated with the building of an American nation. On the vanguard of a new post-atomic world, the meanings of intelligence at Oak Ridge proved to be as tricky and contradictory as ever.

*   *   *

The context of World War II and the postwar period fundamentally reshaped the politics of brainpower in the United States. The federal government's interest in cultivating educational materials that promoted brainpower as a tool for winning the war attached political meaning to ordinary women's, men's, and children's intelligence and expanded the reach of American brainpower internationally. The GI Bill extended educational opportunities to ordinary men who served in the war and threatened the guarding of intelligence against ordinary women and men that was typical in universities such as Harvard. Finally, representations of atomic scientists offered audiences an opportunity to imagine themselves in relation to America's brightest and most able minds while both opening and restricting access to the spaces where these minds had done their most significant work during the war.

Representations of intelligence at Oak Ridge reinforced popular associations of brainpower with subversion, elitism, danger, and social transgression. These depictions were offset by counter-representations emphasizing
the normality of this all-American city; they in turn countenanced new
cultural anxieties about the banality of dangerous minds. The concentration
of brainworkers employed by the United States government at Oak Ridge
assured their inclusion in increasingly narrow definitions of postwar American citizenship, yet representations of this highly intelligent population
also put Oak Ridge's residents on notice: demands that smart women and
men adhere to normative family values, disavow subversive tendencies, and
align with the frontier spirit were promulgated within popular representations of this peculiar community. Efforts to represent intelligence at Oak
Ridge as safe, sanitized, and secure were frustrated by the impossibility of
overlooking the strange, dangerous tendencies of the atomic pioneers and
the portentous work they carried out within the city's cordoned perimeter.
Through the symbolic invocation of suburban architecture, intelligence was
also associated with middle-class values.

Within magazine and newspaper stories the lives of Oak Ridge's residents were mined for clues as to the meanings of brainpower in relation to
national belonging, and representations of intelligence at Oak Ridge reflected the ongoing paradoxes in discussions about the politics of intelligence throughout twentieth-century American popular culture. Even as
scientists' genius was subjected to scrutiny within popular culture representations, the intelligence of Oak Ridge's brainworkers was simultaneously contrasted with the community outside the city as a constructive
alternative to the ignorance of southern rural people, thus cutting off native
southerners from access to the social rewards of brainpower. Ordinary
women and men found themselves in the awkward position of aligning
themselves with common folk who were permanently excluded from the
suburban utopia being cultivated at Oak Ridge or affirming the value of intelligence that threatened to compromise the myths of American equality,
industry, and opportunity. While the paradoxical politics of brainpower at
this moment built upon earlier contradictions in twentieth-century representations, the unique climate of the postwar atomic city introduced an
undercurrent of menace and subversion that the Cold War brought to the
surface with the emergence of a new chapter in the story of brainpower: the
invention of the egghead.

7

Inventing the Egghead: Brainpower in Cold War American Culture

Being an egghead seems to be a station in life to which no one aspires but which everyone would like to think himself natively qualified.

—Charles Frankel, 1956

On November 16, 1957, the *Saturday Evening Post* published an article by Charles Price recounting the peculiar practices of everyday life in his home town of Princeton, New Jersey, a place "where there are so many great thinkers that a man without a Ph.D. is a nonconformist." The gossipy article, assigned the splashy, vaguely anthropological title, "I Live Among the Eggheads," typifies the treatment given eggheads in 1950s America. Price's lavishly illustrated piece—several photographs were accompanied by weirdly zoological captions such as "Professors at play" and "Professors in parley"—sensationalized the explicitly dull lives of Princeton's most ordinary men. "In my town," Price dished, "people are talking about organizing a fourth symphony orchestra; three, apparently, are not enough." The article focused primarily on the excessive braininess of Princeton's ordinary citizens, a highly accomplished assemblage of intellectuals that included physicist Robert Oppenheimer, author John O'Hara, and the anomalous literary critic Richard P. Blackmur, who was "held in awe by Princetonians because he *doesn't* have a college degree." In language that at times lapsed into ethnographic exoticism, Price excavated the minutiae of existence in a town "becoming as well known for its eggheads as Hershey, Pennsylvania, is for its chocolate bars."[1]

How might we account for the explosion of interest in the egghead in Cold War American culture? Why did this particular character take hold at this specific moment, and what accounts for the scorn heaped upon a figure with such a fragile cranium and a pallid complexion? The Cold War egghead refracted cultural fears about the challenges to the American way of life posed by homophile politics, antiracist social movements, and a left that refused to disappear in spite of intimidation tactics, blacklists, and HUAC belligerence. Two texts produced in the 1950s, Frank Fenton's 1954 science-fiction story "The Chicken or the Egghead" and Molly Thacher Kazan's 1957 play *The Egghead*, are particularly useful for considering the fate of intellectuals in the Cold War. Appearing at the height of the McCarthy era, these texts positioned the 1950s intellectual in relation to homosexuality, racial identity, and radical political ideologies and are instructive for understanding the sexual, racial, and radical politics of the egghead in Cold War American culture.

The fascination with eggheads in Cold War popular culture complicates our understanding of a period too easily characterized as anti-intellectual.[2] Though the egghead might have emerged as part of a discourse critical of intellectual elitism, the character was far more complicated than this framework has allowed. Studying the egghead reveals the complex nexus of race, gender, and sexuality at the heart of American representations of intelligence and illustrates the dangerous implications of appealing to the legacy of working-class brainpower at a moment when progressive political movements were being marginalized and subjected to state repression.[3] The emergence of the egghead cast an air of suspicion on those who appeared too smart for their own good by invoking the legacy of brainpower's historical connection to progressive political movements. At the same time that it was conceived as a threatening force, the egghead was represented as a uniquely American curiosity.

Before turning to the specific features that characterized the Cold War egghead, I want to return briefly to Charles Frankel's epigraph that began this chapter. The fundamental paradox that Frankel identifies was irresolvable in Cold War American culture, in part because the egghead signified a broader set of contradictions that dominated the postwar years. The notion that Americans by and large wished to believe themselves "natively" qualified to eggheadedness points to the expansion of exceptionalist language to describe American identity during a period of pitched conflict between the political ideologies of the United States and the USSR. The culture of the Cold War demanded Americans recognize themselves as inherently qualified to export democracy around the globe at the same moment when U.S. citizens were conceived as precariously close to being compromised by subversive menaces. The egghead's fragile shell housed a curious mixture of contradictions concerning American identities, politics, and behavior that was, ironically, nearly impossible to break.

Inventing the Egghead

Before the 1950s, "egghead" was an innocuous term referring to nothing more troubling than a person who possessed a bald, oval head. A Warner Brothers cartoon character bearing the name was featured in such animated films as *Egghead Rides Again*, a 1937 Merrie Melodies short featuring dull-witted man who failed to convince anyone that he was truly a cowboy.[4] By the end of the 1950s, however, the egghead had become an instantly recognizable cultural type whose embodiment bespoke a dangerously subversive disposition and a giant brain.

The first use of the term in reference to an overly intelligent person apparently occured in a Stewart Alsop column from 1952.[5] Alsop was a popular columnist who covered the American political scene with a particularly sharp, no-nonsense approach. In a column about the emerging presidential campaign, Alsop attacked those intellectuals he found superficial for deserting Dwight Eisenhower in favor of Adlai Stevenson simply because the latter candidate possessed greater polish and presented a sophisticated persona. According to one contemporary journalist, Alsop "named them 'eggheads,' inspired presumably by the spectacle of Stevenson's impressive and egg-shaped forehead, distorted to twice its height by one of the humorous tricks that television plays with elevated and shining objects."[6] Another author claimed that Alsop was merely repeating a comment he overheard from a supporter of Stevenson who declared, "I know he has all the eggheads with him, but they aren't enough to elect him."[7]

Though the egghead as such did not appear until 1952, the general character type it described had a number of antecedents. "Whether or not [the term egghead] was suggested by the oval shape of his head," wrote Delmore Schwartz in the *New York Times*, "the significant thing was the necessity for a new word, instead of intellectual, 'longhair,' or 'highbrow.'"[8] The long-hair was a curiosity at a distinct remove from everyday folk; he was elitist, distinguished, and nonpolitical. The "double-dome," a close relative of the "highbrow," was a less commonly used phrase that specifically referred to professors. None of these terms outlived the 1950s, but their legacy included more than their attacks on intelligence through disparaging labels. Each term also emphasized the physical bodies of the figures they characterized, and "longhair" bore the added implication of gender transgression, equating the cultured man with effeminacy and excessive grooming. The overtones of homosexuality in this particular designation were not incidental; the longhair's effeminacy was a particularly significant predecessor to the egghead who was also conceived as queerly feminine.

A signature moment in the evolution of the egghead occurred in October 1956, when *Newsweek* featured an egghead cover story. The image on the magazine's cover featured a white egg donning spectacles of a decidedly old-fashioned, feminine type (Figure 20). The egghead was depicted in noirish shadow and positioned in an asymmetrical composition to the right side of both the magazine's cover and the photograph's borders. This double asymmetry, combined with shadowing and an eerie absence of facial features, rendered the image ominous and vaguely threatening. The headline, positioned like a hastily jotted note at another awkward angle overlapping both the photograph and *Newsweek*'s masthead, read, "The Egghead / Who He Is / Who He Thinks He Is."[9] The enclosed article promised to dissect the egghead in an authoritative way that would disrupt the egghead's own notion of self.

The *Newsweek* cover story attributed the meteoric rise of the egghead to two factors. First, the smartness associated with eggheads was increasingly valuable because "much mechanical progress often creates problems as well as solves them." The egghead was conceived here as a by-product of modernization.[10] Second, the egghead appeared because American intelligence in particular was growing so rapidly. The article observed "the lightning spread of popular education, and with it a striking rise in public tastes. Drugstore book racks, once the undisputed home of Mickey Spillane, now also shelter the paperbound works of Plato, Shakespeare, Freud, and St. Augustine."[11] The egghead, in this definition, became a site of nationalistic pride figured through mass culture consumption.[12]

Such American exceptionalism continued through the author's lengthy recounting of the egghead as a stalwart presence in U.S. history. In seeming contradiction to the claim that the egghead emerged out of the increased

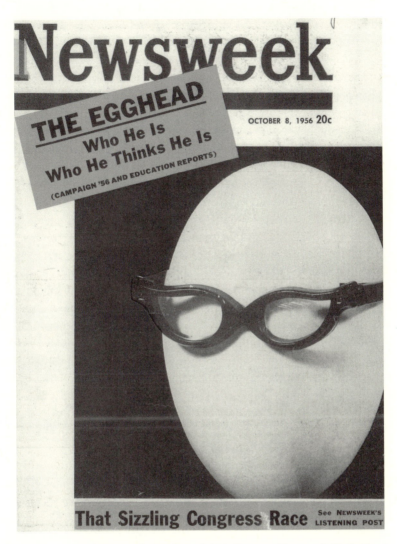

Figure 20. Cover of *Newsweek*, October 8, 1956. Courtesy Newsweek/Daily Beast Company LLC. All rights reserved.

need for smarts brought on by modernization and twentieth-century innovation, the article argued that Jefferson, Madison, Hamilton, and other "founding fathers" could all be considered eggheads.[13] By way of contrast, in the contemporary United States, "an assured social position [for the egghead] was generally absent."[14] The most significant shift in the twentieth-century egghead, then, was the loss of his assured social status. The historical account of the egghead found in the widely circulated *Newsweek* article vacillated between a number of contradictory terms, defining the egghead as historical and timeless, positive and negative, and emerging from the powerful and the masses. The egghead, in other words, engendered a representation of intelligence in American life that was uniquely capable of sustaining mutually incompatible characteristics. The shifty egg depicted on the cover did not elude definition as much as it encompassed a paradox.

In this article, as in many other depictions, four features connect the egghead with Cold War-era debates about American identity. First, the egghead was portrayed as anti-populist. Second, the egghead embodied a racialized, gendered identity. Third, the egghead was represented as queer, both sexually and vis-à-vis social norms. Fourth, the egghead was conceived as politically subversive. Even when celebrated, the egghead was always represented as a transgressive figure. These features crystallized in the figure of the egghead during a transitional moment in U.S. history. It is to these four features that I now turn.

The Egghead as Anti-Populist

One regular feature in representations of the egghead was a criticism of his intellectual elitism. In the context of the 1950s, the expansive rhetoric of anticommunist populism foregrounded the threat that intellectuals posed to American democracy. Widespread associations of eggheads with intellectuals rendered the egghead immediately suspect as anti-populist. Following the end of World War II, as we have seen, higher education was made accessible to greater numbers of Americans than ever before through the GI Bill. Consequently, the ranks of postsecondary students swelled, though these advances disproportionately favored white men.[15] Still, as higher education was made more widely available, intellectuals came to seem an archaic reminder of the closed university doors and ivory towers that had prevented many Americans from pursuing university degrees.[16] Setting up an intellectual class was not only anachronistic, it seemed irrelevant to the newly egalitarian universities.

At the same time, populism was exploding. Historian Michael Kazin has argued that this decade saw the rise of a conservatism that believed a "conspiratorial elite organized both inside government and in the wider culture was forcing Americans into a regimented system that would destroy their livelihoods and tear down their values."[17] In this context, the association of eggheads with an anti-populist persuasion due to their intellectual elitism all but guaranteed the term's opprobrium. "The people of America did not resist the word [egghead]," wrote an author in *The Nation* in 1960. "It seemed to fit their fears and resentments. It illustrated the gap between them and the liberal intellectuals, the gap which rendered both ineffective— and crippled mid-century America."[18]

The populist reaction against intellectuals was, in sum, an important feature in 1950s representations of intelligence. It is this dimension of the popular reaction to the egghead that has been branded anti-intellectualism. This was not, however, the egghead's only feature; the term "anti-intellectual" does not fully encompass the Cold War critique of the egghead, which was not only anti-intellectual but also anti-collectivist, anti-elitist, and anticommunist. These factors were collapsed into anti-intellectualism only at this particular historical moment, and cannot stand apart from the other characteristics of the egghead that appeared with similar frequency in postwar popular culture.

The Egghead Embodied

In a 1955 article in the peer-reviewed journal *Science*, psychologist Harry J. Jerison asserted that humans were distinguishable from lower mammals because of their massive brains. As he examined the proportion of brains to bodies up the evolutionary chain, and citing "the rather common notion that a given level of intelligence for a species is related to a given amount of brain," Jerison determined that higher evolved mammals assumed "a special evolution of the brain in the direction of the development of additional cerebral tissue, the weight of which is independent of the body weight."[19] In other words, the smarter a mammalian species became, the larger the physical mass of its brain in relation to its body. In a typical incident of scientific research reflecting the ideological tenor of the times—while contributing its own expert voice to the expanding discourse on intellectual embodiment—Jerison offered a scientific proof for the egghead. The smarter a species became, the greater its brain grew in relation to its body.

The debate surrounding evolutionary brain size was symptomatic of a wider discussion concerning the embodiment of intelligence in the 1950s. Though the egghead was widely represented as a particular type of intellectual, the term also described a particular form of embodiment. The physical characteristics of the label were predicated upon the aptness of the metaphor for describing a type of body. The egg had few features analogous to those of a human, yet this did not prevent such comparisons from being made. The egghead's smoothness was made phallic, engendering the egghead as male. The egghead's delicate fragility and curvy roundness became feminine features, though not explicitly female. The oval shape of the egg translated into male baldness. And the egg's whiteness was retained as a racial designation.

That the literal egginess of the egghead was being routinely made into a set of embodied characteristics in the 1950s is evidenced by a curious incident following *Newsweek*'s story. The photograph on the magazine's cover on October 15, 1956, the week after the egghead story, featured a closely cropped photograph of Estes Kefauver. When placed next to the photograph of the egghead, the shared features of the egg and Kefauver's head are striking (Figure 21). One *Newsweek* reader even wrote to the magazine noting the disconcerting similarities between the image of the egg and the man.[20] One reason for this remarkable similarity was, of course, the shared compositional features of each photo: the egg and Kefauver were positioned at identical angles; their glasses were similarly oversized for the frame of the photograph; both photographs were cropped so tightly that any extraneous features were completely erased. Yet even adjusting for these obvious compositional overlaps, the fact remains that the Kefauver photograph undeniably resembles the *Newsweek* egghead.

The main corporeal features of the egghead were thus legible despite the obviously metaphorical character of the name. There was no mistaking, for example, the sex of the egghead. There are very few instances in which the term "egghead" was used to refer to women. Charles Price's expose on eggheads in Princeton, for example, did not profile any women at all. This exclusion effectively rendered female intelligence unrepresentable. Though women surely would not have enjoyed being subjected to the unsavory characterizations of the 1950s egghead, their exclusion from representations

Figure 21. Cover of *Newsweek*, October 15, 1956. Courtesy Newsweek/Daily Beast Company LLC. All rights reserved.

must be seen as replicating a deeply patriarchal narrative: women were excluded from the critique of intelligence, thus denying them access to an important form of social empowerment. Male intelligence was represented as dangerous, but female intelligence was conceived as impossible. "Intelligence is an admirable quality," wrote the author of an article in 1954, "but no woman can possess a high degree of sex appeal because of her intellectual accomplishments alone. Men have the capacity to enjoy a woman's mind, but that is not the basis for their falling in love."[21] The egghead resisted women's intellectuality even as it diminished the social value of intellectuals.

A 1957 advertisement for Bonwit's 721 Club, a department store with locations in various parts of New York, offered a stark contrast between men and women through its figuration of the egghead. "Cultured . . ." the ad declared, "to a man, egghead. To a woman, Bonwit's Cultured Pearls in necklaces and earrings."[22] This ad both reinforced notions of male and female difference by noting their divergent definitions of the term "cultured"—men think immediately of cultured people whereas women think of jewelry—but it also implied that the term "egghead" was specifically targeted at men as an insult to be applied to their own sex. The advertisement, and the egghead more generally, suggested that to be a man and an egghead was bad, but to be a woman was to be wholly excluded from the conversation. The woman-as-egghead was visible primarily in her conspicuous absence.

In addition to his maleness, the egghead was almost always represented as white. The whiteness of the egghead in visual depictions was metaphorical just as it was as a racial classification: with eggheads depicted as white men, African Americans were again excluded. Just as with women, the egghead, though overwhelmingly negative as a category, still represented a whole investment in American hierarchies of race and gender. Yet the egghead was also a particular type of white man: he was frequently depicted as an active participant in struggles for racial justice and aligned with black cultural politics.

Among the most compelling appearances of the egghead's racialization might be found in Melvyn Tolson's long poem, *Harlem Gallery*. The poem is a richly textured modernist piece, each page teeming with allusions to texts that only the most highbrow, literate reader would be able to recognize. Tolson, an African American writer, was a politically engaged leftist who was particularly open about his insistence that black writers be encouraged to produce work drawing on both canonical and folkloric sources. As a manifesto for an engaged black intellectualism, *Harlem Gallery* is a veritable egghead extravaganza: Tolson populates his poem with arcane details and esoteric references that show off his literacy and ease with a startlingly broad assortment of texts. Yet the text also expresses the paradoxical relationship of an African American egghead confronted with intellectual culture: the poem's populist character, Hideho Heights, attacks the poet—robust with highbrow allusions—as "a half-white egghead with maggots on the brain."[23] The egghead, even when black, was saddled with signifiers of whiteness. Yet this was whiteness of a particular type: it was interracial, connected with black brainpower, and invested in challenging racial hierarchies.

The egghead's whiteness was occasionally represented as evidence for his squareness. The 1950s saw an intensive examination of the meaning of whiteness in American culture. Norman Mailer's widely discussed (and intensely problematic) essay, "The White Negro," which appeared in 1957, has been described as "a paradigmatic example of the white male investment in African American masculinity."[24] In his essay, Mailer dissected the "hipster" in American life, contrasted with the "Square." "The hipster," according to Mailer, "had absorbed the existential synapses of the Negro, and for practical purposes could be considered a white Negro."[25] African American culture of the 1950s, historian W. T. Lhamon argues, showed Americans "how to come out of the hole."[26] The egghead was white in a decade when this came to signify blandness and an unquestioning acceptance of the status quo. The whiteness of the egghead, in other words, served to further remove him from "the people," or from mass culture, where black contributions were at a premium.

Eggheads represented racial stability in a time when the racial hierarchies in American society were being toppled by the civil rights movement, rock and roll, Ralph Ellison, and the hipster writings of Jack Kerouac and the beatniks.[27] At the same time, however, and in spite of his occasionally square whiteness, the egghead was alternately represented as overly invested in black racial politics. Though his racial composition was assured, the egghead seemed to be sympathetic to blackness in a way that challenged associations of whiteness with conservative racial politics. As we will see in Kazan's play, the egghead was marked by a betrayal of whiteness signified through an overinvestment in black cultural politics.

The paradox engendered by the egghead situates him at the center of a transition in American culture: the egghead represented the stultifying conformity of whiteness, but also challenged the "possessive investment in whiteness" that intelligence unlocked by associating brainpower with the movement for racial justice.[28] In other words, the egghead was represented as white in order to emphasize his dullness, but also to suggest that intelligence moved inexorably toward interracialism. Whether celebrated or maligned, representations of the whiteness of the egghead assured that intelligence would be inextricably associated with contests over race in relation to American identity, and tied in with representations of radical social change.

The Queerness of Eggheads

Though the egghead was generally represented as white and male, he was not the unequivocal heir to the social privilege these categories represented in 1950s America. At a time when conformity was expected of Americans, especially if they hoped to achieve their dreams of social empowerment, representations of the egghead often characterized him as queer.[29] This visibility for the queer egghead was symptomatic of the egghead's perceived social failures but also responded to an increasingly visible homophile movement that was introducing gay politics to the masses.[30] A letter to the editor following *Newsweek*'s profile of the egghead stated unequivocally that he "is a political, economic, and sociological queer."[31] The collapsing of different forms of "queerness" into the egghead—liberal, communist, and homosexual—guaranteed that the egghead would remain on the margins of American political, economic, and social life.

Homosexuality in the 1950s was a deeply contested ground. Though it was not common for gay women and men to publicly declare their homosexuality, there was a moderate visibility for gay men in the arts, for example, and lesbians developed increasingly visible communities in spaces such as bars in working-class communities.[32] Yet the overwhelming tenor of mainstream American responses to homosexuality was decidedly negative, even as organizations such as the Mattachine Society and Daughters of Bilitis formed to challenge this opprobrium. Many articles about the egghead represented him as sensitive, feminine, and sometimes explicitly gay. Perhaps the most vitriolic of such characterizations came from Louis Bromfield, who paraded through countless Cold War-era cultural venues expressing his extreme distaste for the fey qualities of American eggheads. His definition of eggheads in *The Freeman* betrayed his excessive anxiety about the egghead's feminine nature through his thinly veiled homophobic language. "Fundamentally superficial," Bromfield wrote, echoing a common quality ascribed to homosexuals in the 1950s. "Over-emotional and feminine in reactions to any problem. Supercilious and surfeited with conceit and contempt for the experience of more sound and able men. Essentially confused in thought and immersed in mixture of sentimentality and violent evangelism." In his definition, Bromfield repeatedly asserted shared qualities between the egghead and the homosexual, effectively implying—without directly stating—that homosexuality and eggheadedness were synonymous. In fact, Bromfield's entire article read like a series of open taunts directed at gay men: "They dealt, all of them, either in terms of lachrymose sentimentality or shriveled academic abstractions," Bromfield fumed. In his most biting attack on the egghead, he snipped that "the sentimentalist, the secluded professor in his tower of tarnished bargain-priced ivory and the hysterically emotional have all done their share to make the word 'liberal' seem to designate someone who is disappointed, or frustrated, frivolous, sloppy, or shallow."[33]

Bromfield's thinly veiled doublespeak failed to mask the true identity of the egghead to any but the most naïve reader; who but the homosexual could be decried as "shallow," "frustrated," and "frivolous"? In point of fact, Bromfield's nasty comment about "tarnished bargain-priced ivory" seems designed purely to bait gay men who were widely stereotyped in the 1950s as arbiters of taste.[34] As the Bonwit's advertisement implied, the egghead was cultured in such a way as to resemble the tastes of a woman. In this, Bromfield was hardly alone. "Muddled and unhappy," a reader wrote in to Saturday Review, responding to the magazine's profile of eggheads, "they have allowed themselves by shallow emotionalism to be turned into bleeding hearts and crackpot reformers."[35] Again, the egghead encountered the same frustrations—and exhibited the same distasteful qualities—as the homosexual.

These characterizations of the egghead corresponded exactly with persistent representations of Democratic presidential candidate Adlai Stevenson that questioned his "manliness" as well as his sexual orientation. Though there is no evidence that Stevenson engaged in any homosexual activities, J. Edgar Hoover cooked up a false charge that homosexual activity had led to a New York arrest for the presidential candidate.[36] Gossip columnist Walter Winchell's radio show declared that "A vote for Adlai Stevenson is a vote for Christine Jorgensen."[37] And Confidential, the brand-new Hollywood scandal sheet famous for using McCarthy-style insinuation about deviant sexuality among celebrities—and provocatively bearing the teasingly ambiguous tagline, "we name the names"—published an article about unspecified "rumors" dogging Stevenson throughout his campaign.[38]

Broad characterizations of the egghead's queerly feminine tendencies were repeated in a 1956 ad for Donmoor Knit Shirts. The ad featured a photograph of a remarkably well coiffed boy fussily adjusting his thick horn-rimmed glasses over pouting lips. "In Praise of Eggheads," the copy proclaimed. "Not every boy is cut out to be a star fullback or Little League pitcher. Maybe he'll be just as happy as a chess expert, a cellist, or a lepidopterist." Drawn in stark contrast to the manliness of a football star or other athlete, this egghead transgressed proper gender behavior. Though the ad framed its own description as "praise," the copy enthusiastically reassured parents that even their fey little eggheads "tend to look a little more robust in DONMOOR knit shirts." Eggheadedness was valued on the one hand, but on the other it represented a form of gender trouble that needed be resolved with the right attire.[39]

Finally, the 1956 pop song, "Egghead," by Jill Corey, released as a b-side to Corey's moderately well-selling single, "I Love My Baby (My Baby Loves Me)," offered a comical representation of the egghead's failed masculinity. The song was a coy pop number, upbeat and cheerfully eviscerating. Yet rather than presenting the egghead as merely feminine, Corey's winking delivery added a new feature by treating the egghead as sexually incompetent, a trait that, in the song, is connected with his otherwise genius nature:

Egghead
My brainy egghead
You don't know what to do
Or what you ought to do
When we're alone
And lights are down low

You're a genius, you're a whiz
You can win most any quiz
But you're not so smart
When it comes to the heart
You're the biggest fizz there is . . .[40]

Though "Egghead," in a typical bid for radio airplay, veiled its sexual content through references to "the heart," there was little room for ambiguity: the heart was clearly not the primary organ disappointing Corey. The egghead excelled at matters of the mind, but he failed to match his brainy excess with sexual prowess. Though this song did not explicitly brand the egghead as homosexual, he was represented as a heterosexual failure.

In sum, the egghead in the 1950s was embodied as white and male, but he was a white male of a curious sort. The egghead connected intelligence with queer identity and behavior, thus preventing the intelligent American from accessing the rewards of social, political, and cultural power. This characterization collapsed sexual behavior into the anti-populist rhetoric assigned the egghead. Such queer desires introduced another troubling set of behaviors among eggheads, a transgressive political orientation that ranged from highbrow liberalism to rank-and-file Communism.

The Egghead's Subversion

In a cranky letter to the editor in 1958, *New York Times* reader George Strong expressed a criticism of the egghead that was shared by many during the decade. "Creative thought," wrote Strong of the sort of ideas eggheads were inclined to pursue, "has nothing to offer towards the business of moving more freight cars, melting more steel, selling more automobiles. The intellectual is far from being helpful even in aiding his own cause. Can you think of any egghead who did not find fault and was most dissatisfied with the very society which supported him?"[41] For the dyspeptic Mr. Strong, the fundamental problem with the egghead was a no-brainer: his detachment from the forces of capitalism as figured through American industry rendered him subversive. The egghead was so detached from the populist structures of American politics and the day-to-day operations of American industry that he could manage nothing more productive than to take out his frustrations by cooking up nasty theories about the society that sustained him. Strong's argument, especially in its wholesale dismissal of leftist social critique as mere "dissatisfaction," offered a categorical dismissal of egghead anti-Americanism.

As with most of the inflammatory rhetoric assigned subversive Americans during the McCarthy era, the chief criticism leveled at eggheads insinuated their communist tendencies. For some authors, this damning characterization emerged from the actual history of American Communism, which had many adherents—many of them quite intelligent—especially during the 1930s and 1940s. Though eggheads per se did not exist in the 1930s, it took little maneuvering for some to retroactively apply the term to those smarter-than-thou invividuals who had swung to the hard left during the Depression. John Cogley, an otherwise liberal writer who penned a series of articles about eggheads for *Commonweal* in 1952, spearheaded a campaign to cast suspicion on the contemporary eggheads by naming the names of their Communist progenitors. "The most damning argument against the egghead these days," Cogley wrote, "is that from this group came the Soviet-sympathizers, the anti-anti-Communists, the 'agrarian reformer' apologists, etc., who furthered American illusions about Soviet Russia until a few years ago."[42] Cogley insisted that the tendency to be swayed by "dangerous" ideas such as those emerging from the Communist Party was most prevalent among the American eggheads—a finding he established as equally true in the 1930s as the 1950s. For Cogley, the willingness to explore abstract ideas; the desire to improve society through intelligence; the effort to put brains together in the interest of creating a better world were the conditions that both birthed the egghead and caused him to follow a self-destructive path into ideological confusion and political betrayal.

In 1954, Joseph W. Martin, Jr., Speaker of the House, claimed that "left-wing eggheads" were trying to enact policy that would bring about an economic depression so that they could advance their socialist goals.[43] Such red-baiting tactics were commonly employed by Joseph McCarthy, whose fears about eggheads were the stuff of legend, and who was unrelenting in his attacks on Communists.[44] A 1954 *New York Times* article describing McCarthy's red/gay witch-hunt in the face of a mounting criticism noted his immovable conviction that "'eggheads' and 'deluded liberals' were playing into the hands of the communists in demanding curbs on his authority as a communist investigator."[45] A reader wrote into the *Saturday Review* complaiining about eggheads who "dabble in socialism, Communism, or the hand-out state."[46] Still, the deeply ideological deployment of egghead as a term of derision was also subjected to criticism. One reader of the *New York Times* complained that the United States' "whole economic and political attitude is geared to the possibility of war, and any person in public life who dares to speak out against this cancer in our society is immediately branded as a 'communist,' 'egghead,' or 'traitor to his country.'"[47]

Adlai Stevenson seemed wholly bemused—and hopelessly unconcerned—by the associations of eggheads with communist subversion. One of his favorite lines to trot out on the 1952 campaign trail when asked about the popular term he had precipitated was "eggheads of the world, unite! You have nothing to lose but your yolks!" Though his amusing reframing of Marx and Engels's famous conclusion to *The Communist Manifesto* may have succeeded in making light of the egghead craze, it also rewarded the worst fears of conservative critics who were already convinced that liberalism represented communism in democrat's clothing and that eggheads were seeking nothing less than the downfall of the American way of life.

"The Chicken or the Egghead"

In Frank Fenton's 1954 science-fiction story, "The Chicken or the Egghead," Francis Cary, a Hollywood screenwriter and intellectual, is prescribed a pill to become a normal American. Francis's troubled past, which includes authoring a novel critiquing capitalism and an appearance before the House Un-American Activities Committee, is determined to be a result of his eggheadedness, a fate worthy of psychoanalysis. "You are really disturbed because you are an intellectual," his therapist informs him, "and the times are very unfortunate for this type of affliction."[48] Upon taking Dr. Funck's pills, Francis becomes utterly ordinary, a change that frees him to produce a film that becomes the toast of the nation. No longer will he have to contend with his intelligence cutting him off from ordinary men and women. With the aid of this magical nostrum Francis Cary at last becomes an ordinary American.

"The Chicken or the Egghead" appeared in a volume of short stories edited by the popular science-fiction writer Raymond J. Healy, which included several stories that were supposed to be thematically connected. Amid the other stories in *Nine Tales of Space and Time*, Fenton's appears particularly anomalous: it concerned neither space nor time.[49] The story's inclusion in this volume suggests that it was perceived as timely and significant enough for sci-fi audiences to rationalize publication despite its topical discontinuity. Science fiction was a particularly useful genre for exploring intelligence in the United States during the 1950s. Novels and stories often featured intelligent scientists and inventors.[50] They also tended to be critical of the society around them, often setting their narratives in utopian or dystopian futures.[51] In short, the genre was preoccupied with the social meanings of both intelligence and power. It is unsurprising, then, that in the 1950s, the egghead made an appearance.

Frank Fenton was a moderately successful Hollywood actor and screenwriter, writing or co-writing films including *The Sky's the Limit* (1943), *The*

Gay Falcon (1941), and *River of No Return* (1954). Though he was never quite as successful as the writer he described in "The Chicken or the Egghead," many elements of that story were drawn from Fenton's biography. On the surface of it, Frank Fenton's story is a typical rags-to-riches-and-back-again allegory. The protagonist of the story, Francis Cary, lives in a Hollywood studio and makes "a somewhat precarious living" as a screenwriter. Dissatisfied with his philistine writing, he attempts to write a serious book called *The Chicken or the Egghead*, a "novel about the despair of the intellectual, the plight of the egghead." Francis is hopelessly in love with a stunning actress bearing the preposterous screen name Arod Summer, who is quite vapid yet inexplicably attracted to Francis. Though he finds himself irresistibly attracted to her, Francis fears that her "stupidity and ignorance" will prevent him from ever being able to truly love her.[52]

It is only when he is named as a Communist by a fellow screenwriter testifying before HUAC that Francis begins to consider sloughing off his egghead identity. After testifying before the committee—he is innocent of their charges—Francis seeks the counseling of Davison Funck, a jaunty psychiatrist who prescribes him an experimental medicine to alleviate the symptoms of his eggheadedness and replace them with normality, which he defines as "revulsion for those aspirations and aesthetics that the world's philosophers have deemed most admirable in the character of man." Francis takes the pills, and, after several days, produces a screenplay, *The Fall of Carthage*, written expressly for Arod Summer. The distinctly mass-appealing, vulgar film wins an Academy Award for Francis, and he soon becomes the toast of the town. Arod, however, loses interest as he becomes "normal." Eventually, tiring of his normal existence and in despair over losing Arod, Francis stops taking his pills. Though he sacrifices his meteoric success for the return of his eggheaded existence, he does settle on "a kind of bitter satisfaction" he receives in pursuing intellectual life and the final return of Arod to his arms. And, of course, Funck reveals the pills to have been nothing more than "flour and sugar and the power of suggestion."[53]

Several features of this story stand out vis-à-vis the egghead in Cold War American culture; most significantly, Fenton's insistence on opposing eggheads and normal people. The word "normal" takes on a variety of meanings for Fenton. Normal refers to lowbrow taste, identification with the masses, milquetoast political orientation, and a particularly rugged embodiment. Egghead, on the other hand, refers to the reverse: a taste for high culture, elitism, political leftism, and sometimes lanky, sometimes flabby, non-muscular embodiment. Throughout the story, Fenton wavers between judgmental allegorical passages against his egghead's lofty ambition and bitter descriptions of everyone else's stultifying normality. The opposition of these terms, however, is not ultimately beyond resolution: though normal might not always be desirable, Fenton certainly conceives it a valuable corrective to the excessive oddness of the egghead. The end of the story, in which Francis has learned the error of his eggheaded abnormality even as he turns against cooptation by the normal, confirms that the features of the egghead are always set up against society at large. In his abnormality, the egghead is divorced from average Americans and the ideological system that sustains them. He is, regardless of political orientation, un-American.

The relationship between eggheads and communism is explored in detail through several episodes in the story. The first discussion of communism appears in a description of Francis as an egghead that appears at the story's beginning. Just as his particular brand of eggheadedness is indicated in Francis's inability to achieve anything in life beyond membership in a collegiate academic honor fraternity, so it is also implicit in a novel he has written "castigating the capitalist system." Equally damning is the failure of this same novel: it was read by "no more than five hundred people," and, what's more, "the capitalist system was not seriously damaged by his assault."[54] In this early description, then, flirtation with communism signifies Francis's failure to adjust to "normal" society rather than a truly threatening anti-Americanism.

The communism of the egghead in Fenton's story is depicted as a symptom of failure. Francis Cary's communism brands him not only as un-American, but also politically impotent. He is unable to even perform his subversion, and his subversion transforms into perversion. The sexual dimension of this transformation is made especially visible as Francis's greatest success before his normalization appears in the form of a Broadway play—a site containing overtones of homosexuality—exploring "the sex life of the Polish fisherman south of Ventura."[55] Francis's communism brands him as sexually deviant: both as obsessed with prurient subjects (in this case a literal fetishization of the working class in terms of the narrow topic of the play and Francis's concern with sex among workers) and as perverse. "The uneasy notion that he had become eccentric and queer accosted him," Fenton writes of Francis's identity crisis, "so that he even wondered if some latent homosexuality might not be creeping over him in his middle years."[56] Francis's relationship with homosexuality is identical to his relationship with communism: he is attracted to it, but he does not fully adopt its practices.

Communism next appears vis-à-vis the HUAC hearings, referred to in the story as "the Great Communist Conspiracy."[57] Fenton's description of the committee is testily judgmental of both the committee and those forced to testify before it, the latter of whom "appeared scornful and defiant, like the French aristocrats of old, riding in their tumbrels to the guillotine." Francis fears he will be accused of being a communist, a charge he emphatically denies, though he is intensely antagonistic toward those who are conducting the hearings. "A Red," Francis complains to Arod Summer, "a Spic, a Wop, a Hebe, a Pict, a Jute, a Nig. It's a matter of semantics." Though he finds the term distasteful, he is equally scornful of the tendency among intellectuals to venerate the Russian Revolution. "Lenin thought it was a million little paths finally making a human highway," he says. "He neglected to add that it was necessary to pave them with human skulls."[58]

Ironically, Fenton performs a rather difficult feat in his section dealing with the Dies committee: even as he suggests that eggheads are sympathetic to communism, he also contradicts this idea by voicing the counterclaim that communism fails to interest Francis Cary because it is simply too plebeian. "It's for the masses," Francis rants to Arod Summer, "the people, the mobile vulgus. It's a political pitch like trying to get everybody to smoke the same God-damned cigarette. It's another con game and the people are the mark, the big mark."[59] Fenton dismisses communism as a cheap ploy to seduce the masses into un-Americanism. The egghead is thus drawn as overly concerned with mass appeal while remaining completely exiled from mass culture. That these contradictory representational strategies were able to coexist suggests that the egghead was a convenient tool that was speaking just as commonly about impotence and failed masculinity as it was about the specific political circumstances of the day.

Following his being named as a communist by a writer named, not incidentally, Milton Gay, Francis seeks the services of Davison Funck. After taking Funck's pills, Francis writes his screenplay, in which communism again plays a role. He is inspired to write this screenplay while reading a book about Carthage, which he realizes will make a blockbuster film. Rather than pursuing knowledge for knowledge's sake, Francis "visualized his scenes in Technicolor on huge, wide screens." Perhaps more significantly, however, Francis's treatment of the Battle of Carthage draws parallels between the ancient Roman empire and the USSR. Francis's script is set in

Rome, but it likens "ancient Rome to the modern Soviet Russia, inasmuch as both yearned to conquer and enslave the world." This is a key ingredient in the film's success; Francis calculates that the mere suggestion of Soviet treachery will be enough in the Cold War context to resonate with the masses. This proves correct. In this third instance, then, anticommunism is invoked as a symptom of the hysteria of mass culture. Normal Americans are easily satisfied with small morsels of red-baiting, and the mere spectre of Soviet Russia haunts all of mass culture. In this scene from Fenton's story, eggheadedness is defied through red-baiting. Whereas the egghead Francis had excoriated American capitalism, his "chicken" version speaks before presumed anticommunist, pro-American organizations such as "the Committee of Americans for America" and "the Optimists' Club."[60]

Fenton employs communism, then, in a variety of ways: as a symptom of eggheadedness, as a foil to mass culture, as the natural offspring of mass cultural frenzy. The egghead is represented as both attracted to and repelled by communism, but he is overwhelmingly implicated in it. Fenton's ambivalent representation of intelligence as deeply invested in communism while remaining its stalwart friend and foe ultimately reinforces McCarthy-style weapons of insinuation: even those intellectuals who oppose communism are still too close for comfort. Eggheads, then, are those whose critique of American culture skates precariously close to subversion even when earnestly disinclined to support treasonous ideology.

The queer body of the egghead in "The Chicken or the Egghead" is not nearly so ambivalent. From the first, the egghead's body is cast under a cloud of suspicion, a suspicion that is manifest in both the sexual ambiguity discussed above and in terms of the weakness of the egghead. The tension between Francis's brain and his body is what ultimately draws him to Davison Funck and triggers his spiraling descent into mass culture. Fenton refuses to resolve to this tension; ultimately, either the body or the brain must win.

Francis Cary's polarized impulses toward the fulfillment of his bodily and brainy pleasures are first explored in early scenes concerning his relationship with Arod Summer. Cavorting in his study with Summer, Francis "stared at her thoughtfully and wondered why it should matter so much to him that she was a boob, that her stupidity and ignorance were as spectacular as her physical splendor." Francis, in other words, wishes that he could simply appreciate her body, but he cannot stop himself from becoming frustrated by her lack of intelligence. After Summer leaves, Francis "sat down to read in peace, but the perfume of Chanel overcame the prose of Marcel Proust."[61] The appearance of Proust here specifically invokes a specter of homosexuality upon brainy pursuits: Proust's homosexuality is frequently signified in *Remembrance of Things Past* by his languorous satisfaction in maintaining sensual pleasures in his memory.[62] Yet in this scene, the attractions of the brain are not powerful enough to overwhelm the bodily temptations signified through Arod's Chanel, a particularly glamorous *eau de toilette*.

Though Francis presents his communist imbroglio as the chief factor precipitating his visit to Davison Funck, his insecurity about his relationship with Arod is also significant. This insecurity derives from Funck's anxiety about his embodiment. Funck validates these insecurities by defining normality, in part, as one who "earns his bread and board by the sweat of his brow."[63] Echoing the complicated politics of work and identity that informed representations of labor in the 1930s, physical labor was invoked as a key signifier of normal masculinity and American identity.

In a critical scene following his conversion to normality, Francis jumps into a swimming pool at Arod Summer's, a bodily plunge he has never before dared. "He had never been in the pool before," Fenton writes. "His skin was white and the muscles of his long body were soft and flabby." Fenton's pallor signifies his eggheaded embodiment as surely as does his "soft and flabby" body. Yet this embodiment is further described as "lean and angular, his black hair long and awry." Though these descriptions might appear discontinuous, they are used chiefly to differentiate Francis's embodiment from the two dominant bodies found in Hollywood: "the tanned and bemuscled young actors or the brown and potbellied producers."[64] Furthermore, they emphasize the signature features of the egghead's body: he is white, fragile, and feminine.

As Francis achieves Hollywood success and American normality, his body morphs accordingly. He acquires a bulk that is "no longer Lincolnesque" as a result of eating at fine—and rich—establishments. Yet this bodily success is met with a growing lack of interest on the part of Arod Summer. Though Francis's body appears to become more normal, his sexuality does not function alongside it. He does become more firm in answer to his earlier eggheaded fragility ("Firmness became his *modus operandi*"), but he fails to assimilate to his own embodiment.[65] Perhaps because Funck's pills are a sham, effective at psychological games but less so at bodily changes, Francis's essential egghead identity begins to unmask him. Still, the sin of his eggheadedness is redeemed through his sexual longing for Arod Summer. Francis is framed as a sympathetic egghead both because he cannot become normatively embodied and because he retains the proper signifiers of hetero-sexual virility.

In the closing sentences of "The Chicken and the Egghead," Arod Summer finally returns to Francis. The story concludes with a resolution in which Francis has returned to his original identity, only rather than being a full-blown egghead, he is an enlightened Don Juan, cultured and intelligent, yet sensual and libidinal. As Arod returns to him, Francis "swung her aloft in his arms and carried her triumphantly to the bed where all men begin and end."[66] It is, ultimately, Francis's sexual prowess that allows him to re-solve his intellect and his bold heterosexuality. The egghead is again treated as a paradoxical site of marginalization and privilege in equal measure.

Francis Cary exemplifies the egghead's basic characteristics—intellectual achievement, elite taste, political subversion, queer embodiment—yet Fenton's critique of the egghead in American society complicates these characteris-tics through the clunky science-fiction plot device of a strange and magical wonder drug. Though the drug turns out to be the mere power of suggestion—rendering the tale much more of an allegory than a work of science fiction—its effect on Francis's character offers a critique of the egghead that sees his personal shortcomings as failures of will. It is only when Francis's sexual de-sire shapes his choices that he is able to break out of his shell. The implication is that the egghead, though victimized in Cold War American culture, ulti-mately was the victim of his own weakness. By joining the masses of ordinary men the 1950s, the egghead could choose to become normal.

Fenton's ambivalence about how to represent the egghead is instructive. Though he is sympathetic to the plight of the egghead, Fenton fails to sig-nificantly challenge the basic criticisms of intelligence under the sign of an-ticommunist hysteria: its awkward embodiment; its fundamental sexual ambivalence; its unfortunate flirtation with communist ideas. Francis's journey into normality does not legitimize his brainpower, but rather, suc-cessfully teaches him to value the demands of his body above those of his brain. If the central tension in the story pulls between the scent of Chanel or Proust's prose, Francis's lesson is finally to learn that nothing else matters if one achieves sexual possession of their love object and sexual mastery over a malleable and physically attractive woman. The final image of Fenton's story sees Francis proudly tossing and carrying Arod about in a Tarzan-esque climax of chest-beating masculinity. Though he may have eschewed the common ambition of Hollywood, Francis has at last prioritized his body over his brain. Fenton's allegorical defense of the egghead, like so many representations of the egghead in the 1950s, essentially affirmed the criticism of eggheads that he initially sought to disrupt.

The Egghead: A Play by Molly Kazan

Molly Thacher Kazan's play *The Egghead* premiered in October 1957 at New York's Barrymore Theatre after a pre-Broadway tour that included stops in Cleveland, Cincinnati, and Washington. Though she was most famous for her spousal connection to the film director Elia Kazan, Molly Kazan was an ambitious writer on her own. Still, her connection to someone who named names during the McCarthy era put her at the center of the debates about communism during the Cold War. The media also exploited this association by eliciting comments from the outspoken director, who offered patronizing support: "I'm really proud of that girl," he said of her premier, "to think that with four kids . . . and a husband to look after, she nevertheless had the guts and stamina to go through with this project strictly on her own."[67] Kazan's first play received wider notice than it otherwise might have due to her prominent position in glamorous dramatic circles, but *The Egghead* remains important as one of the most complicated representations of the egghead in the Cold War era. For one reviewer, the play was "a story of a typical American viewpoint—be liberal, let a man believe what he wants, stand up for his right to say it, let him be a Communist if he wishes because an American has the right to be wrong."[68] Another reviewer reported that Kazan "spares no vigor in her attacks on misguided campus intellectuals who won't climb out of their ivory towers, besides hitting sleek Red propaganda and racial discrimination."[69]

The play was topical enough to be put in the service of a surprising range of political positions. One audience might read the play as an attack on the un-American silencing during the 1950s red scare; another could see it as an indictment of intellectual culture and an attack on the left. Whatever one's ideological orientation, however, it was impossible to ignore the certainty with which Kazan grouped eggheads and communists together, cultivating a specter of subversion that ultimately dovetailed with the basic parameters of Cold War anticommunism: one's intelligence was proportional to one's subversion. Through this production the forces of anticommunism influenced the politics of intelligence even after the heyday of HUAC was over. Representations of eggheads implied an association of intelligence with subversion that effectively blacklisted brainpower in American culture. Kazan's play also introduced complicated ideas about race and black politics into the discussion of eggheads, alternately positioning African American activists as the pawns of eggheads, academics as dupes of the black left, and white intellectuals as colonizers of black consciousness.

The Egghead begins with a visit by two FBI agents to Hank and Sally Parson's home. Hank is a college professor, Sally his doting wife. The G-Men inquire after one Perry Hall, a former student of Hank's who is suspected of Communist activity at the Trimble Mill, where he is involved in a union-organizing campaign. Perry is an African American man whom Hank was instrumental in helping gain admittance at his college, which, at the time, had a policy of racial exclusion. Hearing of this investigation, Hank proposes inviting Perry to talk in one of his seminars at the university: "I want a controversy," he declares.[70] Sally meanwhile wants all the controversy to go away so she can serve dinner.[71]

The college has become a maelstrom because a student, Porky Wells, anticipating Perry's speech, has informed his father, a man of some influence, of the subversion on campus. Sally, meanwhile, is secretly researching communism, mostly through dusty pamphlets from the 1930s. "They run on about democracy and in the next breath, it's dictatorship," she reports. "You can't be for both! How can you? They're all mixed up!"[72] She becomes convinced that Perry is, in fact, a Communist. Perry arrives at the Parson home that evening. As he reminisces with Hank, most of the discussion involves establishing the eccentric eggheadedness of Hank's life: his ambitious classroom demeanor; his strong defiance against efforts to cancel Perry's talk; his messy study. Hank reads an old poem of Perry's, "Birmingham, Alabama," that he found in his study. Sally harbors many suspicions. Why is Perry a mere union member when he is so involved? Is he avoiding a loyalty oath? Hank asks Perry directly if he is a Communist, claiming he will not allow him to speak if he is a Party member. Perry denies any association with the Party. The situation takes a turn when Essie, the Parsons' sixty-something "Negro woman" housekeeper, appears suddenly and announces to Perry, "I'm glad your Mama isn't here."[73] Once Perry leaves, Sally asks Essie why she was so forward. Essie describes how she knew Perry's mother, through whom she learned of Perry's shadowy past that included use of assumed names such as Charles Henry, who in turn is the author of the same Communist pamphlets Sally had just been reading. Sally becomes furious as she realizes her husband's folly and the vindication of her intuition.

Sally and Hank's colleague, Gottfried, later engage in a pivotal conversation about how one ends up supporting Communists. Sally inquires about her husband: "if he's so brilliant, how could he be so wrong?" She later confronts Hank directly: "Hank," she announces as she discloses what she has learned about Perry, "I am not your little student any more."[74] Perry finally admits he is a Communist and threatens to ruin Hank if he reveals this. Ultimately, Hank gives up his teaching position and learns a valuable lesson.

Kazan's play announced itself as a deeply polarizing work: it was topical and spoke directly to the Cold War concerns that dominated American political discourse when the play appeared. The promotional materials to advertise the play emphasized its timely engagement with contemporary political debates. "Right or Left, You Can Get Seats in the Middle," read one newspaper advertisement.[75] "See Sputnik at 6:05 A.M.," read another, "See 'The Egghead' at 8:40 P.M."[76] The play was announced as a volley in the cultural wars concerning communism in Cold War American culture, invoking the political issues attributed to the left—racial justice, gender equality, free speech—to turn radicalism against itself.

Kazan's characterization of the egghead in her depiction of the hopelessly deluded Hank Parsons exhibits the typical characteristics found in other 1950s representations. The egghead is, first of all, out of touch with reality. In a particularly telling moment, Sally—who is overtly represented as irritated and restricted by her husband's intelligence—dismisses her husband's brain and its disconnection from the "real world" by comparing it to his study: "It's like your study," Sally says. "It needs housecleaning."[77] This seemingly innocuous analogy reveals the main substance of Kazan's critique of intelligence: it creates disorganized, chaotic thought. As a gendered notion, Sally's comment also articulates a critique of intelligence as the site of male dominance: Sally recognizes that it is her job to "houseclean" her husband's mind. Sally confirms the role of wife as housekeeper at the same time that she announces the egghead as a stubborn, deluded male.

Kazan also positions Hank's academic profession as instantiating his racial prejudice. Though he believes his intelligence inoculates him from the gross excesses of American inequality—he was instrumental, after all, in breaking down the racial barriers at his college—Hank is revealed to be a man who is hopelessly prejudiced against most Americans, whom he conceives as unintelligent. "You don't like the younger generation," Sally reveals of Hank, "You think they're going to the dogs. And you don't like Germans— and you don't like Catholics—and you don't like Southerners—! That's quite a list."[78] Aside from his secret hatreds, Hank is presented as deeply antiliberal because he does not believe all humans should be judged equally. "I think that's one thing that set you off on the wrong track," Sally declares, "is you decided way back B.C. that a Negro could do no wrong. And if that isn't prejudice all screwed around and put into reverse—I ask you!"[79] Hank's commitment to free thought and free ideas hardens into an intellectual commitment to racial justice, which becomes dangerous; his willingness to trust Perry Hall suggests that efforts at achieving racial justice cannot succeed unless they are ignorant about racial identity. Kazan's liberalism, then, demands that one "not know" about the race of another; knowledge about race is reframed as weakening liberal defenses.

As the play moves inexorably toward Sally's revelation that Perry Hall is in fact a Communist, the audience comes to realize that it is because he is trying so hard to present himself a thinking man who allows diversity of thought that Hank is able to be duped into being a stooge of the Communists.[80] Sally, who is portrayed as deeply anti-intellectual, is revealed to be a better citizen because she is immersed in nothing but real-world concerns: she does not want a Communist to ruin her life or her dinner. It is precisely her inability to assimilate to the demands of intelligent critique that enables her to correctly identify Perry as the Communist he truly is.

One of the most significant features of *The Egghead* is Kazan's use of gender to frame her dismissal of the eggheads. Throughout the play Sally is maligned by university professors and administrators who dismiss her as charmingly unintelligent. Harvey Robbins, the president of the college, berates Hank for attacking Sally's suspicions about Perry. "Don't bully Sally," Harvey says, echoing Elia Kazan's comments about Molly Thacher Kazan. "She's my favorite girl. How she's maintained her intellectual innocence living with you, I'll never know, but it's one of the most attractive things about her."[81] Harvey's defense of Sally rests on recognition of the failed intellect that makes her resistant to subversive incursion. Sally is celebrated precisely because of women's exclusion from intellectual institutions, and her freedom from ideas enables her to combat the egghead through her domesticity rather than her brainpower. Though Sally reclaims her intelligence by uncovering Perry's hidden Communist Party membership, she functions in the play as a foil to the intellect of the other characters. Her innocence is predicated upon her weak mind.

If gender represents a site of conflict in the play where intelligence fails to fulfill the promises of liberalism, race embodies an intersecting framework for connecting brainpower with progressive politics. Perry Hall is a deeply conflicted character, drawn toward radicalism because of his experience of American racism. "I'm talking America," he says after he has admitted he is a Communist. "I'm talking the Till case. A fourteen-year-old boy murdered in cold blood because he whistled at a white woman."[82] By having Perry utter these lines, Kazan acknowledges that many leftists joined the Communist Party because of their desire to change their racist society.[83] Yet for Kazan, antiracism does not legitimize or even explain Perry's political sympathies. His membership in the Party cannot be justified through social context; his hiding his membership—which was not negotiable during the Cold War owing to the McCarran Act—further evidences Kazan's embittered critique of the insidious subversion of brainpower. Thus one of the play's few block characters is portrayed as hopelessly myopic because of his knowledge of racism, so much so that he is willing to join a party that is actually exploiting him. Perry is dangerous because he is both smart and messianic: "one little nucleus thinks I'm a combination of Einstein and Jesus Christ," Perry says.[84] His anger at American racism does not provide a context for his radicalism as much as it offers a site of potential liberal resolution. Rather than ignoring the racial implications of the egghead, then, Kazan attacks racism as a site where intelligence can further erode American values. One should oppose racism with ignorance because racial knowledge opens the door to Communism.

In contrast to Sally's celebrated naïveté and Perry's misguided intellectual commitment to radical antiracism, Hank Parsons is represented as conflicted and hypocritical. His brain is clouded with too much thinking. Kazan's muddled conclusion to the play sees Hank finally realizing that liberalism is the corrective to all thought. He defends liberalism while suggesting the problem of the egghead is his overinvestment in black politics:

The only thing that was wrong with me was that I wasn't liberal enough! . . . I didn't use my eyes and ears. I didn't use my God damned head! There's nothing wrong with having brains! I didn't use them. I didn't stick to my own principles. I acted out of prejudice. Why, I was insufficiently eggheaded![85]

The message of *The Egghead* is nearly incomprehensible and oddly ambiguous: intelligence is seen as leading to all kinds of problems, particularly when connected to antiracism. Yet the egghead is also celebrated for its potential to answer to the prejudice of black nationalism. The egghead is thus caricatured as both instrumental in subversive, radical politics and self-defeating through this same commitment.

In writing *The Egghead*, Molly Kazan explored several critical dimensions in the debates about eggheads in the 1950s. Her play was deeply immersed in its Cold War context, and though Kazan ultimately decried McCarthyist attacks on free speech, she also offered strong warnings to those who would conceive brainpower as a tool for social change. Though Kazan allowed eggheads some space within American political life, her characters ultimately suggested that intellect was the province of misguided radicals and was destructive to the project of American liberalism.

*   *   *

Molly Kazan's *The Egghead* and Frank Fenton's "The Chicken or the Egghead" both narrowly delimited the range of political critique available to those who attempted to use brainpower as a political weapon. In this regard, their representations of the egghead—both of which were set up as critical of the category itself—reified the limitations this cultural construct placed upon intelligence in American culture. Their cultural texts were deeply invested in Cold War-era attacks on brainpower as potentially subversive. This was articulated through their challenges to American identity formation. Yet their texts reveal the complicated contradictions at the heart of representations of intelligence in the 1950s. Though liberalism seemed to provide a way out of the political tangles radicalism had introduced, efforts at celebrating American liberalism through criticism of brainpower just as often cut off those actors who could have most benefited from a defense of intelligence at this historical moment. African Americans, women, homosexuals, and those whose identities overlapped these categories were each involved in political struggles that needed to call on brainpower to challenge dominant strains of reactionary thought.

The egghead embodied the paradoxes of brainpower in the Cold War by exploiting the contradiction between a cultural desire to possess the social and political power associated with white men and a growing anxiety about the influence of the left, homosexuality, and the black civil rights movement in shaping American life. As the egghead gained traction in Cold War-era popular culture, brainpower was itself constructed as ideologically suspect. What had emerged as a political tool available to a variety of otherwise disenfranchised Americans became tainted with hints of subversion, gender and sexual transgression, and danger to ordinary women and men.

The figuration of the egghead was never simply used to characterize intellectuals as a class. The egghead personified four interlocked characteristics—subversion, queer sexuality, whiteness with uncertain racial alliances, and intelligence—and these were inextricable from broader changes in American Cold War culture precipitated by spreading anxieties about collectivism and communism and a growing recognition of the vulnerability of white heterosexual male privilege. The paradox at the heart of the Cold War construction of eggheads reveals an irresolvable conflict in cultural representations. The egghead functioned to both limit those for whom intelligence was culturally available and to malign those who attempted to advocate education and the expansion of intelligence as a vehicle for social change. Though the populist dimension of this paradox was framed as a liberal political intervention, the climate of the Cold War and the attendant social inequalities in the United States in this period ensured that the popular use of the egghead label served chiefly to restore the ideological hegemony of a virulently white, masculine liberalism. Though alternatives to this model for representing intelligence would appear in later periods, a basic template for diminishing the radical potential of brainpower was now wholly inseparable from sexual, political, and racial ideologies. The contentious language of the egghead cast a wide net, and though counter-representations of intelligence continued to appear and persistently challenged American structures of power, the egghead was freely available as a brooding foil to those who presumed brainpower could be employed to lead the charge of liberation.

Epilogue

Oh man, thought Winsome, an intellectual. I had to pick an
intellectual.

—Thomas Pynchon, *V.*

In 1965, noted historian and public intellectual Christopher Lasch published *The New Radicalism in America*, a weighty tome that surveyed "the
intellectual as a social type" between 1889 and 1963.[1] Coming hot on the
heels of historian Richard Hofstadter's 1964 Pulitzer Prize-winning *Anti-
Intellectualism in American Life*, a groundbreaking work that exposed the
roots and social consequences of American anti-intellectualism, and also
published in the same year as sociologist Lewis Coser's influential *Men of
Ideas*, Lasch's *New Radicalism* confirmed the apparent recent decline in
American intellectual culture, tracking "the life of reason in a world in
which the irrational has come to appear not the exception but the rule."[2]
Lasch, Coser, and Hofstadter together inaugurated a publishing boon for
books dedicated to dissecting the eventual disregard among ordinary
women and men for intellectuals. "The intellectual's relation to the rest of
society is never entirely comfortable," Lasch declared, "but it has not always
been as uncomfortable as it is today in the United States."[3]

Though Lasch recapitulated some of the claims Hofstadter made regarding the long history of U.S. anti-intellectualism, his diagnosis placed
the blame for this crisis less on ordinary Americans' populist tempera-
ment than on intellectuals themselves. Intellectuals, Lasch lamented,
were tolling their own death knell by imagining themselves as "members
of a beleaguered minority." Intellectuals were in trouble not in spite of but
because of their unique position as intellectuals; it was precisely because of
the "sensitivity of intellectuals to attacks on themselves as a groups" that
they found themselves in crisis.[4]

Throughout his book Lasch intones the death of the intellectual class, but he also suggests the recent vintage for even conceiving of intellectuals as a special category. "The word 'intellectual' does not seem to have found its way into American usage much before the turn of the century," he writes. "Before that, most intellectuals belonged to the middle class."[5] Yet the twentieth century did not only introduce the term "intellectual." As we have seen, through popular culture, political organization, and educational initiatives, ordinary women and men in the early decades of the twentieth century pursued a new and exciting set of opportunities and venues to imagine themselves as thinkers. Twentieth-century mass culture instantiated a set of conditions that allowed discourse about intelligence to extend to working-class men and women, and producers of popular cultural texts capitalized on their audience's intellectual aspirations by both rewarding their intelligence and expanding their access to brainpower. These conditions precipitated a Cold War-era backlash that cast suspicion on this thriving American organic intellectual tradition and set the stage for diminishing working-class political movements.

The expansion of brainpower across class, race, and gender lines that had both informed and been shaped by popular culture was all but ignored by 1960s scholars like Hofstadter and Lasch, as they turned to critical self-examination and catalogued the unfortunate circumstances of their own marginalization. As they trained their vision on a perceived wholesale resentment toward intellectuals as a special class outside mainstream society, these scholars successfully reframed Cold War-era attacks on brainpower— attacks that put a long-standing tool of ordinary women and men's political liberation in conservative crosshairs. This scholarly emphasis upon preserving a unique category of intellectuals in turn opened historians to attack by ordinary women and men for attempting to preserve an elitist category, creating a cycle of misunderstanding that continues to manifest in contemporary American life. Though they conceived their efforts as restoring intellectuals to a (perceived) former stature that had been lost, these scholars bracketed off intellect from the brainpower of ordinary women and men and divorced intelligence from working-class cultural politics.

The politics of brainpower in the early twentieth century represented the emergence of organized efforts and expanding venues for cultural representations that foregrounded intellectual tools to advance the social goals and political identities of ordinary women and men. The process of articulating an organic intellectual tradition involved buttressing working-class intelligence through education and popular culture, representing ordinary women and men as intelligent in cultural texts across media, and building solidarity between specialized brainworkers and ordinary Americans. Cultural representations of working-class intelligence dissolved the distinction of intellectuals as a privileged class by positioning their work as always-already a critical component of working people's lives. When the new scholarship in the 1960s pronounced the death of the intellectual class, these same scholars ironically marginalized the voices of ordinary women and men who had redefined intelligence and shaped popular culture to foreground their perspectives and articulate their political identities.

It is curious, then, that the 1960s historians who attempted to resuscitate the reputation of intellectuals and worked to restore them to a place of privilege in the United States imagined their work as functioning in opposition to the same anticommunist impulses that had so effectively cast a shadow of suspicion over intelligence in American culture a decade earlier. Richard Hofstadter, himself a former member of the Communist Party, openly allowed that *Anti-Intellectualism in American Life* "was conceived in response to the political and intellectual conditions of the 1950s"—a moment when the Cold War cultural climate prevented ordinary women and men from accessing the benefits of brainpower that they had been accruing for a half century.[6] It was the 1950s egghead that was the blueprint for the intellectual whose age was imagined to have so recently passed, and it was precisely the emergence of this category and the suspicion it had precipitated that decimated and deflated the organic intellectual tradition.

"Intellectuals of the future," Coser wrote at the close of *Men of Ideas*, "may indeed still play a major role in the United States—if they manage to avoid the twin temptations of total withdrawal and total integration."[7] Integration was a loaded word in the 1960s United States. That Coser summoned integration as an obstacle to restoring the value of intellectuals points to a resistance among liberal intellectual historians of the 1960s to restoring an organic intellectual tradition. The New Left of the 1960s has been remembered for moving progressive politics in the United States out of labor unions and into universities, yet this move was accompanied by an increasingly reified notion of intellectuals as both the essential center of conversations about brainpower and as a marginalized minority whose voices had to be restored if intelligence was going to take root in American political discourse. The occlusion of the origins of the student movement in the 1930s labor movement through the erasure of the Student League for

Industrial Democracy when the organization became Students for a Democratic Society in 1960 points to a broader social trend: the disrespect given
1960s intellectuals, closely aligned with the success of the radical intellectuals who inspired young activists and the calcification of intellectuality from
a set of practices into a marginalized identity, was reimagined during the
decade as characterizing a lengthy disregard for intellectuals in U.S. history,
a revision that drew on the construction of the 1950s egghead as a prece-
dent. Those intellectuals who did find traction in 1960s America—C. Wright
Mills, Herbert Marcuse, Reinhold Niebuhr, to name but a few of the more
prominent among them—also found themselves cast as members of a class
outside the mainstream. "We cannot create a left by abdicating our roles as
intellectuals to become working class agitators or machine politicians, or by
playing at other forms of direct political action," Mills wrote in 1962. "We
can begin to create a left by confronting issues as intellectuals in our work."[8]
The opposition between brainpower and working-class politics was newly
framed by Mills as a matter of charged identity conflict.

Though the subject of the conversation changed with the emergence
of the egghead in the 1950s, the politics of brainpower continued to shape
American culture at various critical moments in the post-1960s United
States. In the beginning of my introduction to this book I recounted the
vigorous debate surrounding charges of stupidity in recent American history. Though the political affiliations of participants in this conversation
have shifted considerably, the allusion to working-class brainpower points
to a growing receptivity on the part of ordinary Americans to the possibility
of returning to a broader conversation drawing on the organic intellectual
tradition to reinvigorate contemporary political culture. The continual appeals to the intelligence of ordinary women and men that emerge regularly
on both the left and the right suggest a resurgence of working-class brainpower that might lie just around the corner.

What begins to emerge when considering the tortuous history of intelligence in American culture is considerably more complicated than that
which those scholars who take as fact the intellectual's decline allow. Though
I have suggested the cultural significance of an organic intellectual tradition for framing working-class politics and popular culture in the
twentieth-century United States, conversations about brainpower that
emerged during those early decades of the American century were characterized more by their paradoxes, stutters, and stops than by any consistent
theorization of what it meant for brainpower to be used as a tool for working-

class liberation. As I have tried to demonstrate throughout this book, competing representations of intelligence could alternately smash the pretensions of an intellectual elite, position ordinary women and men as smarter than experts, appeal to intellectual culture to validate working-class positions, and dismantle intellectual hierarchies. These representations were often uncomfortable and contradictory, sometimes even self-defeating, particularly when the value of intelligence was diminished in order to level the intellectual playing field. Yet even at their most painfully paradoxical, representations of intelligence suggested the potential for brainpower to do important cultural work, claiming a site of political engagement that was uniquely accessible to ordinary women and men and which could radically transform American society using tools that even the poorest could claim as rightful owners.

Regardless how frustratingly counterproductive they could be, the stubborn paradoxes that were inextricable from twentieth-century discussions about and representations of brainpower in the United States kept a conversation about intelligence ongoing, and popular engagement with representations of intelligence persisted in spite of the contradictory impulses that occasionally made them confusing or illegible to those who stood to benefit from them most. Central to my study and, significantly, most peripheral in the studies of intellectual culture that took off in the 1960s was the role of popular culture as a critical site in shaping American ideas about brainpower. The emergence of the mass culture industries precipitated a set of cultural practices that demanded intelligence of producers while targeting ordinary women and men as consumers. Debates about the value of popular culture were inextricable from complicated conversations about the value of brainpower for ordinary Americans. Efforts to defend popular culture were advanced through reference to intelligence, and cultural texts targeting working-class consumers regularly engaged with the politics of brainpower as a central object of discussion.

Whether at Coney Island or in a Chautauqua tent, in newspaper and magazine articles studying Albert Einstein or on radio programs guiding listeners on a tour of Oak Ridge, Tennessee, the relationship between intelligence and social power informed the emerging popular culture of the twentieth century. I have emphasized the emergence of mass culture in this study of brainpower because the growth of the culture industries in the early twentieth century inaugurated a site of critical engagement foregrounding working-class audiences and taste. Working-class leisure was consumed by audiences across social classes, and it was through mass-produced texts that audiences were exposed to the multiple meanings attached to brainpower and the complicated identities that were invoked to characterize smart women and men. These conversations were largely forgotten when 1960s historians prescribed a healthy dose of intellectuals to resolve the social problems of Cold War-era disorder, but they were never abandoned as ordinary women and men continued to imagine themselves as intelligent. Still, rather than building on and expanding the vocabulary of the usable past and reinscribing the organic intellectual tradition in the United States for ordinary women and men, associations of intelligence with eggheadedness were routinely adopted and recapitulated across popular media. Working-class anti-intellectualism was widely apprehended as a foregone conclusion, and efforts to understand the organic intellectual tradition were forestalled.

Rethinking the history of brainpower in American culture as the history of an organic intellectual tradition forces us to rethink narratives that diminish the voices of ordinary women and men in intellectual conversations. Though it is unlikely that many of the women who studied at the Bryn Mawr Summer School would have been comfortable to be identified as intellectuals—let alone have characterized themselves as "beleaguered" members of such a group—they certainly participated in the building of a radical intellectual working class and did their part in shaping the political, cultural, and social meanings of brainpower for working-class women. So, for that matter, did Martin Couney with his baby incubator exhibits, Claude McKay as author of the scandalous *Home to Harlem*, cartoonist McCutcheon who produced a comic about Albert Einstein, and audiences who marveled at the spectacular abilities of Mascot, the arithmetically gifted horse. Their version of brainpower did not separate intellectuals from the masses. Instead, ordinary Americans' participation in working-class movements and amusements was positioned as key to advancing an organic intellectual tradition that paralleled but never truly intersected with the history of "men of ideas" that the 1960s scholars of intellectuals birthed and then buried.

Yet it served many political interests to devalue the intellectual pursuits of ordinary women and men, particularly in the 1950s, a period characterized by various forms of political repression and too often squelched dissent. The politics of brainpower, as we have seen, were essential components of the success of the culture industries throughout the early decades of the twentieth century and functioned as a valuable tool for dismantling hierarchies and advancing political and cultural goals of the working class. The Cold War introduced a game-changing degree of censure against eggheads and intellectuals, but even these were embedded in discursive strategies echoing earlier discussions of brainpower and responsive to ongoing progressive political movements. The egghead was demonized as a special category of Americans, putting organic intellectuals on notice. But the egghead also represented a special category specifically emerging within popular culture that was opposed to organic intellectuals; the figure represented values that took brainpower out of the hands of ordinary women and men and thus disempowered communities that were finding tools for accessing social power and disrupting social hierarchies increasingly scarce.

The fifty years between the turn of the twentieth century and the invention of the egghead saw the emergence of a strikingly diverse variety of representational strategies for conceiving brainpower in American culture. Throughout these decades, intelligence represented a site of conflict that put the concerns of ordinary Americans—especially those who were not profiting from brainwork—at the center of a discourse concerning ideology and identities; class and conflict; and the shifting politics of race, gender, and sexuality. The tension between those who sought to use intelligence to enforce and maintain their power and those who imagined intelligence as a site of empowerment for ordinary women and men simmered below the surface of even the most seemingly innocuous cultural texts and practices. For members of America's working class, brainpower offered both a strategy for accruing cultural capital and a means for destroying capitalism. For women, brainpower could dignify domestic labor, and it could also challenge the structural inconsistencies of patriarchy. For African Americans, brainpower offered a means for affirming the value of a shared history and a tool for shaping a self-determined politics. For immigrants, brainpower presented an arena for incorporation in American society and a mechanism for privileging pluralism. The value of intelligence for ordinary—and often marginalized—Americans was hinged upon brainpower's fluidity and flexibility; its unique capacity for assuming contradictory positions and engendering the paradoxes of identity.

Though its meaning has changed, brainpower continues to command a high premium. As we move farther into the twenty-first century, it might be an appropriate moment to return to the scene over a hundred years ago when amusement parks seamlessly transitioned into working-class universities and audiences sought points of commonality with a disheveled genius whose recently confirmed theory of space and time threatened to throw an entire universe out of balance. In spite of the great obstacles that confront them, ordinary women and men continue to seek intellectual tools to navigate our postmodern world, even as the jealous guarding of brainpower by members of an educated and economically privileged elite persists in threatening the possibility of social equality across race, gender, and class lines. Reclaiming the history of an organic intellectual tradition in American culture represents a starting point for envisioning intelligence as a shared commodity across social classes; wrested from the hands of the intellectuals, there's no telling what the brainpower of the people has the potential to accomplish.

NOTES

Introduction: Or, They Think We're Stupid

Epigraph: Quoted in Jesse L. Hurlbut, *The Story of Chautauqua* (New York: Putnam's Sons, 1921), xvii.

1. Todd Gitlin, "The Renaissance of Anti-Intellectualism," *Chronicle of Higher Education*, December 8, 2000.

2. Mark Crispin Miller, *The Bush Dyslexicon: Observations on a National Disorder* (New York: Norton, 2001), 38.

3. Ann Coulter, *Slander: Liberal Lies About the American Right* (New York: Crown, 2002), 183.

4. Laura Ingraham, *Shut Up and Sing: How Elites from Hollywood, Politics, and the UN Are Subverting America* (Washington, D.C.: Regnery, 2003), 1.

5. Michael Savage, *The Enemy Within: Saving America from the Liberal Assault on Our Schools, Faith, and Military* (Nashville, Tenn.: WND Books, 2003), 105.

6. The framework of anti-intellectualism has been remarkably persistent since the 1963 publication of Hofstadter's epic study of this phenomenon. Richard Hofstadter, *Anti-Intellectualism in American Life* (New York: Knopf, 1963).

7. My definition of brainpower takes on a Foucauldian dimension insofar as it suggests a discursive formation that functions to regulate the dispersal of power within social-historical particularities. Foucault describes how a discourse is formed "whenever, between objects, types of statement, concepts, or thematic choices, one can define a regularity (an order, correlations, positions and functionings, transformations)." Michel Foucault, *The Archaeology of Knowledge*, trans. A. M. Sheridan Smith (New York: Pantheon, 1972), 38. Over the first half of the twentieth century, brainpower assumed the function of both assigning and delimiting social empowerment regulated through access to intellectual tools. Conversations about and representations of disparate topics ranging from amusement parks to radical fiction pointed to an ongoing grappling with the meaning of brainpower for ordinary women and men, in the process shaping the discursive limits of brainpower as a tool for advancing progressive political positions and privileging working-class subjectivities.

8. Closely related to this concept of brainpower is what I term, borrowing from the work of Antonio Gramsci, the organic intellectual tradition. Gramsci, a Marxist

thinker whose work has been particularly influential in the field of cultural studies, delineates two predominant intellectual types: the traditional and the organic intellectuals. The former engaged in pursuits most immediately aligned with the life of the mind: literature, science, philosophy. The latter could be found in any industry, and it was the social conditions surrounding labor that determined which was accorded social status. "In the modern world," Gramsci writes in his *Prison Notebooks*, "technical education, closely bound to industrial labor even at the most primitive and unqualified level, must form the basis of a new type of intellectual." Antonio Gramsci, *Selections from the Prison Notebooks*, ed. and trans. Quintin Hoare and Geoffrey Nowell Smith (New York: International, 1971), 9. As a Marxist critic, Gramsci sought a radical program that promoted conditions cultivating the organic intellectual. Similarly many social reformers in the United States tried to reshape social institutions to privilege the working class, African Americans, women, and other minoritized groups. "The most widespread error of method," Gramsci wrote of scholarship on intellectuals, "seems to me that of having looked for this criterion of distinction in the intrinsic nature of intellectual activities, rather than in the ensemble of the system of relations in which these activities (and therefore the intellectual groups who personify them) have their place within the general complex of social relations" (8). In other words, isolating intellectuals was less a matter of identifying a particular pursuit of knowledge than one of isolating a social function. Thinking about the ways intelligence was represented by and for ordinary women and men—and the role these representations played in shaping working-class social movements—offers a significant channel for exploring an organic intellectual tradition in the United States.

9. Much of the existing work on intelligence in the United States has focused on intelligence testing, a subject that receives relatively little attention in my book. Research on intelligence testing has attempted to trace shifts in the ways scientists have defined intelligence. Since the introduction of the first American intelligence tests—popularized by Henry Herbert Goddard beginning in 1908—psychologists, eugenicists, and behaviorists have tried to gauge the potential for intelligence among both the general population and more narrow subgroups within the United States. Historian JoAnne Brown has argued that intelligence testing represents an effort by psychologists to use "authoritative language to assert professional control over the logic of public education, and, by extension, over the very logic of democratic rule, through the definition of popular conceptions of intelligence." JoAnne Brown, *The Definition of a Profession: The Authority of Metaphor in the History of Intelligence Testing, 1890–1930* (Princeton, N.J.: Princeton University Press, 1992), 4. The scientific community's concern with defining intelligence has been presented to the public as useful for correcting inequities in American society, ensuring equal access to education, and as an excuse for the existence of power differentials. Historians have tended to focus their attention on these aspects of testing. In each case, intelligence testing was conceived

as engaged in American identity, but it was framed as a line of inquiry best answered through the scientific method—and best left to experts.

Recent studies of intelligence testing have emphasized the elaborate ways scientists have sought to gauge, measure, and transcribe cognitive abilities—in effect creating a specialized language to describe something that necessarily defies simple quantification or definition—and have introduced valuable work on the relationship between intelligence testing and American identities, democratic practice, and social distribution of expertise. Within these categories, research into the relationship between intelligence testing and constructions of race has been a particularly contentious site of political intervention. Additionally, public debates about intelligence tests in relation to identity—such as the controversy precipitated by the publication of *The Bell Curve* in 1995—have comprised a significant measure of the discourse surrounding intelligence in the United States. The refusal of the public to align their conceptions of intelligence with scientific demands for standardization and dispassionate observation—evidenced through the ongoing battles about the value of intelligence testing—reinforces the need to include ordinary Americans' definitions of intelligence in academic work on the subject.

At its root, intelligence testing has remained a discourse relating primarily to a specialized scientific audience, and its advocates have assumed that the discourse on intelligence in the United States begins within a specialized academic community. There have been public debates about intelligence testing, but even these have not tended to challenge the notion that the measuring of intelligence is best determined by experts. In some respects, intelligence tests engender an effort to put a scientific imprimatur on a term that has already been defined within mass culture. In other words, intelligence testing represents a particular way intelligence is supposed to be measured by experts, and thus represented an effort on the part of experts to extract intelligence from its popular definition. I am more concerned with how intelligence has been defined by cultural producers within popular culture for mass audiences. Though voices within the scientific community appear in this book, they are generally of concern only when they are being represented within popular culture. I am more concerned with audiences thinking about science by, for example, visiting baby incubator exhibits at Coney Island, a process that essentially turned experimental scientists into circus carneys, than with scientists trying to categorize people according to intelligence or mental aptitude.

On intelligence testing in the American context, see Stephen H. Aby with Martha J. McNamara, *The IQ Debate: A Selective Guide to the Literature* (New York: Greenwood, 1990); Leon Kamin, *The Science and Politics of I.Q.* (Potomac, Md.: Erlbaum, 1974); Henry L. Minton, *Lewis M. Terman: Pioneer in Psychological Testing* (New York: New York University Press, 1988); Leila Zenderland, *Measuring Minds: Henry Herbert Goddard and the Origins of American Intelligence Testing* (New York: Cambridge University Press, 1998). On the specific concerns around racial identity in relation to intelligence, see Douglas Lee Eckberg, *Intelligence and Race: The Origins and Dimensions of the IQ Controversy* (New York: Praeger, 1979); H. J. Eysenck, *The IQ Argument: Race, Intelligence, and Education* (New York: Library Press, 1971); Russell Jacoby and Naomi Glauberman, eds., *The Bell Curve Debate: History, Documents, Opinions* (New York: Times Books, 1995); Richard J. Herrnstein and Charles Murray, *The Bell Curve: Intelligence and Class Structure in American Life* (New York: Free Press, 1994); André Joseph, *Intelligence, IQ, and Race: When, How, and Why They Became Associated* (San Francisco: R&E Research Associates, 1977); David J. Smith, *The Eugenic Assault on America: Scenes in Red, White, and Black* (Fairfax, Va.: George Mason University Press, 1992).

10. See, for example, John Russo and Sherry Lee Linkon, eds., *New Working-Class Studies* (Ithaca, N.Y.: ILR Press, 2005).

11. Michael Denning, *Mechanic Accents: Dime Novels and Working-Class Culture in America* (New York: Verso, 1987).

12. I am using the phrase "culture industries" here to refer to the mechanization, standardization, and corporatization of modern cultural production targeting and constructing mass audiences, a process that accelerated at the turn of the twentieth century. This phrase originated with Theodor Adorno and Max Horkheimer in their defining 1944 work *Dialectic of Enlightenment*. This work influenced the Frankfurt School's analysis of culture with its suggestion that "under monopoly all mass culture is identical, and the lines of its artificial framework begin to show through." *Dialectic of Enlightenment*, trans. John Cumming (New York: Herder and Herder, 1972), 121. Though I do not share the skepticism about audience that by and large defines Frankfurt School approaches to mass culture, I do agree with the basic framework that positions the mass production technology as having fundamentally shaped meaning within modern society (120–67).

13. See Judith A. Adams, *The American Amusement Park Industry: A History of Technology and Thrills* (Boston: Twayne, 1991); Richard Butsch, ed., *For Fun and Profit: The Transformation of Leisure into Consumption* (Philadelphia: Temple University Press, 1990); John T. Cumbler, *Working-Class Community in Industrial America: Work, Leisure, and Struggle in Two Industrial Cities, 1880–1930* (Westport, Conn.: Greenwood, 1979); John F. Kasson, *Amusing the Million: Coney Island at the Turn of the Century* (New York: Hill and Wang, 1978); David Nasaw, *Going Out: The Rise and Fall of Public Amusements* (New York: Basic Books, 1993); Kathy Peiss, *Cheap Amusements: Working Women and Leisure in Turn-of-the-Century New York* (Philadelphia: Temple University Press, 1986); Roy Rosenzweig, *Eight Hours for What We Will: Workers and Leisure in an Industrial City, 1870–1920* (New York: Cambridge University Press, 1983); Susan Strasser, *Satisfaction Guaranteed: The Making of the American Mass Market* (New York: Pantheon, 1989).

14. Richard Ohmann, *Selling Culture: Magazines, Markets, and Class at the Turn of the Century* (New York: Verso, 1996), 14.

15. See Burton J. Bledstein, *The Culture of Professionalism: The Middle Class and the Development of Higher Education in America* (New York: Norton, 1976); Frank Barkley Copley, *Frederick W. Taylor: Father of Scientific Management* (New York: Harper & Bros., 1923); Sudhir Kakar, *Frederick Taylor: A Study in Personality and Innovation* (Cambridge, Mass.: MIT Press, 1970); Daniel Nelson, *Frederick W. Taylor and the Rise of Scientific Management* (Madison: University of Wisconsin Press, 1980), 7.

16. Daniel Nelson, "Scientific Management in Retrospect," in Nelson, *A Mental Revolution* (Columbus: Ohio State University Press, 1992), 5–39, 14. See also Ed Andrew, *Closing the Iron Cage: The Scientific Management of Work and Leisure* (Montreal: Black Rose Books, 1981); Samuel Haber, *Efficiency and Uplift: Scientific Management in the Progressive Era, 1890–1920* (Chicago: University of Chicago Press, 1964).

17. Harry Braverman, *Labor and Monopoly Capital: The Degradation of Work in the Twentieth Century* (New York: Monthly Review Press, 1975).

18. David Montgomery, *Workers' Control in America: Studies in the History of Work, Technology, and Labor Struggles* (Cambridge: Cambridge University Press, 1979), 4.

19. Edward Cubberley, *Public Education in the United States: A Study and Interpretation of American Educational History* (Boston: Houghton Mifflin, 1934), 515–16.

20. Christopher Lasch, *The New Radicalism in America 1889–1963: The Intellectual as a Social Type* (New York: Knopf, 1965), xiii–xiv.

21. Nell Irvin Painter, *Standing at Armageddon: United States, 1877–1919* (New York: Norton, 1987).

22. Charles Frankel, "Definition of the True Egghead," *New York Times Magazine*, October 21, 1956, 14.

Chapter 1. "Aren't We Educational Here Too?": Brainpower and the Emergence of Mass Culture

Epigraph: Horace Traubel, "On Flying over People's Heads," *The Comrade*, August 1903, 242.

1. "Coney Island Revels in a Lidless Sunday," *New York Times*, May 24, 1909.

2. "Coney Must Keep the Law, Mayor Says," *New York Times*, May 21, 1909.

3. "Coney Island Revels in a Lidless Sunday."

4. "Coney Must Keep the Law, Mayor Says."

5. "Coney Island Revels in a Lidless Sunday."

6. "Coney Not Scared About Police," *New York Times*, May 23, 1901.

7. Judith A. Adams, *The American Amusement Park Industry: A History of Technology and Thrills* (Boston: Twayne, 1991), 41–56; John F. Kasson, *Amusing the Million: Coney Island at the Turn of the Century* (New York: Hill and Wang, 1978); Edo McCullough, *Good Old Coney Island, a Sentimental Journey into the Past* (New York: Scribner, 1957).

8. Bruce A. Kimball notes that "studies of the social status of occupations before World War II indicate that professors were highly regarded. Public opinion surveys in the 1920s found that professors were ranked second only to bankers among 'forty-five occupations' that respondents arranged 'in the order of their social standing." *The "True Professional Ideal" in America: A History* (Cambridge, Mass.: Blackwell, 1996), 317.

9. Charles W. Wood, "Coney Island Morality," *The Masses*, October 1917, 26.

10. Glenn Scott Allen, *Master Mechanics and Wicked Wizards: Images of the American Scientist as Hero and Villain from Colonial Times to the Present* (Amherst: University of Massachusetts Press, 2009), 8.

11. "New Coney Dazzles Its Record Multitude," *New York Times*, May 15, 1904.

12. Robert Wilson Neal, "New York's City of Play," *World of To-day* 11 (August 1906), 822.

13. "Incubator Graduates Hold a Reunion," *New York Times*, August 1, 1904.

14. Jeffrey P. Baker, *The Machine in the Nursery: Incubator Technology and the Origins of Newborn Intensive Care* (Baltimore: Johns Hopkins University Press, 1996), 104.

15. Oliver Pilat and Jo Ranson, *Sodom by the Sea: An Affectionate History of Coney Island* (Garden City, N.Y.: Doubleday, Doran, 1941), 192.

16. LeRoy Ashby, *With Amusement for All: A History of American Popular Culture Since 1830* (Lexington: University Press of Kentucky, 2006), 143–218; Martin Paulsson, *The Social Anxieties of Progressive Reform: Atlantic City, 1854–1920* (New York: New York University Press, 1994).

17. Jesse L. Hurlbut, *The Story of Chautauqua* (New York, Putnam's, 1921), x.

18. Sylvia Pettem, *Chautauqua Centennial, Boulder Colorado: A Hundred Years of Programs* (Boulder, Colo.: Book Lode, c. 1997), 29–30.

19. Quoted in "One Idea of Chautauqua," *The Chautauquan*, July 1909, 231.

20. Hurlbut, *The Story of Chautauqua*, x, xiii, ix, xv.

21. See John C. Burnham, ed., *Science in America: Historical Selections* (New York: Holt, Rinehart and Winston, 1971); George H. Daniels, *Science in American Society: A Social History* (New York: Knopf, 1971); Sally Gregory Kohlstedt and Margaret W. Rossiter, *Historical Writing on American Science: Perspectives and Prospects* (Baltimore: Johns Hopkins University Press, 1986); Nathan Reingold, *Science, American Style* (New Brunswick, N.J.: Rutgers University Press, 1991); Marc Rothenberg, *The History of Science and Technology in the United States: A Critical and Selective Bibliography* (New York: Garland, 1982).

22. Edward G. Gordon and Elaine H. Gordon, *Literacy in America: Historic Journey and Contemporary Solutions* (Westport, Conn.: Praeger, 2003); Carl F. Kaestle, Lawrence Helen Damon-Moore, Katherine Tinsley Stedman, and William Vance Trollinger, Jr., *Literacy in the United States: Readers and Reading Since 1880* (New Haven, Conn.: Yale University Press, 1991).

23. T. Brailsford Robertson, "The Cash Value of Scientific Research," *Scientific Monthly*, November 1915, 140.

24. See Glen Scott Allen, *Master Mechanics and Wicked Wizards*.

25. Robertson's claim about the scientist's invisibility is especially bizarre in light of the nineteenth-century interest in scientists. Americans showed an endless capacity for fascination with science and scientists, though primarily in popular forms divorced from any academic context or specialized discourse. See, for example, the Frankenstein tales or the public interest in inventors such as Thomas Edison. Neil Baldwin, *Edison: Inventing the Century* (New York: Hyperion, 1995); Jon Turney, *Frankenstein's Footsteps: Science, Genetics, and Popular Culture* (New Haven, Conn.: Yale University Press, 1998).

26. Richard Ohmann discusses "professional managerial class" consumers of magazines in *Selling Culture: Magazines, Markets, and Class at the Turn of the Century* (New York: Verso, 1996), 118–74.

27. Marcel LaFollette dissects popular notions of "men of science" in *Making Science Our Own: Popular Images of Science, 1910–1955* (Chicago: University of Chicago Press, 1995), 66–77.

28. Jeffrey Melnick, *A Right to Sing the Blues: African Americans, Jews, and American Popular Song* (Cambridge, Mass.: Harvard University Press, 1999), 31.

29. Charles Osborne, "The Scientific Man," arr. Henry E. Pether (New York: T.B. Harms, 1895).

30. In the case of this song, "scientific" seems to refer specifically to an interest in that which could not possibly bring anything to bear on the affairs of the earth. This serves to alienate the scientific man from his surroundings, but also to situate him in a convenient metaphor as one with his "head in the clouds," an excess of imagination at the expense of social concern or individual responsibility.

31. Osborn, "The Scientific Man."

32. Each of these features, it should be noted, would be quite socially alienating, especially the breath of the hapless scientific man. It is left up to the audience to determine if the features have driven him into the scientific life or if the scientific life naturally attracts such characters.

33. Glen Scott Allen dissects these contradictory representations of scientists in his groundbreaking *Master Mechanics and Wicked Wizards*.

34. Jonathan R. Cole and Stephen Cole, *Social Stratification in Science* (Chicago: University of Chicago Press, 1973); Diane Crane, *Invisible Colleges: Diffusion of Knowledge in Scientific Communities* (Chicago: University of Chicago Press, 1972); Warren O. Hagstrom, *The Scientific Community* (New York: Basic Books, 1965); Daniel J. Kevles, *The Physicists: The History of a Scientific Community in America* (New York: Knopf, 1978); Derek J. deSolla Price, *Little Science, Big Science* (New York: Columbia University Press, 1963).

35. "Reverence and Blasphemy," *Good Morning*, May 15, 1919, 23.

36. Women working in scientific occupations were nearly invisible in popular culture and wrote very few articles about science in popular magazines. At least through the 1940s, LaFollette argues, female readers were instructed that "if you choose a career in science, you will be one among few, the work will be hard and lonely, and popular opinion will most likely regard you as an abnormal woman." *Making Science*, 79.

37. "If It's Funny—Laugh," *Half-Century*, December 1917, 17.

38. Electric lights were not only a nineteenth-century invention, they had become, by the dawn of the twentieth century, a source of great amusement and wonder. By 1917 they were widely available in many homes, through electrification was still limited to certain areas of the United States. Malcolm MacLaren, *The Rise of the Electrical Industry During the Nineteenth Century* (Princeton, N.J.: Princeton University Press, 1943); David E. Nye, *Electrifying America: Social Meanings of a New Technology, 1880–1940* (Cambridge, Mass.: MIT Press, 1990); Harold C. Passer, *The Electrical Manufacturers, 1875–1900* (Cambridge, Mass.: Harvard University Press, 1953).

39. Daniel Nelson, *Frederick W. Taylor and the Rise of Scientific Management* (Madison: University of Wisconsin Press, 1980).

40. Frank Barkley Copley, *Frederick W. Taylor: Father of Scientific Management* (New York: Harper & Bros, 1923); Sudhir Kakar, *Frederick Taylor: A Study in Personality and Innovation* (Cambridge, Mass.: MIT Press, 1970); Nelson, *Frederick W. Taylor*, 7.

41. "Before 1910," Daniel Nelson writes, "Taylor and his followers used various labels to describe their work. At the instigation of Louis Brandeis, they agreed to employ the term *scientific management*, one of the phrases they had used informally. For the next twenty years scientific management meant the ideas and techniques of Taylor, his disciples, and those who followed in their footsteps." Nelson, *Frederick W. Taylor*, 3.

42. Horace Bookwalter Drury, *Scientific Management: A History and Criticism* (New York: Columbia University Press, 1915), 20.

43. Frederick Winslow Taylor, *The Principles of Scientific Management* (New York: Harper & Bros., 1911), 6.

44. Frederick M. Feiker, "What Scientific Management Is," in *How Scientific Management Is Applied* (Chicago: A. W. Shaw, 1915), 10.

45. Samuel Haber explains: "Science had a luster all its own. For a generation in which most people believed that progress was written into the laws of the universe, true and good often seemed to be indistinguishable. Science, which was a more certain form of the true, could also appear as a more rigorous form of the good. The very fruitfulness of science seemed to substantiate this. Furthermore, for the engineers, science was the passkey into their new profession." Samuel Haber, *Efficiency and Uplift: Scientific Management in the Progressive Era, 1890–1920* (Chicago: University of Chicago Press, 1964), 11.

46. Taylor, *Principles*, 97.

47. Unsurprisingly, workers were loathe to pick up on the "scientific" aspects of scientific management. Taylor himself acknowledged in his testimony before Congress in 1912 that "very serious objection has been made to the use of the word 'science' in this connection." He then went on to validate his use of the term by referring to a definition by a professor at MIT, effectively relying, once again, upon popular understandings of the authority of scientists to validate his own work. Frederick W. Taylor, *Scientific Management: Comprising Shop Management . . .* (New York: Harper & Bros., 1947), 41.

48. Christine Frederick, *Efficient Housekeeping; or, Household Engineering, Scientific Management in the Home* (Chicago: American School of Home Economics, 1915); Christine Frederick, *The New Housekeeping: Efficiency Studies in Home Management* (New York: Doubleday, 1913); Mary Pattison, *Principles of Domestic Engineering, or the What, Why and How of a Home* (New York: Trow Press, 1915).

49. Frederick, *Efficient Housekeeping*, 15.

50. Janice Williams Rutherford, *Selling Mrs. Consumer: Christine Frederick and the Rise of Household Efficiency* (Athens: University of Georgia Press, 2003).

51. On the devaluation and definition of women's work at this time, see Julie Matthei, *An Economic History of Women in America: Women's Work, the Sexual Division of Labor, and the Development of Capitalism* (New York: Schocken, 1982); John L. Rury, *Education and Women's Work: Female Schooling and the Division of Labor in Urban America, 1870–1930* (Albany: State University of New York Press, 1991).

52. Pattison, *Principles of Domestic Engineering*, 1.

53. William G. Bowen, Martin A. Kurzweil, and Eugene M. Tobin, *Equity and Excellence in American Higher Education* (Charlottesville, University of Virginia Press, 2005), 14.

54. Daniel A. Clark, *Creating the College Man: American Mass Magazines and Middle-Class Manhood, 1890–1915* (Madison: University of Wisconsin Press, 2010).

55. Christopher Lasch, *The New Radicalism in America 1889–1963: The Intellectual as a Social Type* (New York: Knopf, 1965), xiv.

56. Ed Gardenier and Edwin S. Brill, "There's a Lot of Things You Never Learn at School," (New York: Doty and Brill, 1902).

57. Ed Wynn, *The Freshman and the Sophomore*, 1907, Rare Books and Special Collections Division, American Memory Project, 2.

58. C. G. and C. B. MacArthur, "The Menace of Academic Distinctions," *Scientific Monthly*, May 1916, 461.

59. "A Spokesman for the Brotherhood," *The Masses*, December 1916, 11.

60. William J. Robinson, *Dr. Robinson's Voice in the Wilderness*, July 1919, 35.

61. *Half-Century*, May 1917, 14.

62. *Good Morning*, October 1, 1919, 12.

63. "The College President," *Good Morning*, May 22, 1919, 37.

64. The connection between knowledge and sexuality is discussed in Helen Lefkowitz Horowitz, *Rereading Sex: Battles over Sexual Knowledge and Suppression in Nineteenth-Century America* (New York: Knopf, 2002).

65. Harry B. Smith, "Watch the Professor," from *The Tattooed Man* (New York: Witmark and Sons, 1907).

66. Some songs, such as "And They Say He Went To College," represented college students as quite dense, but even these songs recognized the irony of a less than stellar brain on a college campus. E. P. Moran and Seymour Furth, "And They Say He Went to College" (New York: Shapiro, 1907).

67. Jack Mahoney, "He's a College Boy. A Rollicking Rah! Rah! Rah! Song," music by Theodore Morse (New York: Theodore Morse Music, 1909).

68. On representations of women in college see Shirley Marchalonis, *College Girls: A Century in Fiction* (New Brunswick, N.J.: Rutgers University Press, 1995); Lynn Peril, *College Girls: Bluestockings, Sex Kittens, and Co-eds, Then and Now* (New York: Norton, 2006). On women in higher education see Helen S. Astin, ed., *Some Action of Her Own: The Adult Woman and Higher Education* (Lexington, Mass.: Lexington Books, 1976); Barbara M. Soloman, *In the Company of Educated Women: A History of Women and Higher Education in America* (New Haven, Conn.: Yale University Press, 1985).

69. Bowen et al., *Equity and Excellence*, 25.

70. "Universities, Colleges, and Technological Schools, School Year 1907," in *Statistical Abstracts of the United States 1908* (Washington, D.C.: GPO, 1908), 113, fig. 56; "Universities, Colleges, and Schools of Technology," in *Statistical Abstracts of the United States 1915* (Washington, D.C.: GPO, 1915), 103, fig. 67.

71. J. R. Shannon, "Co-Ed," music by J. S. Zamecnik (Cleveland: Sam Fox, 1914).

72. In spite of its reduction of female intelligence to seductive charms, the song also represented a site of conflicted sexual progressivism: the women in these songs were pursuing knowledge and sexual pleasure together.

73. Reprinted in *Half-Century*, October 1916, 10.

74. Rayford Logan, *The Negro in American Life and Thought: The Nadir, 1877–1901* (New York: Dial Press, 1954).

75. Alfred A. Moss, Jr., *The American Negro Academy: Voice of the Talented Tenth* (Baton Rouge: Louisiana State University Press, 1981); Charles M. Payne and Adam Green, *Time Longer Than Rope: A Century of African American Activism, 1850–1950* (New York: New York University Press, 2003), 141–399; Jeffrey B. Perry, ed., *A Hubert Harrison Reader* (Middletown, Conn.: Wesleyan University Press, 2001); Arnold Rampersad, *The Art and Imagination of W. E. B. Du Bois* (Cambridge, Mass.: Harvard University Press, 1976); Raymond Wolters, *Du Bois and His Rivals* (Columbia: University of Missouri Press, 2002), 1–142.

76. W. E. B. Du Bois, *The Souls of Black Folk* (Chicago: McClurg, 1903; Modern Library Edition, 1996), 91.

77. Hubert Harrison, *The Voice*, January 1919, 176.

78. Chandler Owen, "What Will Be the Real Status of the Negro After the War?" *Messenger*, March 1919, 13.

79. Katherine E. Williams, editorial, *Half-Century*, August 1916, 3.

80. Cyril A. Crichlow, "Knowledge and Understanding," *Half-Century*, September 1917, 3.

81. Theodore Kornweibel, Jr., *No Crystal Stair: Black Life and the* Messenger, *1917–1928* (Westport, Conn.: Greenwood, 1975).

82. Frank Wentworth, "The Times and Their Tendencies," *Comrade*, January 1905, 4.

83. Appeal Book Department advertisement from *Wayland's Monthly*, November, 1915.

84. George Cotkin has described how Socialists popularized science in the early decades of the twentieth century. "The Socialist Popularization of Science in America, 1901 to the First World War," *History of Education Quarterly* 24, 2 (Summer 1984): 201–14. This process curiously concluded following the successful Russian revolution of 1917. Cotkin finds that the Socialist push to popularize science dissipated when radicals could point to a contemporary historical reality—an immediate experience—rather than abstracted theories. Cotkin writes that "the need to popularize science and to base Marxism on a language of science had diminished, because after the Bolshevik seizure of power in 1917 American theorists finally had a model of a successful revolution. The revolution allowed Americans to jettison their analogies between Marxist theory and natural science and to replace them with the more powerful and current example of a 'scientific' revolution led by that scientist of the revolution, as they liked to say, the practical engineer Lenin." Cotkin, "Socialist Popularization," 211.

85. John Spargo, review of John Phin, *The Shakespeare Cyclopaedia and New Glossary*, *Comrade*, February 1903, 115.

86. Review of *Social Freedom*, by Elsie Clews Parsons, *The Masses*, June 1916, 24–25.

87. Backward and Forward, *Why?*, March 1913, 6.

88. The relationship between gender and politics in the Progressive Era is dissected in Kevin P. Murphy's *Political Manhood: Red Bloods, Mollycoddles, and the Politics of Progressive Era Reform* (New York: Columbia University Press, 2008).

Chapter 2. The Force of Complicated Mathematics: Einstein Enters American Culture

Epigraph: William Carlos Williams, "St. Francis Einstein of the Daffodils [First Version]," in *The Collected Poems of William Carlos Williams*, ed. A. Walton Litz and Christopher MacGowan (New York: New Directions, 1986), 130.

1. "Einstein's Idea Puzzles Harding, He Admits as Scientist Calls," *New York Times*, April 26, 1921.

2. On Einstein's entry into American culture see Loren R. Graham, "Einstein's Reception," in *Albert Einstein, Historical and Cultural Perspectives: The Centennial*

Symposium in Jerusalem, ed. Gerald Holton (Princeton, N.J.: Princeton University Press, 1982), 107–36; Alan J. Friedman and Carol C. Donley, *Einstein as Myth and Muse* (New York: Cambridge University Press, 1985).

3. From a speech quoted in David Kennedy, *Over Here: The First World War and American Society* (New York: Oxford University Press, 1980), 46.

4. No historical or biographical study of Wilson's life and presidency is complete without accounting for this shift, but his transformation received its most exhaustive treatment in Patrick Devlin, *Too Proud to Fight: Woodrow Wilson's Neutrality* (New York: Oxford University Press, 1974).

5. Kennedy, *Over Here*, 14.

6. See, for example, James R. Mock and Cedric Larson, *Words That Won the War: The Story of the Committee on Public Information, 1917–1919* (Princeton, N.J.: Princeton University Press, 1939).

7. Kennedy, *Over Here*, 66.

8. "Einstein Sees Boston; Fails on Edison Test," *New York Times*, May 18, 1921.

9. See especially James Malcolm Bird, ed., *Einstein's Theories of Relativity and Gravitation; A Selection of Material from the Essays Submitted in the Competition for the Eugene Higgins Prize of $5,000* (New York: Scientific American, 1921); Max Born, *Einstein's Theory of Relativity* (New York: Dutton, 1922); Charles Lane Poor, *Gravitation Versus Relativity: A Non-Technical Explanation of the Fundamental Principles of Gravitational Astronomy and a Critical Examination of the Astronomical Evidence Cited as Proof of the Generalized Theory of Relativity* (New York: Putnam, 1922); J. W. N. Sullivan, *Three Men Discuss Relativity* (New York: Knopf, 1926).

10. Bird, *Einstein's Theories*, 2.

11. "Eclipse Showed Gravity Variation," *New York Times*, November 6, 1919.

12. "Lights All Askew in the Heavens," *New York Times*, November 10, 1919.

13. Charles Lane Poor, "Jazz in the Scientific World," *New York Times*, November 16, 1919.

14. Carla Waechter, letter, *New York Times*, November 17, 1919.

15. "Princeton Honors Fuss Dr. Einstein," *Evening Bulletin—Philadelphia*, May 10, 1921.

16. Edwin Slosson, *Easy Lessons in Einstein: A Discussion of the More Intelligible Features of the Theory of Relativity* (New York: Harcourt, Brace and Howe, 1920), v. The McCutcheon referenced here is the prolific Chicago cartoonist John T. McCutcheon, who was particularly fond of mocking know-it-all experts.

17. Morris R. Cohen, "Einstein's Theory of Relativity," *New Republic*, January 21, 1920, 228.

18. Editorial, *Campus* (City College of New York), April 26, 1921; quoted in József Illy, *Albert Meets America: How Journalists Treated Genius During Einstein's 1921 Travels* (Baltimore: Johns Hopkins University Press, 2006), 115.

19. "Psychopathic Relativity," *New York Times*, April 5, 1921.

20. On the origins of American exceptionalism, see Jonathan M. Hansen, *The Lost Promise of Patriotism: Debating American Identity, 1890–1920* (Chicago: University of Chicago Press, 2003); Hans Kohn, *American Nationalism: An Interpretative Essay* (New York: Macmillan, 1957); Wilbur Zelinsky, *Nation into State: The Shifting Symbolic Foundations of American Nationalism* (Chapel Hill: University of North Carolina Press, 1988).

21. Morris R. Cohen, "Roads to Einstein," *New Republic*, July 6, 1921, 174.

22. This defense of the United States in the context of "western" values resonates with the imperialist project described in Edward Said, *Culture and Imperialism* (New York: Knopf, 1993).

23. Bird, *Einstein's Theories*, 10, 11–12.

24. "Joys and Sorrows of the Einstein Editor," *Scientific American*, November 6, 1920.

25. Kenneth W. Payne, "Einstein on Americans," *New York Times*, July 10, 1921.

26. On the growth of a consumer culture in the United States during this period, see Susan Porter Benson, *Counter Cultures: Saleswomen, Managers, and Customers in American Department Stores, 1890–1940* (Urbana: University of Illinois Press, 1986); Stewart Ewen, *Captains of Consciousness: Advertising and the Social Roots of Consumer Culture* (New York: McGraw-Hill, 1976); Roland Marchand, *Advertising the American Dream: Making Way for Modernity, 1920–1940* (Berkeley: University of California Press, 1985). For the roots of this trend at the turn of the century, with particular attention to magazine consumption, nothing compares with Richard Ohmann's comprehensive *Selling Culture: Magazines, Markets, and Class at the Turn of the Century* (New York: Verso, 1996).

27. "Kindred Studies Up on Einstein Theory," *New York Times*, May 17, 1921.

28. "Lights All Askew," *New York Times*, 17.

29. The overreach in this author's effort to frame the theory of relativity in vernacular terms is particularly striking since the "fact" he cites is true only in a vacuum. "Einstein Here with Weizmann to Aid Zionism," *New York Call*, April 3, 1921.

30. "Einstein Expounds His New Theory," *New York Times*, December 3, 1919.

31. I am using the word "populist" here following Michael Kazin in his expansive updating of Hofstadter's formative thesis from 1955: as shorthand for a rhetorical strategy that opposes elite or concentrated interests with the will of the people, inevitably favoring the latter. Richard Hofstadter, *The Age of Reform; From Bryan to F.D.R.* (New York: Knopf, 1955); Michael Kazin, *The Populist Persuasion: An American History* (New York: Basic Books, 1995).

32. "Topics of the Times; Amateurs Will Be Resentful," *New York Times*, November 11, 1919.

33. "Topics of the Times; Disturbers of Minds Unpopular," *New York Times*, September 6, 1920.

34. "Topics of the Times; His Offense Can Be Imagined," *New York Times*, August 9, 1922.

35. The rhetoric of Americanism as a response to the Bolshevik revolution is discussed in Alan Dawley, *Struggles for Justice: Social Responsibility and the Liberal State* (Cambridge, Mass.: Harvard University Press, 1991), 218–53. See also Roberta Strauss Feuerlicht, *America's Reign of Terror: World War I, the Red Scare, and the Palmer Raids* (New York: Random House, 1971); Lloyd C. Gardner, *Safe for Democracy: The Anglo-American Response to Revolution, 1913–1923* (New York: Oxford University Press, 1984); Edwin P. Hoyt, *The Palmer Raids, 1919–1920: An Attempt to Suppress Dissent* (New York: Seabury, 1969); Julian F. Jaffe, *Crusade Against Radicalism: New York During the Red Scare, 1914–1924* (Port Washington, N.Y.: Kennikat, 1972); Robert K. Murray, *Red Scare: A Study in National Hysteria, 1919–1920* (Minneapolis: University of Minnesota Press, 1955).

36. Jane Burbank, *Intelligentsia and Revolution: Russian Views of Bolshevism, 1917–1922* (New York: Oxford University Press, 1986); Michael David-Fox, *Revolution of the Mind: Higher Learning Among the Bolsheviks, 1918–1929* (Ithaca, N.Y.: Cornell University Press, 1997).

37. Poor, *Gravitation Versus Relativity*, v.

38. Poor, "Jazz in the Scientific World."

39. Although he is specifically concerned with the ideological meanings attached to movie stars, film scholar Richard Dyer's analysis of stars might be usefully applied to other famous celebrities—among whom Einstein must be counted—as well. Dyer writes: "From the perspective of ideology, analyses of stars, as images existing [as] media texts, stress their structured polysemy, that is, the finite multiplicity of meanings and affect they embody and the attempt so to structure them that some meanings and affects are foregrounded and others are masked or displaced. The concern of such textual analysis is then not to determine the correct meaning and affect, but rather to determine what meanings and affects can legitimately be read in them." Richard Dyer, *Stars* (London: British Film Institute, 1979), 3.

In the case of Einstein, his media construction is divorced from both his actual biography and his scientific theory, just as a movie star is detached from her real life and abilities (though these might be relevant).

40. On the tension surrounding national identities following World War I, see Gary Gerstle, *American Crucible: Race and Nation in the Twentieth Century* (Princeton, N.J.: Princeton University Press, 2001), 81–127; Michael Ignatieff, *Blood and Belonging: Journeys into the New Nationalism* (New York: Farrar, Straus, and Giroux, 1994), 5–6; Matthew Frye Jacobson, *Barbarian Virtues: The United States Encounters Foreign Peoples at Home and Abroad, 1876–1917* (New York: Hill and Wang, 2000).

41. "Lights All Askew," *New York Times.*

42. "Einstein Explains 2 Phases of Theory," *New York American*, April 3, 1921.

43. "Lodge Pays Tribute to Einstein Theory," *New York Times*, February 9, 1920.

44. "Aladdin Einstein," *Freeman*, April 27, 1921, 153.

45. "Einstein Finds America 'Solid,'" *New York Evening Post*, April 8, 1921.

46. On race, Jewishness, and immigrant identities in American history, see Matthew Frye Jacobson, *Whiteness of a Different Color: European Immigrants and the Alchemy of Race* (Cambridge, Mass.: Harvard University Press, 1998).

47. "Einstein Here with Weizmann," *New York Call*.

48. Edwin F. Slosson, "Einstein's Reception," *Independent*, April 16, 1921, 401.

49. On this subject see David A. Hollinger, *Science, Jews, and Secular Society: Studies in Mid-Twentieth-Century American Intellectual History* (Princeton, N.J.: Princeton University Press, 1996).

50. Slosson, "Einstein's Reception," 401.

51. Edwin F. Slosson, "Einstein's Theory," *Independent*, December 20, 1919, 100. Slossen's characterization of Einstein as being a Swiss Jew was an effort to correct perceptions of him as German. On the anti-German sentiment in the United States in the years following American entry into World War I, see Phyllis Keller, *States of Belonging: German-American Intellectuals and the First World War* (Cambridge, Mass.: Harvard University Press, 1979); Frederick C. Luebke, *Bonds of Loyalty: German-Americans and World War I* (Dekalb: Northern Illinois University Press, 1974); Richard O'Connor, *The German-Americans: An Informal History* (Boston: Little, Brown, 1968), 344–452; La Vern J. Rippley, "Ameliorated Americanization: The Effect of World War I on German-Americans in the 1920s," in Frank Trommler and Joseph McVeigh, eds., *America and the Germans: An Assessment of a Three-Hundred-Year History* (Philadelphia: University of Pennsylvania Press, 1985), 217–31; La Vern J. Rippley, *The German-Americans* (Boston: Twayne, 1976), 180–95.

52. Nancy Gentile Ford, *Americans All! Foreign-Born Soldiers in World War I* (College Station: Texas A&M University Press, 2001), 24. Ford has written about the positions of Jews toward World War I, noting especially that "eventually, over 250,000 Jews served in the United States military . . . Jewish American leaders even tied their war effort to 'Americanization' issues, and concluded that only the 'un-Americanized Jew' would fear the war, since they would inadvertently connect the American draft with the Russian draft." She goes on to quote from "The Jew Is No Slacker," *Sunday Jewish Courier*, June 9, 1918: "When the Jew becomes Americanized, however, he then becomes entirely different. Then he understands that the Constitution of the United States gives all citizens of the country equal rights, and that this country affords every inhabitant equal opportunity. Then he who originally was a 'slacker' is among the first to volunteer, and on the field of battle he is the renowned hero" (*Americans All!*, 37). This intensive rallying behind Americanization and the war was certainly important in determining how Einstein's Jewish identity was conceived in early representations.

53. "Dr. Einstein Found America Anti-German," *New York Times*, July 2, 1921.

54. On changing immigration policies in the United States, see Keith Fitzgerald, *The Face of the Nation: Immigration, the State, and the National Identity* (Stanford, Calif.: Stanford University Press, 1996); Desmond King, *Making Americans: Immigration, Race, and the Origins of the Diverse Democracy* (Cambridge, Mass.: Harvard University Press, 2000).

55. "Einstein Expounds His New Theory," *New York Times*, December 3, 1919.

56. On the alien as immigrant, see Rachel Rubin and Jeffrey Melnick, *Immigrants in Popular Culture: An Introduction* (New York: New York University Press, 2006), 1–2.

57. "Just What It Is," *Boston Evening Transcript*, May 17, 1921.

58. Mae Ngai, *Impossible Subjects: Illegal Aliens and the Making of Modern America* (Princeton, N.J.: Princeton University Press, 2004).

59. Einstein could embody various kinds of immigrants: threatening, welcome, assimilable, unassimilable, etc. Still, the unique challenges confronting non-European immigrants (especially from Asian nations) were not addressed through Einstein. By "archetypal immigrant" I mean to highlight the variety of subject positions Einstein was made to inhabit through popular representation; I do not intend to suggest that he actually represented the diverse identities and experiences of American immigrants during this period. His reception in American culture was contingent on the recognizability of his immigrant status as a potential citizen; many immigrants did not have this option available, especially after the passage of the 1924 Johnson-Reed Act. Einstein was an archetypal immigrant insofar as archetypes were invested in representing immigrants as potential citizens. See Mae Ngai's work for further discussion of these points.

60. "Baseball Makes U.S. Concentrate, Asserts Scientist Einstein," *Hartford Daily Courant*, May 23, 1921.

61. The quest to assimilate Einstein into American life is symptomatic of the investment many Americans felt in excluding non-Americans from civic discourse, a feature that dovetails with the nativism being circulated after World War I. See John Higham, *Strangers in the Land: Patterns of American Nativism, 1860–1925* (New Brunswick, N.J.: Rutgers University Press, 1955).

62. "Baseball Makes U.S. Concentrate," *Hartford Daily Courant*.

63. The specific identities Einstein embodied—Swiss, German, Jewish—were significant here, but the fact that he was not an actual immigrant (it was his ideas that were migrating, not his body) meant that he was used in early days to discuss general concerns about immigration, though these implied European immigration—as opposed to emigration from nations such as Mexico or China, treated as "special cases"—as immigrant groups who could be collapsed into invisible bodies. This gave way later to specific concerns about Einstein himself as a Jewish immigrant from Germany when he arrived in the U.S. in 1921. On Mexican immigration, see David G. Gutiérrez, *Walls and Mirrors: Mexican Americans, Mexican Immigrants, and the Politics of Ethnicity* (Berkeley: University of California Press, 1995); George Sanchez, *Becoming Mexican American: Ethnicity, Culture, and Identity in Chicano Los Angeles, 1900–1945* (New York: Oxford University Press, 1993). On migration from China during the period of exclusion, see Erika Lee, *At America's Gates: Chinese Immigration During the Exclusion Era, 1882–1943* (Chapel Hill: University of North Carolina Press, 2003); Ronald T. Takaki, *Strangers from a Different Shore: A History of Asian Americans* (Boston: Little, Brown, 1989); Birgit Zinzius, *Chinese America: Stereotype and*

Reality; History, Present and Future of the Chinese Americans (New York: P. Lang, 2004). On European immigrants and the visibility of immigrant bodies, see especially Jacobson, *Whiteness of a Different Color.*

64. *Oxford English Dictionary*, 2nd ed., s.v. "Long-hair."

65. "Einstein Tells Why He Can't Explain," *Boston Daily Globe*, May 18, 1921.

66. "Princeton Honors Fuss Dr. Einstein," *Evening Bulletin—Philadelphia*, May 10, 1921.

67. "Baseball Makes U.S. Concentrate," *Hartford Daily Courant.*

68. "Einstein's Music Excels Science in Wife's Opinion," *New York American*, April 3, 1921.

69. "Einstein Here," *Cleveland Press*, May 25, 1921.

70. "How Einstein, Thinking in Terms of the Universe, Lives from Day to Day," *New York Evening Post*, March 26, 1921.

71. "Einstein Sails for Liverpool," *New York Call*, May 31, 1921.

72. "Baseball Makes U.S. Concentrate," *Hartford Daily Courant.*

73. "Einstein Here with Weizmann," *New York Call.*

74. "Einstein Tells Why He Can't Explain," *Boston Daily Globe.*

75. "Einstein Here."

76. Vera Weizmann and DavidTutaev, *The Impossible Takes Longer: The Memoirs of Vera Weizmann, Wife of Israel's First President, as Told to David Tutaev* (London: Hamilton, 1967), 102.

77. "The Adventure of Professor Einstein and the Hat," *Campus* (City College of New York), June 4, 1921, quoted in Illy, *Albert Meets America*, 281.

78. "Einstein Counted Wrong," *New York Times*, July 13, 1924.

79. "How Einstein, Thinking in Terms of the Universe, Lives from Day to Day."

80. "Prof. Einstein Here, Explains Relativity," *New York Times*, April 3, 1921.

Chapter 3. Knowledge Is Power: Women, Workers' Education,
and Brainpower in the 1920s

Epigraph: Unattributed poem, *Spring Magazine: Affiliated Summer Schools for Women Workers in Industry*, April 1929, 11, Box 3, American Labor Education Service (ALES) Records, 1927–1962, 5225, Kheel Center for Labor-Management Documentation and Archives, M. P. Catherwood Library, Cornell University (hereafter Kheel Center).

1. American Federation of Labor Workers Education Bureau (WEB), *Workers' Education Directory*, Printed Ephemera Collection on Organizations, Box 109, Folder: Workers Education Bureau, n.d., Tamiment Library and Robert F. Wagner Labor Archives.

2. On the formation of the ILGWU, see Louis Levine, *The Women's Garment Workers: A History of the I.L.G.W.U.* (New York: B.W. Huebsch, 1924); Lazare Teper, *The Women's Garment Industry* (New York: Educational Department, ILGWU, 1937).

3. Levine, *Women's Garment Workers*, 485.

4. The Amalgamated Clothing Workers of America, for example, followed the IL-GWU in developing its Educational Department. Robert Joseph Schaefer, "Educational Activities of the Garment Unions, 1890–1948: A Study in Workers' Education in the International Ladies' Garment Workers' Union and the Amalgamated Clothing Workers of America in New York City," Ph.D. dissertation, Columbia University, 1951, 74.

5. Ryllis Alexander Goslin and Omar Pancoast Goslin, *Growing Up: 21 Years of Education with the International Ladies' Garment Workers' Union* (New York: ILGWU-ED, 1938), Box 1, ILGWU Education Department Files, 1920–1979, 5780/166, Kheel Center.

6. Quoted in Levine, *Women's Garment Workers*, 495.

7. Harry J. Carman, *The International Ladies' Garment Workers' Union and Workers' Education*, reprinted from *Workers' Education*, February 1926, 5, ILGWU Education Department Files, 1920–1979, 5780/166, Kheel Center.

8. Fannia M. Cohn, *The Educational Work of the International Ladies' Garment Workers' Union*, Report submitted to the conference of the Workers Education Bureau of America, April 2, 1921, 2. Box 1, ILGWU Education Department Files, 1920–1979, 5780/166, Kheel Center.

9. Goslin and Goslin, *Growing Up*.

10. Quoted in Schaefer, "Educational Activities of the Garment Unions," 11, n. 1.

11. Nancy Cott, *The Grounding of Modern Feminism* (New Haven, Conn.: Yale University Press, 1987), 6.

12. T. R. Adam, *The Worker's Road to Learning* (New York: American Association for Adult Education, 1940), 32.

13. *Workers' Education Year Book 1924* (New York: WEB, 1924), 55.

14. On women in the labor movement see Mari Jo Buhle, "Socialist Women and the 'Girl Strikes,' Chicago, 1910," *Signs* 1 (1976): 1039–51; Elizabeth Faue, *Community of Suffering and Struggle: Women, Men, and the Labor Movement in Minneapolis, 1915–1945* (Chapel Hill: University of North Carolina Press, 1991); Pauline Newman, "How Women Forged Early Union," *Allied Industrial Worker* 19 (August 1976): 7; Annelise Orleck, *Common Sense & a Little Fire: Women and Working Class Politics in the United States, 1900–1965* (Chapel Hill: University of North Carolina Press, 1995).

15. Horace M. Kallen, *Education, the Machine and the Worker: An Essay in the Psychology of Education in Industrial Society* (New York: New Republic, 1925), xi.

16. Will Herberg, "Jewish Labor Movement in the United States: Early Years to World War I," *Industrial and Labor Relations Review* 5, 4 (1953): 501–23; Irving Howe, *World of Our Fathers: The Journey of the East European Jews to America and the Life They Found and Made* (New York: Harcourt Brace, 1976).

17. David A. Hollinger, *Science, Jews, and Secular Culture: Studies in Mid-Twentieth-Century American Intellectual History* (Princeton, N.J.: Princeton University Press, 1996); Howe, *World of Our Fathers*.

18. Cohn, *The Educational Work of the International Ladies' Garment Workers' Union*, 2, 9.

19. On cultural capital, see Pierre Bourdieu, *Distinction: A Social Critique of the Judgement of Taste*, trans. Richard Nice (London: Routledge and Kegan Paul, 1984).

20. By way of contrast, one might consider that the American Peoples Schools used the motto, "Education as a Joyous Adventure." American Peoples Schools, Printed Ephemera Collection on Organization, Box 9, Folder: American Peoples Schools, 1934, undated, Tamiment Library and Robert F. Wagner Labor Archives.

21. Cohn, *Educational Work of the International Ladies' Garment Workers' Union*, 8.

22. On M. Carey Thomas, see Helen Lefkowitz Horowitz, *The Power and Passion of M. Carey Thomas* (New York: Knopf, 1994).

23. Karyn L. Hollis, *Liberating Voices: Writing at the Bryn Mawr Summer School for Women Workers* (Carbondale: Southern Illinois University Press, 2004), 16.

24. Rita Heller, "Blue Collars and Bluestockings: The Bryn Mawr Summer School for Women Workers, 1921–1938," in *Sisterhood and Solidarity: Workers' Education for Women, 1914–1984*, ed. Joyce L. Kornbluh and Mary Frederickson (Philadelphia: Temple University Press, 1984), 107–45.

25. Hilda Worthington Smith, *Women Workers at the Bryn Mawr Summer School* (New York: Affiliated Summer Schools for Women Workers in Industry and American Association for Adult Education, 1929), 125.

26. Bryn Mawr Summer School Pamphlet, 1929, Box 2, WEB Records, 1921–1951, 5277, Kheel Center.

27. Letter from industrial worker, n.d, Box 2, Folder 15, ALES Records, 1927–1962, 5225, Kheel Center.

28. Smith, *Women Workers at the Bryn Mawr Summer School*, 11.

29. Brigid O'Farrell and Joyce L. Kornbluh, *Rocking the Boat: Union Women's Voices, 1915–1975* (New Brunswick, N.J.: Rutgers University Press, 1996), 21.

30. One of the fundamental conflicts among labor leaders and between organized labor and unorganized workers was about the tendency for big craft unions to promote themselves as worthy by positioning their rank and file as model citizens. This tendency often left out African American and unskilled workers and succeeded in setting up a set of expectations for workers that demanded they conform to middle-class behavior. The greatest challenge to these demands was found in the briefly prominent Industrial Workers of the World. The Congress of Industrial Organizations later formed to organize unskilled workers, and much of the energy that made the CIO successful emerged from the passionate radicalism of workers in the garment industries. On the exclusions of the AFL, see Bruce Nelson, *Divided We Stand: American Workers and the Struggle for Black Equality* (Princeton, N.J.: Princeton University Press, 2001). On immigrants and the labor movement, see Joan Younger Dickinson, *The Role of the Immigrant Women in the U.S. Labor Force, 1890–1910* (New York: Arno Press, 1980); A. T. Lane, *Solidarity or Survival? American Labor and European Immigrants, 1830–1924* (New York: Greenwood, 1987). On the Wob-

blies, see Patrick Renshaw, *The Wobblies: The Story of Syndicalism in the United States* (Garden City, N.Y.: Doubleday, 1967). On the CIO, see Robert H. Zieger, *The CIO, 1935–1955* (Chapel Hill: University of North Carolina Press, 1995).

31. Illustration from 1939 pamphlet for the BMSS, Box 3, ALES Records, 1927–1962, 5225, Kheel Center.

32. Quoted in O'Farrell and Kornbluh, *Rocking the Boat*, 21.

33. Sorell Balazowsky, "Student Impression of Bryn Mawr," Box 1, Folder 45, WEB Records, 1921–1951, 5277, Kheel Center.

34. On the concerns about the relationship between workers and management, see the discussion of scientific management in David Montgomery, *The Fall of the House of Labor: The Workplace, the State, and American Labor Activism, 1865–1925* (New York: Cambridge University Press, 1987), 9–57.

35. Quoted in Hilda Worthington Smith, Foreword, in Bryn Mawr Summer School for Women Workers in Industry, *The Workers Look at the Stars* (New York: Vineyard Shore, 1927), 3.

36. Unsigned letter from Bryn Mawr student, 1927, Box 2, Folder 15, ALES Records, 1927–1962, 5225, Kheel Center.

37. Minne Hoskins, letter written August 2, 1929, Box 1, Folder 45, WEB Records, 1921–1951, 5277, Kheel Center.

38. Smith, *Women Workers at the Bryn Mawr Summer School*, 38, 93, 129.

39. Ibid., 69.

40. Ibid., 17.

41. O'Farrell and Kornbluh, *Rocking the Boat*, 22.

42. Loretta Gregoire, letter to Lucretia, August 2, 1929, Box 1, Folder 45, WEB Records, 1921–1951, 5277, Kheel Center.

43. Beatrice Kercher, letter, n.d., Box 1, Folder 45, WEB Records, 1921–1951, 5277, Kheel Center.

44. Helen Brooks, letter, n.d. [1929?], Box 1, Folder 45, WEB Records, 1921–1951, 5277, Kheel Center. Bryn Mawr began accepting African American students in 1926.

45. Tessie Frankalangia, "Bryn Mawr," *Spring Magazine of the United Summer Schools for Women Workers in Industry*, 1930, 22. Box 3, ALES Records, 1927–1962, 5225, Kheel Center.

46. Quoted in "The Field of Workers' Education Activities of the Districts," *Spring Magazine of the United Summer Schools for Women Workers in Industry*, 1930, 36–37. Box 3, ALES Records, 1927–1962, 5225, Kheel Center.

47. Smith, *Women Workers at the Bryn Mawr Summer School*, 141.

48. Schaefer, "Educational Activities of the Garment Unions."

49. J. B. Salutsky, "The Labor Education Program and Activities of the Amalgamated Clothing Workers of America," *Workers Education in the United States: Report of Proceedings First National Conference on Workers Education in the United States* (New York: Workers Education Bureau, 1921), 54–55, Box 2, WEB Records, 1921–1951, 5277, Kheel Center.

50. Amalgamated Clothing Workers of America, "A Brief Outline of Activities Contemplated by the Educational Department," [1920?], Amalgamated Clothing and Textile Workers Union Printed Ephemera Collection, Box 4, Folder: National Education Department/Education Department, 1939–1958, n.d., Tamiment Library and Robert F. Wagner Labor Archives.

51. Spencer Miller, Jr., "Our Fifteenth Anniversary," *Workers' Education*, October 1936, 1; "Brief Chronology of the Workers Education Bureau of America," *Workers' Education*, October 1936, 40.

52. Quoted in Adam, *The Worker's Road to Learning*, 16.

53. Schaefer, "Educational Activities of the Garment Unions," 111–12.

54. Adam, *The Worker's Road to Learning*, 20.

55. Schaefer, "Educational Activities of the Garment Unions," 123–24.

56. On the centralization of the AFL and its consequences, see James Oliver Morris, *Conflict Within the AFL: A Study of Craft Versus Industrial Unionism, 1901–1938* (Ithaca, N.Y.: Cornell University Press, 1958); Philip Taft, *The A. F. of L. in the Time of Gompers* (New York: Harper, 1957).

57. "The Organization of a National Workers' Education Bureau," in *Workers Education in the United States*, 112.

58. Algernon Lee, "Methods of Mass Education," in *Workers Education in the United States*, 114.

59. Frank B. Metcalfe, secretary-treasurer of Workers' College of Milwaukee, to Spencer Miller, Box 1, ILGWU Education Department Files, 1920–1979, 5780/166, Kheel Center.

60. Broadus Mitchell, *How To Start Workers' Study Classes: A Primer to Promote Workers' Education*, Workers' Educational Pamphlet Series 1 (New York: Workers Education Bureau, 1922), 15.

61. Spencer Miller, address before the Forty-Third Convention of the AFL, October 3, 1924, at Portland, Oregon, Box 2, WEB Records, 1921–1951, 5277, Kheel Center.

62. Spencer Miller, Jr., "The Promise of Workers Education," *Workers Education Year Book 1924*, 17–29, 23.

63. *Workers Education Year Book 1924*, 34, 65.

64. "We Hope You Will Join," Affiliated School for Workers, n.d.. Quotation is attributed to a student at the Wisconsin Summer School. Printed Ephemera Collection on Organizations, Box 1, Folder: Affiliated Schools for Workers, 1935–1939, Tamiment Library and Robert F. Wagner Labor Archives.

Chapter 4. "The Negro Genius": Black Intellectual Workers
in the Harlem Renaissance

Epigraph: Hubert Harrison, *When Africa Awakes: The "Inside Story" of the Stirrings and Strivings of the New Negro in the Western World* (New York: Porro Press, 1920), 125.

1. Benjamin Brawley, *The Negro Genius: A New Appraisal of the Achievement of the American Negro in Literature and the Fine Arts* (New York: Dodd, Mead, 1937), 9.

2. The important trajectory of uplift ideology in black political and social formations is discussed most fully in Kevin Gaines, *Uplifting the Race: Black Leadership, Politics, and Culture in the Twentieth Century* (Chapel Hill: University of North Carolina Press, 1996).

3. For general studies of history and historiographic criticism of the Harlem Renaissance, see Houston A. Baker, Jr., *Modernism and the Harlem Renaissance* (Chicago: University of Chicago Press, 1987); James De Jongh, *Vicious Modernism: Black Harlem and the Literary Imagination* (Cambridge: Cambridge University Press, 1990), 1–70; Brent Hayes Edwards, *The Practice of Diaspora: Literature, Translation, and the Rise of Black Internationalism* (Cambridge, Mass.: Harvard University Press, 2003); Barbara Foley, *Spectres of 1919: Class and Nation in the Making of the New Negro* (Urbana: University of Illinois Press, 2003); Nathan Irvin Huggins, *Harlem Renaissance* (New York: Oxford University Press, 1971); George Hutchinson, *The Harlem Renaissance in Black and White* (Cambridge, Mass.: Harvard University Press, 1995); David Levering Lewis, *When Harlem Was in Vogue* (New York: Knopf, 1981); William J. Maxwell, *New Negro, Old Left: African-American Writing and Communism Between the Wars* (New York: Columbia University Press, 1999).

4. Brawley, *Negro Genius*, 9.

5. Quoted in Henry Louis Gates, "The Trope of a New Negro and the Reconstruction of the Image of the Black," *Representations* 24 (Autumn 1988), 136.

6. Gail Bederman, *Manliness and Civilization: A Cultural History of Gender and Race in the United States, 1880–1917* (Chicago: University of Chicago Press, 1995).

7. The explicitly political dimensions of Harlem Renaissance cultural production are discussed most fully in Foley, *Spectres of 1919*; Hutchinson, *Harlem Renaissance in Black and White*; Maxwell, *New Negro, Old Left*.

8. On the maleness of the New Negro, see especially Hazel V. Carby, *Race Men* (Cambridge, Mass.: Harvard University Press, 2000).

9. Sexual identities have been conceived by recent scholars as significant to shaping the Harlem Renaissance. See Eric Garber, "A Spectacle in Color: The Lesbian and Gay Subculture of Jazz-Age Harlem," in Martin Duberman, Martha Vicinus, and George Chauncey, eds., *Hidden from History: Reclaiming the Gay and Lesbian Past* (New York: New American Library, 1989), 318–33; Gary Edward Holcomb, *Claude McKay, Code Name Sasha: Queer Black Marxism and the Harlem Renaissance* (Gainesville: University Press of Florida, 2007); Richard Bruce Nugent, *Gay Rebel of the Harlem Renaissance: Selections from the Work of Richard Bruce Nugent*, ed. Thomas H. Wirth (Durham, N.C.: Duke University Press, 2002); A. B. Christa Schwarz, *Gay Voices of the Harlem Renaissance* (Bloomington: Indiana University Press, 2003); Shane Vogel, *The Scene of Harlem Cabaret: Race, Sexuality, Performance* (Chicago: University of Chicago Press, 2009).

10. Gaines, *Uplifting the Race*, 21.

11. Henry Louis Gates, Jr., and Gene Andrew Jarrett, eds., *The New Negro: Readings on Race, Representation, and African American Culture, 1892–1938* (Princeton, N.J.: Princeton University Press, 2007).

12. Booker T. Washington, *Up from Slavery* (New York: Signet Classic, 2000), 142; W. E. B. Du Bois, "The Talented Tenth," in *The Negro Problem: A Series of Articles by Prominent American Negroes of Today*, ed. Booker T. Washington et al. (New York: J. Pott, 1903), 33–75, 33.

13. W. E. B. Du Bois, *The Souls of Black Folk* (Chicago: McClurg, 1903; Modern Library Edition, 1996), 109.

14. W. E. B. Du Bois, "Returning Soldiers," *The Crisis* 18, 1 (May 1919), 14.

15. George S. Schuyler, "The Rise of the Black Internationale," *The Crisis* 45, 8 (August 1938), 277.

16. See Judith Vivian Branzburg, "Women Novelists of the Harlem Renaissance: A Study in Marginality," Ph.D. dissertation, University of Massachusetts, 1983; Gloria T. Hull, *Color, Sex, and Poetry: Three Women Writers of the Harlem Renaissance* (Bloomington: University of Indiana Press, 1987); Sharon L. Jones, *Rereading the Harlem Renaissance: Race, Class, and Gender in the Fiction of Jessie Fauset, Zora Neale Hurston, and Dorothy West* (Westport, Conn.: Greenwood, 2002); Cherene Sherrard-Johnson, *Portraits of the New Negro Woman: Visual and Literary Culture in the Harlem Renaissance* (New Brunswick, N.J.: Rutgers University Press, 2007); Cheryl A. Wall, *Women of the Harlem Renaissance* (Bloomington: University of Indiana Press, 1995).

17. Fannie Barrier Williams, "The Intellectual Progress of the Colored Women of the United States Since the Emancipation Proclamation," in *The World's Congress of Representative Women*, ed. May Wright Sewall (Chicago: Rand, McNally, 1894) 696–711, 700.

18. Horace Mann Bond, "Intelligence Tests and Propaganda," *The Crisis* 28, 2 (June 1924), 61–64, 61.

19. J. A. Rogers, "Who Is the New Negro, and Why?" *Messenger* 9, 3 (March 1927): 93, 68, 93.

20. Harrison, *When Africa Awakes*, 123.

21. See Jeffrey B. Perry, *Hubert Harrison: The Voice of Harlem Radicalism, 1883–1918* (New York: Columbia University Press, 2009).

22. Harrison, *When Africa Awakes*, 123.

23. Ibid., 134, 127.

24. Ibid., 124, 125–26, 125.

25. Ibid., 126–27.

26. Michael David-Fox, *Revolution of the Mind: Higher Learning among the Bolsheviks, 1918–1929* (Ithaca, N.Y.: Cornell University Press, 1997).

27. Harrison, *When Africa Awakes*, 127, 128.

28. Carl Van Vechten, *Nigger Heaven* (New York: Knopf, 1926). See also Leon Coleman, *Carl Van Vechten and the Harlem Renaissance: A Critical Assessment* (New York: Garland, 1998); Justin D. Edwards, "Carl Van Vechten's Sexual Tourism in Jazz Age Harlem," in Jay Bochner and Edwards, *American Modernism Across the Arts* (New York: Peter Lang, 1999), 167–84; Bruce Kellner, *Carl Van Vechten and the Irreverent Decades* (Norman: University of Oklahoma, 1968); Edward G. Lueders, *Carl Van Vechten* (New York: Twayne, 1965); Dorothy Stringer, *"Not Even Past": Race, Historical Trauma, and Subjectivity in Faulkner, Larsen, and Van Vechten* (New York: Fordham University Press, 2010).

29. Quoted in Maxwell, *New Negro, Old Left*, 56. This form of "inspectin'" was especially significant at a moment when the Chicago School was informing sociological studies of black life. Martin Bulmer, *The Chicago School of Sociology: Institutionalization, Diversity, and the Rise of Sociological Research* (Chicago: University of Chicago Press, 1984).

30. Alain Locke, *The New Negro* (New York: Albert and Charles Boni, 1925), 9.

31. Claude McKay, *Home to Harlem* (New York: Harper & Bros., 1928); Wallace Thurman, *Infants of the Spring* (New York: Macaulay, 1932); Richard Wright, "Blueprint for Negro Writing," *New Challenge* 2, 2 (Fall 1937): 53–65. On slumming literature see Chad Heap, *Slumming: Sexual and Racial Encounters in American Nightlife, 1885–1940* (Chicago: University of Chicago Press, 2009); Scott Herring, *Queering the Underworld: Slumming, Literature, and the Undoing of Lesbian and Gay History* (Chicago: University of Chicago Press, 2007).

32. W. E. B. Du Bois, "Books," *The Crisis* 33, 2 (December 1926), 81.

33. Lewis, *When Harlem Was in Vogue*, 181.

34. "The Negro in Art; How Shall He Be Portrayed; A Symposium," *The Crisis* 31, 5 (March 1926): 219–220, 219.

35. DuBose Heyward, *Porgy* (New York: George H. Doran, 1925).

36. Lewis, *When Harlem Was in Vogue*, 157–58.

37. "The Negro in Art: How Shall He Be Portrayed; A Symposium," *The Crisis* 32, 1 (May 1926): 35–36, 35.

38. "The Negro in Art," *The Crisis* (March 1926): 220.

39. Ibid.

40. "The Negro in Art: How Shall He Be Portrayed; A Symposium," *The Crisis* 31, 6 (April 1926): 278–80, 278. 279.

41. "The Negro in Art: How Shall He Be Portrayed; A Symposium," *The Crisis* 32, 2 (June 1926), 72.

42. Louis Fremont Baldwin, *From Negro to Caucasian, Or How the Ethiopian Is Changing His Skin* (San Francisco: Pilot, 1929); *Passing*, 116. On Passing see Steven J. Belluscio, *To Be Suddenly White: Literary Realism and Racial Passing* (Columbia: University of Missouri Press, 2006); Juda Bennett, *The Passing Figure: Racial Confusion in Modern American Literature* (New York: Peter Lang, 1996); M. Giulia Fabi, *Passing and the Rise of the African American Novel* (Urbana: University of Illinois Press, 2001);

Elaine K. Ginsberg, ed., *Passing and the Fictions of Identity* (Durham, N.C.: Duke University Press, 1996); Lori Harrison-Kahan, *The White Negress: Literature, Minstrelsy, and the Black-Jewish Imaginary* (New Brunswick, N.J.: Rutgers University Press, 2011); Kathleen Pfeiffer, *Race Passing and American Individualism* (Amherst: University of Massachusetts Press, 2003); Gayle Wald, *Crossing the Line: Racial Passing in Twentieth-Century U.S. Literature and Culture* (Durham, N.C.: Duke University Press, 2000).

43. Jessie Redmon Fauset, *Plum Bun: A Novel Without a Moral* (New York: Stokes, 1928; Boston: Beacon Press, 1990), 48.

44. Ibid., 13.

45. France, ironically, was also invoked during this period as a space for encountering both intellectual cultures and black diasporic identities. Edwards, *The Practice of Diaspora.*

46. Fauset, *Plum Bun*, 37.

47. Ibid., 106, 274, 211, 114, 209.

48. Ibid., 133, 209.

49. Thurman, *Infants of the Spring*, 36, 35.

50. Locke, *The New Negro*, 7, 8, 9–10, 13.

51. Deborah E. McDowell, introduction to Fauset, *Plum Bun*, xxvi.

52. On intimacy in Harlem Renaissance literature, see especially Vogel, *The Scene of Harlem Cabaret.*

53. W. E. B. Du Bois, "The Browsing Reader: Two Novels," *The Crisis* 35, 2 (June 1928): 202.

54. Vogel, *The Scene of Harlem Cabaret*, 132–66.

55. Michael B. Stoff, "Claude McKay and the Cult of Primitivism," in *The Harlem Renaissance Remembered: Essays Edited with a Memoir*, ed. Arna Bontemps (New York: Dodd, Mead, 1972) 126–46, 126.

56. McKay, *Home to Harlem*, 1.

57. McKay's communism is discussed at length in Holcomb, *Claude McKay*; Maxwell, *New Negro, Old Left*; and James Edward Smethurst, *The New Red Negro: The Literary Left and African American Poetry, 1930–1946* (New York: Oxford University Press, 1999).

58. McKay, *Home to Harlem*, 32, 130.

59. Ibid., 133.

60. Wayne Cooper, *Claude McKay: Rebel Sojourner of the Harlem Renaissance* (Baton Rouge: Louisiana State University Press, 1987), 235.

61. McKay, *Home to Harlem*, 164.

62. Ibid., 139, 155, 157.

Chapter 5. "We Have Only Words Against": Brainworkers and Books in the 1930s

Epigraph: Thomas H. Beck, William L. Chery, and Charles Colebaugh, "Trust Brains," *Collier's*, May 19, 1934, 66.

1. David M. Kennedy, *Freedom from Fear: The American People in Depression and War, 1929–1945* (New York: Oxford University Press, 1999); Richard Lowitt and Maurine Beasley, eds., *One Third of a Nation: Lorena Hickok Reports on the Great Depression* (Urbana: University of Illinois Press, 1981); William E. Leuchtenburg, *Franklin D. Roosevelt and the New Deal* (New York: Harper & Row, 1963).

2. Max Ascoli, *Intelligence in Politics* (New York: Norton, 1936); Paul William Ward, *Intelligence in Politics: An Approach to Social Problems* (Chapel Hill: University of North Carolina Press, 1931).

3. Michael Denning, *The Cultural Front: The Laboring of American Culture in the Twentieth Century* (New York: Verso, 1996); Lawrence W. Levine and Cornelia R. Levine, *The People and the President: America's Conversation with FDR* (Boston: Beacon Press, 2002); Bill Mullen and Sherry Linkon, eds., *Radical Revisions: Rereading 1930s Culture* (Urbana: University of Illinois Press, 1996); Hugh Wilford, *The New York Intellectuals: From Vanguard to Institution* (New York: Manchester University Press, 1995)

4. Ascoli, *Intelligence in Politics*, 14.

5. John Dos Passos, *The Big Money*, 525. References to *U.S.A.* are to the single-volume edition. However, since each novel is paginated separately, I will cite the title and page of the novel. John Dos Passos, *U.S.A.* (New York: Modern Library, 1937).

6. The relationship between language, politics, and American identity had been discussed by H. L. Mencken in *The American Language: A Preliminary Inquiry into the Development of English in the United States* (New York: Knopf, 1919).

7. Rexford G. Tugwell, *The Brains Trust* (New York: Viking, 1968); Samuel I. Rosenman, *Working with Roosevelt* (New York: Harper, 1952); Elliot A. Rosen, *Hoover, Roosevelt, and the Brains Trust: From Depression to New Deal* (New York: Columbia University Press, 1977).

8. In part, this perception of Communism was due to the CPUSA's adopting of a Popular Front strategy cooperation with New Deal reform efforts. On the centrality of the Communist Party in 1930s radicalism, see Fraser M. Ottanelli, *The Communist Party of the United States: From the Depression to World War II* (New Brunswick, N.J.: Rutgers University Press, 1991). On the specific contours of the party during the Depression, see also Michael Brown et al., eds., *New Studies in the Politics and Culture of U.S. Communism* (New York: Monthly Review Press, 1993); Albert Fried, *Communism in America: A History in Documents* (New York: Columbia University Press, 1997); Andrew Hemingway, *Artists on the Left: American Artists and the Communist Movement, 1926–1956* (New Haven, Conn.: Yale University Press, 2002); Robin D. G. Kelley, *Hammer and Hoe: Alabama Communists During the Great Depression* (Chapel Hill: University of North Carolina Press, 1990). Earlier, during the so-called "Third Period" spanning 1929–1935, the CPUSA adopted their Black Belt thesis that stated black women and men living in those regions of the South where they were denied voting rights constituted an oppressed nation. In response to this sort of call to action, African Americans such as Paul Robeson adopted a new position as cultural ambas-

sadors, positioning themselves as members of their race who transcended cultural lines and reinstated a democratic discourse into a racial dialogue that had historically quieted black voices. See Gerald Horne, "The Red and the Black: The Communist Party and African-Americans in Historical Perspective," in Brown et al., *New Studies*, 199–238; Mark Naison, *Communists in Harlem During the Depression* (Urbana: University of Illinois Press, 1983). On women in radical politics during this period, see Rosalyn Baxandall, "The Question Seldom Asked: Women and the CPUSA," in Brown et al., *New Studies*, 141–62; Constance Coiner, *Better Red: The Writing and Resistance of Tillie Olsen and Meridel Le Sueur* (New York: Oxford University Press, 1995); Denning, *Cultural Front*, 295–309.

9. Leuchtenberg, *Franklin D. Roosevelt*, 41–42.

10. "Brain Trusts for Literature," *The Saturday Review of Literature*, December 2, 1933, 304.

11. Kennedy, *Freedom from Fear*, 124; Leuchtenberg, *Franklin D. Roosevelt*, 32–33.

12. Ascoli, *Intelligence in Politics*, vii.

13. Tugwell, *The Brains Trust*, 3–11.

14. James Kieran, "Baruch Acclaims Roosevelt as Sound," *New York Times*, September 6, 1932.

15. James Kieran, "Farley to Go West with Roosevelt," *New York Times*, September 9, 1932.

16. Rosenman, *Working with Roosevelt*, 58.

17. See Tugwell, *The Brains Trust*, 3–11.

18. It is a supreme irony, then, that the brain trust was itself quite concerned with antitrustism. See Alonzo L. Hamby, *For the Survival of Democracy: Franklin Roosevelt and the World Crisis of the 1930s* (New York: Free Press, 2004), 357–58.

19. Sean Dennis Cashman, *America in the Age of Titans: The Progressive Era and World War I* (New York: New York University Press, 1988), 6–44; George Evans, Jr., *Business Incorporations in the United States, 1800–1943* (New York: National Bureau of Economic Research, 1948); James Weinstein, *The Corporate Ideal in the Liberal State, 1900–1918* (Boston: Beacon Press, 1968).

20. "The Hullabaloo over the 'Brain Trust,'" *Literary Digest*, June 3, 1933, 8.

21. Quoted in ibid.

22. Albert W. Atwood, "Government by Professors," *Saturday Evening Post*, October 14, 1933, 88.

23. Carl Dolmetsch, *The Smart Set: A History and Anthology* (New York: Dial Press, 1966). See also Catherine Keyser, *Playing Smart: New York Women Writers and Modern Magazine Culture* (New Brunswick, N.J.: Rutgers University Press, 2010).

24. Advertisement for Mennen Brushless Shave, *Saturday Evening Post*, October 14, 1933, 91.

25. Advertisement for De Soto, *The Saturday Evening Post,* January 7, 1933, 40.

26. Beck, Chery, and Colebaugh, "Trust Brains," 66.

27. Quoted in "The 'Left Wing,'" *New York Times*, May 7, 1933.

28. Arthur Krock, "'Brain Trust's' Visions Astound the French," *New York Times*, April 27, 1933.

29. Daniel T. Rodgers, *Atlantic Crossings: Social Politics in a Progressive Age* (Cambridge, Mass.: Belknap Press of Harvard University Press, 1998).

30. "'Plot': A Brain Trustee Talked; Dr. Wirt Writes a Letter About Communism and Revolution," *Newsweek*, March 31, 1934, 8.

31. Regin Schmidt, *Red Scare: FBI and the Origins of Anti-Communism in the United States, 1919–1943* (Copenhagen: Museum Tusculanum Press, University of Copenhagen, 2000), 324–60.

32. Wirt's plan, otherwise known as the "work-study-play" system, was roundly critized in a 1912 article by John Franklin Bobbitt from *Elementary School Teacher* as essentially indoctrinating children into modern business practice. The system fell out of favor by 1920. Given his sympathy to the managerial revolution, it is unsurprising that Wirt would take exception to the popularity of the brain trust. Ellwood P. Cubberley, *Public Education in the United States: A Study and Interpretation of American Educational History* (1919; Boston: Houghton Mifflin, 1962), 530–32; John Taylor Gatto, *The Underground History of American Education: An Intimate Investigation into the Prison of Modern Schooling* (New York: Oxford Village Press, 2000), 187–88.

33. "'Plot,'" *Newsweek*, 8.

34. Griffin Fariello, *Red Scare: Memories of the American Inquisition; An Oral History* (New York: Norton, 1995); Joel Kovel, *Red Hunting in the Promised Land: Anticommunism and the Making of America* (New York: Basic Books, 1994); Murray B. Levin, *Political Hysteria in America: The Democratic Capacity for Repression* (New York: Basic Books, 1971); Robert K. Murray, *Red Scare: A Study of National Hysteria, 1919–1920* (Minneapolis: University of Minnesota Press, 1955); Regin Schmidt, *Red Scare.*

35. "Dr. Wirt's 'Exposure' of the Brain Trust," *Literary Digest*, April 7, 1934, 10.

36. Oswald Garrison Villard, "The Communistic Brain Trust," *Nation*, April 4, 1934, 377.

37. "The Brain Trust," *New Republic*, June 7, 1933, 85.

38. Ibid., 86.

39. Producerism as a major theme in American representations is an important topic in Erika Doss, *Benton, Pollock, and the Politics of Modernism: From Regionalism to Abstract Expressionism* (Chicago: University of Chicago Press, 1991). See also Steven J. Ross, *Workers on the Edge: Work, Leisure, and Politics in Industrializing Cincinnati, 1788–1890* (New York: Columbia University Press, 1985), 3.

40. Melissa Dabakis, *Visualizing Labor in American Sculpture: Monuments, Manliness, and the Work Ethic, 1880–1935* (Cambridge: Cambridge University Press, 1999); Erika Doss, "Toward an Iconography of American Labor: Work, Workers, and the Work Ethic in American Art, 1930–1945," *Design Issues* 13, 1 (Spring 1997): 53–66; Erika Doss, "Looking at Labor: Images of Work in 1930s America," *Journal of Decorative and Propaganda Arts* 24 (Spring 2002): 198–229; Michael Kimmel, *Manhood in*

America: A Cultural History (New York: Free Press, 1996); Barbara Melosh, *Engendering Culture: Manhood and Womanhood in New Deal Public Art and Culture* (Washington, D.C.: Smithsonian Institute Press, 1991), 83–109; Jonathan Weinberg, *Male Desire: The Homoerotic in American Art* (New York: Abrams, 2004), 58–81.

41. The signature moment in this alliance appeared with the signing of the pamphlet, *Culture and the Crisis*, by the League of Professional Groups for Foster and Ford. This document laid out a program for revolutionary cultural production. Daniel Aaron has remarked on the significance of this document that "if the picture of cultural dissolution conjured up by the pamphlet was hardly novel in 1932, the fact that fifty-three writers and artists, many of them well known, were prepared to renounce their bourgeois allegiances, to affiliate as 'brain workers' with the only other class they deemed worthy of respect—'the muscle workers'—this was indeed unprecedented in American history." Daniel Aaron, *Writers on the Left: Episodes in American Literary Communism* (New York: Harcourt Brace, 1961), 197; League of Professional Groups for Foster and Ford, *Culture and the Crisis: An Open Letter to the Writers, Artists, Teachers, Physicians, Engineers, Scientists, and Other Professional Workers of America* (New York: Workers Library Publishers, 1932). See also Denning, *Cultural Front*, 423–25.

42. "Brain Workers Need Little Food," *Literary Digest*, October 4, 1930, 18.

43. "Brain-Fag, Body-Fag," *Commonweal*, May 12, 1933, 32–33.

44. On workers as citizens, see Lizabeth Cohen, *Making a New Deal: Industrial Workers in Chicago, 1919–1939* (New York: Cambridge University Press, 1990); Gary Gerstle, *Working-Class Americanism: The Politics of Labor in a Textile City, 1914–1960* (New York: Cambridge University Press, 1989).

45. George Bodoni, "Shaving and Brain Activity," *New Masses*, March 24, 1936, 20.

46. Bruce Barton, *The Man Nobody Knows: A Discovery of Jesus* (Indianapolis: Bobbs-Merrill, 1925).

47. Gerald Weales, "Popular Theatre of the Thirties," *Tulane Drama Review* 11 (Summer 1967): 51–69, 52.

48. Harold Rome, music and lyrics, *Pins and Needles* (1937).

49. On public libraries as sites of civic engagement, see Sidney H. Ditzion, *Arsenals of a Democratic Culture* (New York: American Library Association, 1947); Michael Harris, ed., *Reader in American Library History* (Washington, D.C.: National Cash Register Company, 1971); Carleton B. Joeckel, *The Government of the American Public Library* (Chicago: University of Chicago Press, 1935); C. Seymour Thompson, *Evolution of the American Public Library, 1653–1876* (Washington, D.C.: Scarecrow Press, 1952).

50. Joyce L. Kornbluh, *A New Deal for Workers' Education: The Workers' Service Program, 1933–1942* (Urbana: University of Illinois Press, 1987).

51. Gary Gerstle defines civic nationalism as the idea that "the United States was a divine land where individuals from every part of the world could leave their troubles,

start life anew, and forge a proud, accomplished, and unified people." Promoting brainpower in the 1930s often promoted civic nationalism. Gary Gerstle, *American Crucible: Race and Nation in the Twentieth Century* (Princeton, N.J.: Princeton University Press, 2001), 3.

52. Francis V. O'Connor, ed., *Art for the Millions: Essays from the 1930s by Artists and Administration of the Works Progress Administration Federal Art Project* (Greenwich, Conn.: New York Graphic Society, 1973); Jonathan Harris, *Federal Art and National Culture: The Politics of Identity in New Deal America* (New York: Cambridge University Press, 1995).

53. Ennis Carter, *Posters for the People: Art of the WPA* (Philadelphia: Quirk Books, 2008); Christopher DeNoon, *Posters of the WPA* (Los Angeles: Wheatley Press, 1987).

54. On Orozco, see Laurance P. Hurlburt, *The Mexican Muralists in the United States* (Albuquerque: University of New Mexico Press, 1989); Alma Reed, *Orozco* (New York: Oxford University Press, 1956); Desmond Rochfort, *Mexican Muralists: Orozco, Rivera, Siqueiros* (London: L. King, 1993), 83–120. An early version of evolutionary depictions mapping the ascent from ape to human had appeared in a crude form in 1863, but such depictions had become streamlined and were widely circulated in the 1920s. Evolutionary charts were firmly implanted in American popular culture by the time the FAP poster appeared. See Constance Areson Clark, "Evolution for John Doe: Pictures, the Public, and the Scopes Trial Debate," *Journal of American History* 87, 4 (March 2001): 1275–1303.

55. John S. Brubacher and Willis Rudy, *Higher Education in Transition: A History of American Colleges and Universities, 1636–1956* (New York: Harper, 1956); Colin B. Burke, *American Collegiate Populations: A Test of the Traditional View* (New York: New York University Press, 1982); David O. Levine, *The American College and the Culture of Aspiration, 1915–1940* (Ithaca, N.Y.: Cornell University Press, 1986).

56. Daniel Rodgers, *Atlantic Crossings*. See also Elizabeth Borgwardt, *A New Deal for the World: America's Vision for Human Rights* (Cambridge, Mass.: Belknap Press of Harvard University Press, 2005); James Kloppenberg, *Uncertain Victory: Social Democracy and Progressivism in European and American Thought 1870–1920* (New York: Oxford University Press, 1986); Peter Flora and Arnold J. Heidenheimer, eds., *The Development of Welfare States in Europe and America* (New Brunswick, N.J.: Transaction, 1981).

57. On constructivism, see Natalia L. Adaskina, "Constructivist Fabrics and Dress Design," *Journal of Decorative and Propaganda Arts* 5 (Summer 1987): 144–59; Christina Kiaer, *Imagine No Possessions: The Socialist Objects of Russian Constructivism* (Cambridge, Mass.: MIT Press, 2005); Christina Lodder, *Russian Constructivism* (New Haven, Conn.: Yale University Press, 1983).

58. Alan Dawley, *Changing the World: American Progressives in War and Revolution* (Princeton, N.J.: Princeton University Press, 2003); Ian Tyrrell, *Woman's World/ Woman's Empire: The Women's Christian Temperance Union in International Perspective, 1880–1930* (Chapel Hill: University of North Carolina Press, 1991); Leila Rupp,

Worlds of Women: The Making of an International Women's Movement (Princeton, N.J.: Princeton University Press, 1997).

59. Rodin's sculpture was commissioned by the French government in 1880. Various versions were produced between 1880 and Rodin's death in 1917. The homoerotic virility of the work was widely discussed during this time. A 1907 book noted that "the muscularity of the man is intruded on the notice, causing the profane to scoff and to query why a thinker needs such brawn." The WPA poster's invocation of the debates about brains and bodies engendered through the stature of the sculpture could not have been mere coincidence: Frederick Lawton, *The Life and Work of Auguste Rodin* (New York: Scribner's, 1907), 108. See also Jacques de Caso and Patricia B. Sanders, *Rodin's Sculpture: A Critical Study of the Spreckels Collection* (San Francisco: Fine Arts Museums of San Francisco, 1977), 130–38; Albert Elsen, *Rodin* (New York: The Museum of Modern Art, 1963); Albert Elsen, *Rodin's* Thinker *and the Dilemmas of Modern Public Sculpture* (New Haven, Conn.: Yale University Press, 1985).

60. Robin D. G. Kelley, *Race Rebels: Culture, Politics, and the Black Working Class* (New York: Free Press, 1994), 103–28; Bill V. Mullen, *Popular Fronts: Chicago and African American Cultural Politics* (Urbana: University of Illinois Press, 1999); William J. Maxwell, *New Negro, Old Left: African-American Writing and Communism Between the Wars* (New York: Columbia University Press, 1999).

61. Hemingway, *Artists on the Left*, 64–65.

62. The relationship between Popular Front ideology and racial identity is a major concern in Michael Denning's *Cultural Front*. See especially 323–61.

63. This bears strong resonances of the World War II Double V campaign. Beth T. Bates, "'Double V for Victory' Mobilizes Black Detroit, 1941–1946," in *Freedom North: Black Freedom Struggles Outside the South, 1940–1980*, ed. Jeanne Theoharis and Komozi Woodward, with Matthew Woodward (New York: Palgrave Macmillan, 2003), 17–39.

64. On connections between military enlistment and citizenship, see Christopher Capozzola, *Uncle Sam Wants You: World War I and the Making of the Modern American Citizen* (New York: Oxford University Press, 2008); Cecilia Elizabeth O'Leary, *To Die For: The Paradox of American Patriotism* (Princeton, N.J.: Princeton University Press, 1999).

65. The Schomburg Center for Research in Black Culture originally opened in Harlem as the "Negro Division" of the New York Public Library in 1925. Beginning with a major donation in the following year, the Center became a major repository for materials relating to black life and culture. Kwame Anthony Appiah and Henry Louis Gates, Jr., eds., *Africana: The Encyclopedia of the African and African American Experience* (New York: Oxford University Press, 2005), s.v. "Schomburg Center for Research in Black Culture."

66. This was the essence of what Du Bois advocated in his work related to education, especially the essays collected in W. E. B. Du Bois, *The Education of Black People: Ten*

Critiques, 1906–1960, ed. Herbert Aptheker (Amherst: University of Massachusetts Press, 1973).

67. See Mark Seltzer, *Bodies and Machines* (New York: Routledge, 1992); Terry Smith, *Making the Modern: Industry, Art, and Design in America* (Chicago: University of Chicago Press, 1993); Cecelia Tichi, *Shifting Gears: Technology, Literature, and Culture in Modernist America* (Chapel Hill: University of North Carolina Press, 1987).

68. On the anxiety produced by modernization and technology in industry, see Martha Banta, *Taylorized Lives: Narrative Productions in the Age of Taylor, Veblen, and Ford* (Chicago: University of Chicago Press, 1993).

69. *Modern Times,* directed by Charles Chaplin (Warner Brothers: 1936).

70. These representations paralleled the depictions of working-class bohemian intellectuals described in Hutchins Hapgood, *The Spirit of Labor* (New York: Duffield, 1907).

71. Ernest Hemingway, *The Sun Also Rises* (1926; New York: Scribners, 1954), 17.

72. Ann Douglas has discussed how Hemingway and his contemporaries used blunt language to articulate the alienation of modern life. Ann Douglas, *Terrible Honesty: Mongrel Manhattan in the 1920s* (New York: Farrar, Straus, 1995).

73. James T. Farrell, "A Note on Contemporary Letters," *Earth,* February 1931, 2–5, 4.

74. On the politics of tough language in the radical tradition, see Rachel Rubin, *Jewish Gangsters of Modern Literature* (Urbana: University of Illinois Press, 2000); Alan M. Wald, *Trinity of Passion: The Literary Left and the Antifascist Crusade* (Chapel Hill: University of North Carolina Press, 2007), 16–45.

75. Denning uses the phrase "the cultural front" to describe the leftist politics of cultural production in the 1930s and 1940s. See Denning, *The Cultural Front.* The political culture that developed in the 1930s is also discussed in important works including James Burkhart Gilbert, *Writers and Partisans: A History of Literary Radicalism in America* (New York: Wiley, 1968); Richard H. Pells, *Radical Visions and American Dreams: Culture and Social Thought in the Depression Years* (New York: Harper & Row, 1973); Warren Susman, *Culture as History: The Transformation of American Society in the Twentieth Century* (New York: Pantheon, 1984). For a particularly negative assessment of this period, none approaches the vitriol of Robert Warshow, "The Legacy of the 30s: Middle Class Culture and the Intellectual's Problem," *Commentary* 4 (December 1947).

76. Ernest Hemingway, *For Whom the Bell Tolls* (New York: Scribner, 1940).

77. On intellectual culture on the left, see Judy Kutulas, *The Long War: The Intellectual People's Front and Anti-Stalinism, 1930–1940* (Durham, N.C.: Duke University Press, 1995).

78. Jack Conroy, *The Disinherited* (1933; New York: Hill and Wang, 1963); Dos Passos, *U.S.A.*; Edmund Wilson, *To the Finland Station: A Study in the Writing and Acting of History* (New York: Farrar, Straus, 1932).

79. Fielding Burke, *Call Home the Heart: A Novel of the Thirties* (1932; Old Westbury, N.Y.: Feminist Press, 1983), 308. Citations are to the Feminist Press edition.

80. Robert Cantwell, *Land of Plenty* (1934; Carbondale: Southern Illinois University Press, 1971), 3, 8, 13.

81. Ibid., 14, 15.

82. The *Menorah Journal* was a Jewish monthly created in 1906 by Henry Hurwitz as a mouthpiece for the Menorah Society, a Jewish group that began in 1906 at Harvard University. The journal was radicalized around 1923 and remained a prominent organ of left-wing—often Trotskyist, or anti-Stalinist—thought until 1931, during which years the editors and sponsors moved in and out of membership in the Communist Party. The magazine's contributors during these years comprised a veritable *Who's Who* of leftist intellectuals and renegades in the 1930s: the poet Kenneth Fearing, the artist Louis Lozowick, novelist and essayist Michael Gold, all with Elliot Cohen at the helm. As was common in the period of intensive leftist political activities, the contributors to the journal were largely sympathetic to the goals and ideology of the CPUSA, but their political sympathies were often more closely allied with the anti-Stalinist left. Alan M. Wald, *The New York Intellectuals: The Rise and Decline of the Anti-Stalinist Left from the 1930s to the 1980s* (Chapel Hill: University of North Carolina Press, 1987), 27–50.

83. Paula Rabinowitz, *Labor and Desire: Women's Revolutionary Fiction in Depression America* (Chapel Hill: University of North Carolina Press, 1991), 138, 139.

84. Tess Slesinger, *The Unpossessed* (New York: Simon and Schuster, 1934; New York: New York Review Books, 2002), 28. Citations are to the New York Review Books edition unless otherwise noted.

85. Ibid., 61.

86. Slesinger, *The Unpossessed*, 194; 74.

87. Jonathan Ned Katz, *Gay/Lesbian Almanac* (New York: Carroll and Graf, 1983), 575.

88. H. T. Tsiang, *The Hanging on Union Square* (New York: Tsiang, 1935), 73, 78.

89. Ibid.

90. On working-class identity and homosexuality, see Peter Boag, *Same-Sex Affairs: Constructing and Controlling Homosexuality in the Pacific Northwest* (Berkeley: University of California Press, 2003); George Chauncey, *Gay New York: Gender, Urban Culture, and the Making of the Gay Male World, 1890–1940* (New York: Basic Books, 1994); Elizabeth Lapovsky Kennedy and Madeline D. Davis, *Boots of Leather, Slippers of Gold: The History of a Lesbian Community* (New York: Routledge, 1993).

91. Max Eastman, *Venture* (New York: A. & C. Boni, 1927), 1.

92. Slesinger, *The Unpossessed*, 301.

93. Tsiang, *Hanging*, 32.

94. Richard Wright, *Native Son* (New York: Harper & Bros., 1940).

95. Richard Wright, "How 'Bigger' Was Born," reprinted in *Twentieth-Century Interpretations of Native Son: A Collection of Critical Essays*, ed. Houston A. Baker, Jr. (Englewood Cliffs, N.J.: Prentice-Hall, 1972), 21–47, 30.

96. Ibid., 34.

97. Irving Howe, "Black Boys and Native Sons," in Baker, *Twentieth-Century Interpretations*, 63–70, 64.

98. For general criticism on *Native Son*, see Robert A. Bone, *The Negro Novel in America* (New Haven, Conn.: Yale University Press, 1958), 140–52; Graham Clarke, "Beyond Realism: Recent Black Fiction and the Language of 'The Real Thing,'" *Black American Literature Forum* 16, 1 (1982): 43–48, 43; Joyce Ann Joyce, *Richard Wright's Art of Tragedy* (Iowa City: University of Iowa Press, 1986), 103–4; Dorothy S. Redden, "Richard Wright and *Native Son*: Not Guilty," in *Bigger Thomas*, ed. Harold Bloom (New York: Chelsea House, 1990), 73–82, 75–76; Laura E. Tanner, "The Narrative Presence in *Native Son*," in Bloom, ed., *Bigger Thomas*, 127–42, 138–39.

99. Edward Margolies, *Native Sons* (Philadelphia: Lippincott, 1968), 80; Richard Sullivan, afterword to 1961 edition of *Native Son* (New York: Signet), 396.

100. Judith Giblin Brazinsky, "The Demands of Conscience and the Imperatives of Form: The Dramatization of *Native Son*," *Black American Literature Forum* 18, 3 (1984): 106–9, 107; John M. Reilly, "Giving Bigger a Voice: The Politics of Narrative in *Native Son*," in Kenneth Kinnamon, ed., *New Essays on Native Son*, 35–62 (New York: Cambridge University Press, 1990), 58–60; Paul N. Siegel, "The Conclusion of Richard Wright's *Native Son*," *PMLA* 79 (1974): 517–23.

101. Reilly, "Giving Bigger a Voice," 60.

102. Barbara Foley, *Radical Representations: Politics and Form in U.S. Proletarian Fiction, 1929–1941* (Durham, N.C.: Duke University Press, 1993), 321. Foley describes the basic structure of such novels: "In texts of this genre, naïve protagonists, usually young, encounter various trials that enable them to test their mettle. They undergo apprenticeships in the lessons of life and emerge older and wiser. Their careers serve the functions of synecdochic commentary, for they are 'types' representing broader lineaments of their time and place. Yet bildungsroman heroes are usually set apart from their peers by a number of distinctive traits—looks, intelligence, ambition. They are at once ordinary and extraordinary" (321). The irony of the proletarian bildungsroman is that the genre was generally representative of "the classic form of the bourgeois novel" (321). In relying on such a bourgeois model, radical authors confronted the tension at the center of their ideology: they needed to offer a vision of a revolutionary working class who has resolved the dialectic of theory and practice and become aware of itself as a class, yet this needed to happen outside bourgeois institutions. The radical novel thus had to resolve both the content and the form of the bildungsroman. By both using and disrupting the expectations of the bildungsroman, radical writers could imagine a cultural context in which self-exploration was inextricable from a rising political consciousness. The proletarian intellectual was an ideal character for exploring such a contradictory impulse: she or he was both of the people and outside the masses.

103. The form of *U.S.A.* challenged the bourgeois structure of the novel by situating the reader as a worker. In April, 1936, *Esquire* published an excerpt from the

"Camera Eye" sections of *U.S.A.* Though *Esquire* had published Dos Passos in many previous issues, this particular instance was unusual in that it began with an editor's note explaining how to read this work of "semi-fiction." To start, the note instructed, "do not insist upon making consecutive sense of every phrase and sentence as you go along. The effect is as cumulative as that of music or painting. Second, remember that this is the verbal equivalent of the inclusive technique of photography, registering apparently irrelevant and even distracting detail for the sake of achieving a complete atmospheric approximation of reality." Editor's Note, John Dos Passos, "The Camera Eye," *Esquire*, April, 1936, 51. These instructions for reading the piece are instructive for a number of reasons. First, they attempt to relate the prose structure of Dos Passos to innovation in other media: painting, photography, and music. Though this appeal to modernism offers insight into the motivations of the editors, it was unlikely to wash with readers, since formal challenges in music and visual art had not themselves been wholly embraced, even by the 1930s. Additionally, the appeal to modernism in painting hardly works in relation to the social realist impulses of Dos Passos, since the modernism in painting had moved away from representation and into abstraction, a movement reversed in radical literature. Lastly, the comparison with photography might have been seen as quite opposite to the comparison with modern painting. Even as the instructions attempted to underscore the "artiness" of Dos Passos's prose, the photographer might be seen as more a technician, and in the 1930s photography was often confused with a documentary impulse. By extension, the reader must adopt the gaze of the photographer, becoming, in effect, the technician/writer. In other words, the instructions were less useful for understanding the article and more for positioning readers themselves as proletarian cognoscenti.

104. On the formal innovations of Dos Passos, see Jean-Paul Sartre, *Literary Essays* (New York: Philosophical Library, 1957), 88–96.

105. Dos Passos, *The 42nd Parallel*, 297, 82.

106. Dos Passos, *The Big Money*, 93.

107. Dos Passos, *1919*, 12,16.

108. Dos Passos, *The 42nd Parallel*, 301–2.

109. Dos Passos, *The Big Money*, 436.

110. Dos Passos, *The 42nd Parallel*, 62, 139, 175, 213.

Chapter 6. Dangerous Minds: Spectacles of Science in the Postwar Atomic City

Epigraph: Daniel Lang, "The Atomic City," *New Yorker*, September 29, 1945, 48.

1. Jay Walz, "Atom Bombs Made in Three Hidden 'Cities,'" *New York Times*, August 7, 1945.

2. On atomic culture in the U.S., see Paul Boyer, *By the Bomb's Early Light: American Thought and Culture at the Dawn of the Atomic Age* (Chapel Hill: University of North Carolina Press, 1985); Morton Grodzins, Eugene Rabinowtch, eds., *The Atomic*

Age: Scientists in National and World Affairs; Articles from the Bulletin of the Atomic Scientists 1945-1962 (New York: Basic Books, 1963); Margot A. Henriksen, *Dr. Strangelove's America: Society and Culture in the Atomic Age* (Berkeley: University of California Press, 1997).

3. On the relationship between postwar citizenship and family, see Judith E. Smith, *Visions of Belonging: Family Stories, Popular Culture, and Postwar Democracy, 1940-1960* (New York: Columbia University Press, 2004).

4. *Handbook on Education and the War* (Washington, D.C.: Government Printing Office, 1943), xiii, xv.

5. *Our Country's Call to Serve: Education and National Defense Series, Pamphlet No. 1* (Washington, D.C.: Government Printing Office, 1941), 3.

6. *Our Country's Call*, 17.

7. *What the Schools Can Do: Education and National Defense Series, Pamphlet No. 4* (Washington, D.C.: Government Printing Office, 1942), 1.

8. See, for example, Robin Kelley, *Race Rebels: Culture, Politics, and the Black Working Class* (New York: Free Press, 1994) 161–81; David M. Kennedy, *Freedom from Fear: The American People in Depression and War, 1929-1945* (New York: Oxford University Press, 1999), 746–97; Shane White and Graham White, *Stylin': African American Expressive Culture from Its Beginnings to the Zoot Suit* (Ithaca, N.Y.: Cornell University Press, 1998).

9. *Our Country's Call*, 19.

10. *Practicing Democracy in the College: Education and National Defense Series, Pamphlet 8* (Washington, D.C.: Government Printing Office, 1942), 25.

11. Edgar J. Fisher, "International Education in Wartime," *South Atlantic Bulletin* 8, 1 (April 1942): 1, 7–8. Dugan's organization was primarily concerned with promoting student exchange programs. It is noteworthy that the program brought only 35 students from Latin America to the United States in the 1938–1939 school year; by 1941–1942, that number had risen to 220, largely due to the contributions of the U.S. Division of Cultural Relations of the Department of State (7).

12. Rachel Davis-Du Bois, "Peace and Intercultural Education," *Journal of the Sociology of Education* 12, 7 (March 1939): 418–24.

13. Daniel A. Clark, "'The Two Joes Meet, Joe College, Joe Veteran': The G.I. Bill, College Education, and Postwar American Culture," *History of Education Quarterly* 38, 2 (Summer 1998): 165–89; Keith Olson, "The G.I. Bill and Higher Education: Success and Surprise," *American Quarterly* 25, 5 (December 1973): 596–610. On African Americans and higher education, see Hilary Herbold, "Never a Level Playing Field: Blacks and the GI Bill," *Journal of Blacks in Higher Education* 6 (Winter 1994): 104–8.

14. Keith W. Olson, *The G.I. Bill, the Veterans, and the Colleges* (Lexington: University Press of Kentucky, 1974), 1–24.

15. Suzanne Mettler, *Soldiers to Citizens: The G.I. Bill and the Making of the Greatest Generation* (New York: Oxford University Press, 2005), 18.

16. Mettler, *Soldiers to Citizens*, 11. See also 144–62.

17. Margot Canaday, "Building a Straight State: Sexuality and Social Citizenship Under the 1944 G.I. Bill," *Journal of American History* 9, 3 (2003).

18. Clark, "Two Joes Meet."

19. James B. Conant, "Annual Report of the President of the University," *Harvard Alumni Bulletin*, February 3, 1945, 286; James B. Conant, "Annual Report of the President of the University," *Harvard Alumni Bulletin*, January 22, 1944, 244. Quoted in Olson, *G.I. Bill*, 33.

20. Theodore Rockwell III, "Frontier Life Among the Atom Splitters," *Saturday Evening Post*, December 1, 1945, 46.

21. "Atom City into Open City," *Senior Scholastic*, April 9, 1949, 13.

22. On the development of the military laboratories and residential community at Oak Ridge, see Peter B. Hales, *Atomic Spaces: Living on the Manhattan Project* (Urbana: University of Illinois Press, 1997); Charles W. Johnson and Charles O. Jackson, *City Behind a Fence: Oak Ridge, Tennessee, 1942–1946* (Knoxville: University of Tennessee Press, 1981); Leland Johnson, *Oak Ridge National Laboratory: The First Fifty Years* (Knoxville: University of Tennessee Press, 1994); Robert S. Norris, *Racing for the Bomb: General Leslie R. Groves, the Manhattan Project's Indispensable Man* (South Royalton, Vt.: Steerforth Press, 2002), 187–229. Oak Ridge was one of three communities created for the development of the atomic bomb. The other two, which I do not consider here, were Los Alamos, New Mexico, and Hanford, Washington.

23. On containment in the Cold War, see Elaine Tyler May, *Homeward Bound: American Families in the Cold War Era* (New York: Basic Books, 1988); Alan Nadel, *Containment Culture: American Narrative, Postmodernism, and the Atomic Age* (Durham, N.C.: Duke University Press, 1995). On containment as military strategy, see Thomas H. Etzold and John Lewis Gaddis, *Containment: Documents on American Policy and Strategy, 1945-1950* (New York: Columbia University Press, 1978); John Lewis Gaddis, *Strategies of Containment: A Critical Appraisal of Postwar American National Security Policy* (New York: Oxford University Press, 1982).

24. On postwar suburban development, see Rosalyn Baxandall and Elizabeth Ewen, *Picture Windows: How the Suburbs Happened* (New York: Basic Books, 2000); Kenneth Jackson, *Crabgrass Frontier: The Suburbanization of the United States* (New York: Oxford University Press, 1985); Barbara Mae Kelly, *Expanding the American Dream: Building and Rebuilding Levittown* (Albany: State University of New York Press, 1993).

25. Johnson and Jackson, *City Behind a Fence*, 66, 112–18.

26. "Birthplace of the Atomic Bomb," *Architectural Record*, September, 1945, 12.

27. Rockwell, "Frontier Life Among the Atom Splitters," 45. It is significant that the growth of roads and the difficulties of traveling by automobile should figure prominently here, since this was a major component of postwar American industry. Cotten Seiler, *Republic of Drivers: A Cultural History of Automobility in America* (Chicago: University of Chicago Press, 2008).

28. Bruce J. Schulman has described the postwar influx of manufactures in the South in his important work, *From Cotton Belt to Sunbelt: Federal Policy, Economic Development, and the Transformation of the South, 1938–1980* (New York: Oxford University Press, 1991).

29. Daniel Lang, "The Atomic City," *New Yorker*, September 29, 1945, 50.

30. Elizabeth Edwards, "'City of the Atomic Bomb' Has Library," *Library Journal*, September 15, 1945, 812.

31. Daniel Lang, "The Atomic City," 48.

32. Louis Falstein, "Oak Ridge: Secret City," *New Republic*, November 12, 1945, 636.

33. On gender in the postwar years, see Joanne Meyerowitz, ed., *Not June Cleaver: Women and Gender in Postwar America, 1945–1960* (Philadelphia: Temple University Press, 1994).

34. Though the term "military-industrial complex" did not appear until the end of the 1950s, the respect allocated for scientists working on government military projects is detailed in Hughes, *The Manhattan Project*. On the frontier in American culture, see Henry Nash Smith, *Virgin Land: The American West as Symbol and Myth* (Cambridge, Mass.: Harvard University Press, 1950). On gender and "frontier rhetoric," see Suzanne Clark, *Cold Warriors: Manliness on Trial in the Rhetoric of the West* (Carbondale: Southern Illinois University Press, 2000).

35. "Birthplace of the Atomic Bomb," 11–12.

36. "Twilight over Oak Ridge," *New York Times*, December 16, 1945.

37. On national security in American Cold War culture, see Robert J. Corber, *In the Name of National Security: Hitchcock, Homophobia, and the Political Construction of Gender in Postwar America* (Durham, N.C.: Duke University Press, 1993); Craig Eisendrath, ed., *National Insecurity: U.S. Intelligence After the Cold War* (Philadelphia: Temple University Press, 2000); Benjamin O. Fordham, *Building the Cold War Consensus: The Political Economy of U.S. National Security Policy, 1949–1951* (Ann Arbor: University of Michigan Press, 1998); Michael J. Hogan, *A Cross of Iron: Harry S. Truman and the Origins of the National Security State, 1945–1954* (New York: Cambridge University Press, 1998). On the ideology of containment, which was articulated by George Kennan in 1947, see James Burnham, *Containment or Liberation? An Inquiry into the Aims of United States Foreign Policy* (New York: John Day, 1953); Elizabeth Edwards Spalding, *The First Cold Warrior: Harry Truman, Containment, and the Remaking of Liberal Internationalism* (Lexington: University Press of Kentucky, 2006).

38. Henry J. Taylor, "Industrial Super-Marvels Behind the Atom Bomb," *Reader's Digest*, August, 1948, 19.

39. Falstein, "Oak Ridge: Secret City," 635.

40. "The Oak Ridger," *Newsweek*, November 8, 1948, 58.

41. Daniel Lang, "Career at Y-12," *New Yorker*, February 2, 1946, 46.

42. Rockwell, "Frontier Life Among the Atom Splitters," 46.

43. "Atom City into Open City," 13. This concern was also made visible in the persistent conversations about espionage and spies during the Cold War. John Earl Haynes, *Early Cold War Spies: The Espionage Trials That Shaped American Politics* (New York: Cambridge University Press, 2006); Michael Kackman, *Citizen Spy: Television, Espionage, and Cold War Culture* (Minneapolis: University of Minnesota Press, 2005); Athan Theoharis, *Chasing Spies: How the FBI Failed in Counterintelligence But Promoted the Politics of McCarthyism in the Cold War Years* (Chicago: Ivan Dee, 2002).

44. Lang, "Career at Y-12," 51.

45. Rockwell, "Frontier Life Among the Atom Splitters," 29.

46. Richard B. Gehman, "Oak Ridge Witch Hunt," *New Republic*, July 5, 1948, 12.

47. On surveillance of bodies in the Cold War, see Katherine Hauser, "George Tooker, Surveillance, and Cold War Sexual Politics," *GLQ* 11, 3 (2005): 391–425.

48. "Birthplace of the Atomic Bomb," 10.

49. On the scientific theory behind atomic energy in American culture, see Brian Bologh, *Chain Reaction: Expert Debate and Public Participation in American Commercial Nuclear Power, 1945–1975* (New York: Cambridge University Press, 1991).

50. On paranoia in American culture and politics, see Richard Hofstadter, *The Paranoid Style in American Politics, and Other Essays* (New York: Knopf, 1965); Timothy Melley, *Empire of Conspiracy: The Politics of Paranoia* (Ithaca, N.Y.: Cornell University Press, 2000); Dana Polan, *Power and Paranoia: History, Narrative, and the American Cinema, 1940–1950* (New York: Columbia University Press, 1986).

51. Lang, "The Atomic City," 48.

52. On individualism in the 1940s, see David Riesman, *The Lonely Crowd: A Study of the Changing American Character* (New Haven, Conn.: Yale University Press, 1950).

53. "Spreading the Know-How," *Time*, October 28, 1946, 65.

54. May, *Homeward Bound*, 94.

55. Falstein, "Oak Ridge: Secret City," 637.

56. The meanings of containment—particularly in their sexual and familial dimensions—is also discussed in Nadel, *Containment Culture*.

57. Rockwell, "Frontier Life Among the Atom Splitters," 19.

58. Falstein, "Oak Ridge: Secret City," 635.

59. Louis Falstein, "The Men Who Made the A-Bomb," *New Republic*, November 26, 1945, 708.

60. "Youth in the Atomic Age," *School Review*, June 1946, 319–20.

61. Warner Ogden, "The Ridge Kids vs. The Atom," *New York Times*, June 2, 1946.

62. "Yak-Ac," *Time*, April 8, 1946, 52.

63. Warner Ogden, "The A-Bomb's Home," *New York Times*, April 14, 1946.

64. Stephanie Coontz, *The Way We Never Were: American Families and the Nostalgia Trap* (New York: BasicBooks, 1992); May, *Homeward Bound*; Lisa McGirr, *Suburban Warriors: The Origins of the New American Right* (Princeton, N.J.: Princeton University Press, 2001).

65. "Oak Ridge: Life Where the Bomb Begins," *Newsweek*, August 5, 1946, 32.

66. Lang, "The Atomic City," 49.

67. "City of Safe Drivers," *Business Week*, August 3, 1946, 20.

68. This demand for order and safety anticipated the representations of normalcy found in the immensely popular and influential study, Robert S. Lynd and Helen Merrell Lynd, *Middletown: A Study in American Culture* (New York: Harcourt, Brace, 1929).

69. George O. Robinson, *The Oak Ridge Story: The Saga of a People Who Share in History* (Kingsport, Tenn.: Southern Publishers, 1950), 47–48.

70. Taylor, "Industrial Super-Marvels Behind the Atom Bomb," 22.

71. "Hot Factory," *Time*, February 27, 1950, 65.

72. Lang, "The Atomic City," 47.

73. "Oak Ridge: Life Where the Bomb Begins," 32.

74. Lang, "The Atomic City," 48.

75. Sidney Shalett, "The Atom Smashers at Play," *Saturday Evening Post*, May 3, 1947, 12.

76. Ibid.

77. American movies were also very influential in perpetuating ideas about scientists. See Christopher Frayling, *Mad, Bad, and Dangerous? The Scientist and the Cinema* (London: Reaktion Books, 2005).

78. There were, of course, intelligent women working at Oak Ridge, a fact that disrupted some efforts at conceiving the atomic city as a masculine gendered space. Yet these women were often depicted in popular culture as representing an opposed identity to the intelligence of the men. Daniel Lang, for example, offhandedly—and rather dismissively—described "girls out of college supervising girls out of high school who stand in front of a dial watching to see if a needle jumps from zero to ten" (Lang, "The Atomic City," 47). Theodore Rockwell's account of his guided tour of Oak Ridge described his horror at the "girls" controlling some of the machines in the plants: "when a machine is put into a girl's hands with no fundamental explanation, and she is able by a casual twist of a coded dial to command thousands of horsepower without even realizing it, it gives you a strange feeling. You are afraid that someday this titanic force, having bowed to a brain which had bared its secrets with awe and respect, will mutiny against the indifferent girl who dared to toy so aimlessly with unimpressive dials of her control cubicle" ("Frontier Life Among the Atom Splitters," 48). The women who were educated, intelligent scientists were not represented in the popular media. Efforts to reframe women scientists at Oak Ridge—albeit within the familiar frontier narrative—have been undertaken, but they have focused on recent women, rather than recovering women of the past. See Oak Ridge National Laboratory, *Pioneer Women: Pushing the Frontiers of Science and Engineering at Oak Ridge National Laboratory* (Oak Ridge, Tenn.: Oak Ridge National Laboratory, 1995).

79. Falstein, "The Men Who Made the A-Bomb," 707.

80. Ibid., 707–8.

81. "Oak Ridge: Life Where the Bomb Begins," 32.

82. Lang, "The Atomic City," 49.

83. Ibid., 47–48.

84. Lang did not offer the possibility, of course, that his patron might in fact be signifying the distance between his world and her own: her metaphor might be read as an absurd—even campy—comment on the expectation that a Southern resident would both yearn for and fail to understand northern urban life. On complicated politics of the "hillbilly," see Anthony Harkins, *Hillbilly: A Cultural History of an American Icon* (New York: Oxford University Press, 2004); J. W. Williamson, *Hillbillyland: What the Movies Did to the Mountains and What the Mountains Did to the Movies* (Chapel Hill: University of North Carolina Press, 1995); Rachel Rubin, "Voice of the Cracker: Don West Reinvents Appalachia," in Bill V. Mullen and James Smethurst, *Left of the Color Line: Race, Radicalism, and Twentieth-Century Literature of the United States* (Chapel Hill: University of North Carolina Press, 2003), 205–22.

85. Falstein, "Oak Ridge: Secret City," 636.

86. "How Oak Ridge Street Program Grew," *American City*, April 1948, 102.

87. Robinson, *The Oak Ridge Story*, 50.

88. Lang, "The Atomic City," 48.

89. Falstein, "The Men Who Made the A-Bomb," 707.

90. Lang, "The Atomic City," 48.

91. "Oak Ridge—'Reconverted,'" *Business Week*, August 3, 1946, 19–21, 19.

92. Rockwell, "Frontier Life Among the Atom Splitters," 48.

93. Williamson, *Hillbillyland*, 2–3.

94. Falstein, "The Men Who Made the A-Bomb," 707.

95. Lang, "The Atomic City," 50.

96. Rockwell, "Frontier Life Among the Atom Splitters," 28.

97. Johnson and Jackson, *City Behind a Fence*, 112–118.

98. "Oak Ridge: Life Where the Bomb Begins," 32.

99. Falstein, "Oak Ridge: Secret City," 635.

100. Falstein, "Oak Ridge: Secret City," 637.

101. Lang, "The Atomic City," 50.

102. Morris Green, "Uncle Sam's Problem City," *American City*, August, 1953, 93.

103. "Atomic Cities' Boom," *Business Week*, December 18, 1948, 65–72, 65.

104. Lang, "The Atomic City," 50.

105. Falstein, "Oak Ridge: Secret City," 637.

106. "Atomic Cities' Boom," 65–66.

107. Lang, "The Atomic City," 50.

108. Jean Lowrie, "The Library—Nerve Center of the School," *Wilson Library Bulletin*, 426–27.

109. Rockwell, "Frontier Life Among the Atom Splitters," 45.

110. Lang, "The Atomic City," 51.

111. Ibid.

112. Falstein, "Oak Ridge: Secret City," 637.

113. Lang, "The Atomic City," 50.

114. Falstein, "Oak Ridge: Secret City," 637.

115. Lang, "The Atomic City," 50.

116. Robinson, *The Oak Ridge Story*, 53–55.

117. Rockwell, "Frontier Life Among the Atom Splitters," 45.

118. Falstein, "Oak Ridge: Secret City," 636.

Chapter 7. Inventing the Egghead: Brainpower in Cold War American Culture

Epigraph: Charles Frankel, "Definition of the True Egghead," *New York Times Magazine*, October 21, 1956, 14.

1. Charles Price, "I Live Among the Eggheads," *Saturday Evening Post*, November 16, 1957, 42, 43, 146, 42.

2. The anti-intellectual framework has been most persuasively advanced in Richard Hofstadter, *Anti-Intellectualism in American Life* (New York: Knopf, 1963).

3. I am using liberalism here to denote a generally agreed-upon definition that emerged following the expansion of federal government in the 1930s: a commitment to capitalism and democracy standing against Communism, a recognition that a strong federal government was necessary to safeguard American liberty, and a belief in incremental social change. I am also sensitive, however, to the ways in which historians such as William H. Chafe have argued that "the term *liberal* has altered over time." The historiography on conservatism has undergone a similar shift toward acknowledging the historical contingencies of political categories. The tension I am trying to highlight in this chapter centers on a moment marked by struggles over defining and implementing a "liberal consensus" that sought, again using Chafe's words, "to develop a liberal ideology that incorporates both the rights of individuals and the importance of collective identities on people's lives and fortunes" in the midst of international and national struggles over political, racial, gender, and sexual identities. Though the term *liberalism* might obscure as much as it reveals, I contend that it is impossible to write about the political world during the Cold War without acknowledging the immense influence of liberalism on the shape of American culture, society, and politics. I also conceive this chapter as contributing to the ongoing investigations into the origins and meanings of postwar liberalism: I contend that the irresolvable paradoxes of the egghead were instrumental in shaping a version of liberalism that placed a premium on white male privilege and diminished the value of intellectuals in Cold War political culture. William H. Chafe, *The Achievement of American Liberalism: The New Deal and Its Legacies* (New York: Columbia University Press, 2003), xii, xviii.

4. Joe Adamson, *Tex Avery, King of Cartoons* (1975; New York: Da Capo, 1985), 208–9. Though the precise meaning of an egghead would change in the 1950s, it is significant that the implications of failed masculinity appear in this prefiguration.

5. Joseph Alsop and Stewart Alsop, *The Reporter's Trade* (New York: Reynal, 1958), 188; Joseph W. Alsop with Adam Platt, *"I've Seen the Best of It": Memoirs* (New York: Norton, 1992), 341; Robert W. Merry, *Taking On the World: Joseph and Stewart Alsop—Guardians of the American Century* (New York: Viking, 1996), 236.

6. Harrison Smith, "The Egghead Problem," *Saturday Review*, February 21, 1953, 24.

7. Arthur Krock, "Ideas Live, Men Die," *New York Times*, October 2, 1955.

8. Delmore Schwartz, "Survey of Our National Phenomena," *New York Times*, April 15, 1956.

9. *Newsweek*, October 8, 1956.

10. This historical argument dovetails with Bledstein's history of professionalism that would appear later. Burton J. Bledstein, *The Culture of Professionalism: The Middle Class and the Development of Higher Education in America* (New York: Norton, 1976).

11. "Eggheads: Cracking the Enigma," *Newsweek*, October 8, 1956, 53–57, 57.

12. Though the egghead was supposed to be a negative force in society, then, he was also a signifier of America's educational achievement. On the roots and rise of American nationalism in the 1950s, see especially Richard M. Fried, *The Russians Are Coming! The Russians Are Coming! Pageantry and Patriotism in Cold-War America* (New York: Oxford University Press, 1998); William L. O'Neill, *American High: The Years of Confidence, 1945–1960* (New York: Free Press, 1986). See also John Fousek, *To Lead the Free World: American Nationalism and the Cultural Roots of the Cold War* (Chapel Hill: University of North Carolina Press, 2000); Matthew S. Hirshberg, *Perpetuating Patriotic Perceptions: The Cognitive Function of the Cold War* (Westport, Conn.: Praeger, 1993).

13. "Eggheads: Cracking the Enigma," 53.

14. Ibid., 55.

15. Hilary Herbold, "Never a Level Playing Field: Blacks and the GI Bill," *Journal of Blacks in Higher Education* 6 (Winter 1994): 104–8.

16. On representations of education under the G.I. Bill, see Christopher P. Loss, "'The Most Wonderful Thing Has Happened to Me in the Army': Psychology, Citizenship, and American Higher Education in World War II," *Journal of American History* 92, 3 (December 2005): 864–91.

17. Michael Kazin, *The Populist Persuasion: An American History* (New York: Basic Books, 1995), 167.

18. Michael Novak, "The Brain Curtain," *The Nation*, December 10, 1960, 454.

19. Harry J. Jerison, "Brain to Body Ratios and the Evolution of Intelligence," *Science*, April 1, 1955, 449.

20. Alvin O. Collins, letter, *Newsweek*, November 5, 1956, 6.

21. Lee Graham, "Ten Secrets of Sex Appeal," *Coronet*, March, 1954, 35.

22. Advertisement for Bonwit's 721 Club, *New York Times*, December 17, 1957.

23. M. B. Tolson, *Harlem Gallery* (New York: Twayne, 1965), 139.

24. Andrea Levine, "The (Jewish) White Negro: Norman Mailer's Racial Bodies," *MELUS* 28 (Summer 2003): 59–82, 59; Norman Mailer, "The White Negro: Superficial Reflecitons on the Hipster," in *Advertisements for Myeslf* (New York: Putnam's, 1959), 337–58.

25. Mailer, *Advertisements for Myself*, 341.

26. W. T. Lhamon, *Deliberate Speed: The Origins of a Cultural Style in the American 1950s* (Washington, D.C.: Smithsonian Institution Press, 1990), 67.

27. Ralph Ellison, *Invisible Man* (New York: Random House, 1952); Jack Kerouac, *On the Road* (New York: Signet, 1957).

28. George Lipsitz, *The Possessive Investment in Whiteness: How White People Profit from Identity Politics* (Philadelphia: Temple University Press, 1998).

29. On conformity, nonconformity, and anticommunism in the 1950s, see Terry Christensen and Peter J. Haas, *Projecting Politics: Political Messages in American Film* (New York: M.E. Sharpe, 2005) 109–24; Leerom Medovoi, *Rebels: Youth and the Cold War Origins of Identity* (Durham, N.C.: Duke University Press, 2005).

30. On the 1950s homophile and gay rights movement see John D'Emilio, *Sexual Politics, Sexual Communities: The Making of a Homosexual Minority in the United States, 1940–1970* (Chicago: University of Chicago Press, 1983); Marcia M. Gallo, *Different Daughters: A History of the Daughters of Bilitis and the Rise of the Lesbian Rights Movement* (New York: Carrol and Graf, 2006); Daniel Hurewitz, *Bohemian Los Angeles and the Making of Modern Politics* (Berkeley: University of California Press, 2007); Martin Meeker, *Contacts Desired: Gay and Lesbian Communications and Community, 1940s–1970s* (Chicago: University of Chicago Press, 2006).

31. Joseph A. Keough, letter, *Newsweek*, November 5, 1956, 6.

32. Gavin Butt, *Between You and Me: Queer Disclosures in the New York Art World, 1948–1963* (Durham, N.C.: Duke University Press, 2005); Elizabeth Lapovsky Kennedy and Madeline D. Davis, *Boots of Leather, Slippers of Gold: The History of a Lesbian Community* (New York: Routledge, 1993); Michael S. Sherry, *Gay Artists in Modern American Culture: An Imagined Conspiracy* (Chapel Hill: University of North Carolina Press, 2007).

33. Louis Bromfield, "The Triumph of the Egghead," *The Freeman*, December 1, 1952, 158, 159.

34. Jonathan Dollimore, "Post/Modern: On the Gay Sensibility, or the Pervert's Revenge on Autheniticity," in *Camp: Queer Aesthetics and the Performing Subject*, ed. Fabio Cleto, 221–36 (Ann Arbor: University of Michigan Press, 1999).

35. Percy W. Brown, Letter to the Editor, *Saturday Review*, March 28, 1953, 24.

36. David K. Johnson, *The Lavender Scare: The Cold War Persecution of Gays and Lesbians in the Federal Government* (Chicago: University of Chicago Press, 2004), 121.

37. Jorgensen was an ex-G.I. who had the first publicly acknowledged male-to-female surgical sex change in the United States. Joanne Meyerowitz, *How Sex Changed: A History of Transsexuality in the United States* (Cambridge, Mass.: Harvard University Press, 2002), 51–97.

38. Johnson, *Lavender Scare*, 121.

39. Advertisement for Donmoor Knit Shirts, *New York Times*, April 8, 1956.

40. Jill Corey with Jimmy Carroll and His Orchestra, "Egghead," by Hoffman, Manning, and Story (Columbia, 1956).

41. George Strong, letter, *New York Times*, May 4, 1958.

42. John Cogley, "Eggheads, Soft-Boiled," *Commonweal*, November 28, 1952, 190.

43. "Martin Condemns Talk of a Slump," *New York Times*, January 24, 1954.

44. See David M. Oshinsky, *A Conspiracy So Immense: The World of Joe McCarthy* (New York: Free Press, 1983); Thomas C. Reeves, *The Life and Times of Joe McCarthy, A Biography* (New York: Stein and Day, 1982).

45. W. H. Lawrence, "McCarthy Defends His Methods and Defies Critics 'High or Low,'" *New York Times*, March 18, 1954.

46. Percy W. Brown, letter, *Saturday Review*, March 28, 1953, 21.

47. Susan Faulkner, letter, *New York Times*, November 13, 1954.

48. Frank Fenton, "The Chicken or the Egghead," in *9 Tales of Space and Time*, ed. Raymond J. Healy (New York: Henry Holt, 1954), 220.

49. Healy weakly justified including of Fenton's story by referring to "psychiatry, political theory, sociology, and magic drugs" as the story's "science-fiction elements," even as he acknowledged (or hoped) that the story "will soon be widely discussed in a variety of circles not necessarily devoted to science fiction." Raymond J. Healy, introduction to Fenton, "The Chicken or the Egghead," 211.

50. John Huntington, *Rationalizing Genius: Ideological Strategies in the Classic American Science Fiction Short Story* (New Brunswick, N.J.: Rutgers University Press, 1989).

51. Thomas D. Clareson, *Some Kind of Paradise: The Emergence of American Science Fiction* (Westport, Conn.: Greenwood Press, 1985); Lester del Rey, *The World of Science Fiction: 1926–1976: The History of a Subculture* (New York: Garland, 1980).

52. Fenton, "The Chicken or the Egghead," 213, 214, 216.

53. Ibid., 221, 236.

54. Ibid., 213–14.

55. Ibid., 214. On homosexuality and broadway musicals, see John M. Clum, *Something for the Boys: Musical Theater and Gay Culture* (New York: St. Martin's Press, 1999); D. A. Miller, *Place for Us: Essay on the Broadway Musical* (Cambridge, Mass.: Harvard University Press, 1998).

56. Fenton, "The Chicken or the Egghead," 216.

57. Ibid., 217. On HUAC, see Walter Goodman, *The Committee: The Extraordinary Career of the House Committee on Un-American Activities* (Baltimore: Penguin, 1968); Kenneth O'Reilly, *Hoover and the Un-Americans: The FBI, HUAC, and the Red Menace* (Philadelphia: Temple University Press, 1983).

58. Fenton, "The Chicken or the Egghead," 218.

59. Ibid., 218.

60. Ibid., 227, 235.

61. Ibid., 216, 217.

62. Marcel Proust, *Remembrance of Things Past*, trans. C.K. Scott Moncrieff and Terence Kilmartin (1934; New York: Random House, 1981). See also Emily Eells, *Proust's Cup of Tea: Homoeroticism and Victorian Culture* (Burlington, Vt.: Ashgate, 2002); Gregory Woods, "High Culture and High Camp: The Case of Marcel Proust," in *Camp Grounds: Style and Homosexuality*, ed. David Bergman, 121–143 (Amherst: University of Massachusetts Press, 1993); Eve Sedgwick, *Epistemology of the Closet* (Berkeley: University of California Press, 1990), 213–51.

63. Fenton, "The Chicken or the Egghead," 222.

64. Ibid., 225, 226.

65. Ibid., 229, 231.

66. Ibid., 237.

67. Lewis Funke, News and Gossip of the Rialto, *New York Times*, October 6, 1957.

68. Dale Stevens, "'The Egghead' Has Warmth, Wit," clipping in Van Zandt (Porter) Papers, 1952–1967, Box 2, Billy Rose Theatre Collection at New York Public Library for the Performing Arts.

69. Review in *Variety*, September 18, 1957.

70. Molly Thacher Kazan, *The Egghead* (New York: Dramatists Play Service, 1958), 31.

71. On the narrow domestic expectations for many women in the 1950s, see Coontz, *The Way We Never Were*; Eugenia Kaledin, *Mothers and More: American Women in the 1950s* (Boston: Twayne Publishers, 1984); May, *Homeward Bound*.

72. Kazan, *Egghead*, 39.

73. Ibid., 56.

74. Ibid., 63.

75. Advertisement for *The Egghead* in *New York Times*, October 16, 1957.

76. Advertisement for *The Egghead* in *New York Times*, October 17, 1957.

77. Kazan, *Egghead*, 66.

78. Ibid.

79. Ibid.

80. On the popular interpretation of Communists as tricking their adherents, see Harvey Klehr, *The Secret World of American Communism* (New Haven, Conn.: Yale University Press, 1995); Harvey Klehr, *The Soviet World of American Communism* (New Haven, Conn.: Yale University Press, 1998).

81. Kazan, *Egghead*, 27.

82. Ibid., 62.

83. See Robin D. G. Kelley, *Hammer and Hoe: Alabama Communists During the Great Depression* (Chapel Hill: University of North Carolina Press, 1990); William J. Maxwell, *New Negro, Old Left: African-American Writing and Communism Between the Wars* (New York: Columbia University Press, 1999); Mark Naison, *Communists in Harlem During the Depression* (Urbana: University of Illinois, 1983); Cedric J. Robinson,

Black Marxism: The Making of the Black Radical Tradition (Totowa, N.J.: Totowa, 1983); Mark Solomon, *The Cry Was Unity: Communists and African Americans, 1919–1936* (Jackson, University Press of Mississippi, 1998).

84. Kazan, *Egghead*, 69.

85. Ibid., 78.

Epilogue

Epigraph: Thomas Pynchon, *V. A Novel* (Philadelphia: Lippincott, 1963), 127.

1. Christopher Lasch, *The New Radicalism in America 1889–1963: The Intellectual as a Social Type* (New York: Knopf, 1965).

2. Richard Hofstadter, *Anti-Intellectualism in American Life* (New York: Knopf, 1963); Louis Coser, *Men of Ideas* (New York: Free Press, 1965); Lasch, *New Radicalism*, xvii.

3. Lasch, *New Radicalism*, ix.

4. Ibid., x.

5. Ibid.

6. Hofstadter, *Anti-Intellectualism*, 3.

7. Coser, *Men of Ideas*, 360.

8. Irving Louis Horowitz, "The Unfinished Writings of C. Wright Mills: The Last Phase," *Studies on the Left* 3 (Fall 1963): 10.

INDEX

Page numbers in italics refer to illustrations.

ACKNOWLEDGMENTS

Completing this book would have been impossible without the support of a generous and engaging intellectual community. Bruce Schulman and Patricia Hills in the American and New England Studies program at Boston University offered endless editorial comments and scholarly advice. Marilyn Halter and Nina Silber were also attentive readers. I received financial support from a Boston University Humanities Foundation award and a fellowship from the New York University Tamiment Library's Center for the Study of the Impact of the Cold War on the United States. A two-year Modern Intellectual History fellowship at Boston University provided further assistance. This book was made possible through generous publication subvention support provided by the University of Massachusetts Boston, Office of the Vice Provost for Research and Dean of Graduate Studies.

The capable and generous staff at the archives I visited during the research stage of this project allowed me to discover far more material than I could have anticipated. In particular I would like to thank the staff at the Kheel Center for Labor-Management Documentation and Archives at Cornell University, the Tamiment Library and Robert F. Wagner Labor Archives at New York University, the Howard Gottlieb Archival Research Center at Boston University, the Schlesinger Library at Radcliffe, the Boston Public Library, and the New York Public Library for their resourcefulness.

My academic home in the American Studies department at the University of Massachusetts Boston is a joyous place to teach and produce scholarship. My colleagues Lynnell Thomas, Judith Smith, Marisol Negrón, Bonnie Miller, Phil Chassler, Jeff Melnick, Paul Atwood, Patricia Roub, and Shirley Tang, have been unfailingly supportive of my work and career. I cannot imagine having completed this project without such a strong community surrounding me. Rachel Rubin offered important feedback and provided significant mentorship at several critical stages of this book's production. She has been an indispensable resource throughout the process of writing and revising. Shauna Lee Manning has provided many forms of assistance – thank you. I would also like to thank all the brilliant UMass Boston students who have enriched me both professionally and intellectually.

Over the years I have been lucky enough to count Ross Barrett, Gillian Mason, Carney Maley, Desirée Garcia, Salomé Aguilera Skvirsky, Susan Tomlinson, and Molly Geidel among my colleagues. They have strengthened my work, and their own stimulating and exciting academic projects have made me proud to consider them academic peers. My colleagues during the two years I taught in History and Literature at Harvard University spurred me forward in this work. Particular thanks go to Jeanne Follansbee, Jill Lepore, Robin Bernstein, Kim Reilly, Katherine Stebbins-McCaffrey, and Seo-Young Chu. Over the course of those two years I had the honor of teaching and advising one of the most remarkable students I've encountered. Pat Chesnut was never afraid to challenge me but always enthusiastic about learning; it would be difficult to enumerate all the ways working with him made me a better teacher and scholar.

Many folks outside these institutions have been crucial and deserve extra thanks. So thanks to Cheryl Higashida, Gary Holcomb, Jószef Illy, James Smethurst, Dayo Gore, Julia Mickenberg, Paula Rabinowitz, Chris Vials, and Alan Wald. Other friends have been incalculably important to me, especially Allison Lentino, Cindy Staton, David Stankiewicz, Shauna Peck Slome, Melissa Mack, Jason Dionne, and Utah Nickel: I am grateful for you. Phoebe Sung and Peter Buer are two of the smartest and most creatively inspiring people I've ever known. Thanks also to David Mislin, Michael Borum, Chris Castellani, Dan Samson, Tony Paine, Christopher Vyce, Stephanie Vyce, and Danielle Coriale.

Bob Lockhart at the University of Pennsylvania Press has been an amazing editor, lending both his editorial talent and sympathetic ear as needed. I have been lucky to work with an editor whose dedication to his work is matched only by his skill and discernment. I would also like to thank Jim O'brien for his expert enduring.

My family in New Hampshire, especially my parents, brother and sister-in-law, and Joan Scott, asked many challenging questions about this project, but they never doubted me. Their confidence in my ability to finish, while not always deserved, was invariably appreciated. Vivien Clark made my time in New York interesting and enjoyable. I am lucky to also consider myself part of the extended Halley family, a joyous group that never fails to revive my spirits. I wish my uncle Bill were alive to accept a copy of this book;

his crotchety New Hampshire contrarianism inspired me from childhood to today.

Brian Halley lived with me during the entire process of researching and writing this book. His willingness to offer his talented editorial guidance and analytical eye without becoming frustrated by my belligerence is a testament to both his professional skills and strength of character. He is my partner and best friend, and I am proud to acknowledge that this book would be unimaginable without him.

* * *

An earlier version of Chapter 7 originally appeared as "Inventing the Egghead: The Paradoxes of Brainpower in Cold War American Culture," *Journal of American Studies* 45, 2 (2011). Copyright © Cambridge University Press 2010, reprinted with permission.